Barcode Back

MW01120310

Young Adult Offenders

This latest volume in the Cambridge Criminal Justice Series focuses upon young adults and their treatment in the criminal justice system. The subject is very topical because there is increasing evidence that a rigid distinction between 'youth' and 'adulthood' is not appropriate in modern societies. For example, important developmental tasks such as finishing one's education, finding regular work and the foundation of one's own family are now completed later than in former times; neuropsychological brain functions are still developing beyond age 18; and desistance from criminal offending occurs most rapidly in early adulthood.

Despite such evidence, the United Kingdom and other countries have largely neglected policies for young adult offenders in comparison with young people under 18. Although there seems to be no general transnational solution for this problem, there is a clear need for differentiation. This book brings together leading authorities in the field to analyse theoretical, empirical and policy issues relating to this neglected group of people, exploring different approaches to both crime prevention and offender treatment. It will be of interest to researchers, practitioners and policy makers in the fields of criminology, criminal justice, prisons, probation, forensic psychology and psychiatry, sociology, education and social work.

Friedrich Lösel is Director of the Institute of Criminology at the University of Cambridge and Professor of Psychology at the University of Erlangen-Nuremberg, Germany.

Sir Anthony Bottoms is Emeritus Wolfson Professor of Criminology at the University of Cambridge and Honorary Professor of Criminology at the University of Sheffield.

David P. Farrington is Professor of Psychological Criminology at the Institute of Criminology, University of Cambridge, and Adjunct Professor of Psychiatry at the Western Psychiatric Institute and Clinic, University of Pittsburgh.

Cambridge Criminal Justice Series

Published in association with the Institute of Criminology at the
University of Cambridge

1. **Community Penalties**
   Change and challenges
   Edited by Anthony Bottoms, Loraine Gelsthorpe and Sue Rex

2. **Ideology, Crime and Criminal Justice**
   A symposium in honour of Sir Leon Radzinowicz
   Edited by Anthony Bottoms and Michael Tonry

3. **Reform and Punishment**
   The future of sentencing
   Edited by Sue Rex and Michael Tonry

4. **Confronting Crime**
   Crime control policy under New Labour
   Edited by Michael Tonry

5. **Sex Offenders in the Community**
   Managing and reducing the risks
   Edited by Amanda Matravers

6. **The Effects of Imprisonment**
   Edited by Alison Liebling and Shadd Maruna

7. **Hearing the Victim**
   Adversarial justice, crime victims and the state
   Edited by Anthony Bottoms and Julian V. Roberts

8. **Young Adult Offenders**
   Lost in transition?
   Edited by Friedrich Lösel, Anthony Bottoms and David P. Farrington

Young Adult Offenders

Lost in transition?

**Edited by Friedrich Lösel,
Anthony Bottoms and
David P. Farrington**

 Routledge
Taylor & Francis Group

LONDON AND NEW YORK

First published 2012 by Routledge
2 Park Square, Milton Park, Abingdon, Oxon, OX14 4RN

Simultaneously published in the USA and Canada
by Routledge
711 Third Avenue, New York, NY 10017

Routledge is an imprint of the Taylor & Francis Group, an informa business

British Library Cataloguing in Publication Data
A catalogue record for this book is available from the British Library

Library of Congress Cataloging in Publication Data
Friedrich Lösel, Anthony Bottoms, and David P. Farrington.
   Young adult offenders: lost in transition? edited by Friedrich Lösel,
   Anthony Bottoms, and David P. Farrington.
   p. cm. – (Cambridge criminal justice series)
   1. Juvenile delinquents. 2. Juvenile delinquents–Rehabilitation.
   3. Juvenile justice, Administration of. 4. Young adults.
   I. Lösel, Friedrich. II. Bottoms, A. E.
   III. Farrington, David P.
HV9069.Y62 2012
364.36–dc23   2011033409

ISBN: 978-1-84392-271-1 (hbk)
ISBN: 978-0-203-12851-0 (ebk)

Typeset in Times New Roman
by Sunrise Setting Ltd, Torquay, UK

Contents

vi *Contents*

List of figures

List of tables

Contributor biographies

Rob Allen is an independent researcher and co-founder of Justice and Prisons (www.justiceandprisons.org). He chaired the Barrow Cadbury Trust T2A Alliance from 2008 until 2011 and was Director of the International Centre for Prison Studies (ICPS) at King's College London from 2005 until 2010. Prior to joining ICPS, he ran Rethinking Crime and Punishment, an initiative set up by the Esmée Fairbairn Foundation to change public attitudes to prison, and before that was Director of Research and Development at the National Association for the Care and Resettlement of Offenders (NACRO). He was also a member of the Youth Justice Board from 1998 to 2006 and chaired CLINKS, the umbrella group for the criminal justice voluntary sector from 2005 until 2010. He has written widely on youth and criminal justice, including *From Punishment to Problem Solving* (2006), *Justice Reinvestment: A New Approach to Crime and Justice* (2007) and *Last Resort – Exploring the Reduction in Child Imprisonment* (2011).

Monica Barry is Senior Research Fellow at the School of Law, Strathclyde University, and Honorary Senior Research Fellow at the Scottish Centre for Crime and Justice Research. Her research interests centre on criminal justice policy, desistance from crime, youth policy and the impact of youth transitions on offending behaviour. She is the author of *Youth Offending in Transition: The Search for Social Recognition* (2006), editor of *Youth Policy and Social Inclusion: Critical Debates with Young People* (2005) and joint editor with Fergus McNeill of *Youth Offending and Youth Justice* (2009).

Sir Anthony Bottoms is Emeritus Wolfson Professor of Criminology at the University of Cambridge and Honorary Professor of Criminology at the University of Sheffield. He is also a Fellow of the British Academy. During his academic career, his interests within criminology have been wide ranging, but in more recent years he has focused especially on issues relating to social order and legal compliance, setting up the Sheffield Desistance Project with Joanna Shapland, which aims to explain more fully why even recidivist offenders frequently reduce their offending during their early twenties.

Frieder Dünkel has been Professor of Criminology and Head of the Department of Criminology at the University of Greifswald in Germany since 1992. Prior to this he was a research fellow at the Max-Planck-Institute for Foreign and International Penal Law at Freiburg i. Br. He has coordinated various national and international research projects and has organized numerous conferences on juvenile justice and prison law. He plays an active role in several international and national organisations, including the Council of Europe and UNICEF. His key research interests lie in the fields of penology, prison law, human rights, criminal policy, youth crime and youth justice and he has published widely in these fields.

David P. Farrington, OBE, is Professor of Psychological Criminology at the Institute of Criminology, Cambridge University, and Adjunct Professor of Psychiatry at the Western Psychiatric Institute and Clinic, University of Pittsburgh. His major research interest is in developmental criminology and he is Director of the Cambridge Study in Delinquent Development; a prospective longitudinal survey of over 400 London males from age 8 to age 48. In addition to the 550 published journal articles and book chapters on criminological and psychological topics, he has published over 80 books, monographs and government publications.

Alison Liebling is Professor of Criminology and Criminal Justice and Director of the Prisons Research Centre at the University of Cambridge's Institute of Criminology. She has published several books, including *Prisons and their Moral Performance* (2004) and the *Prison Officer and the Effects of Imprisonment* (2005), as well as many articles in criminological journals. She is also General Editor of the international journal *Punishment and Society* and is on the editorial board of the Oxford University Press Clarendon Series in Criminology. She has recently completed a comparative study of public and private sector prisons as well as a repeat study of staff–prisoner relationships in a maximum security prison.

Friedrich Lösel is Director of the Institute of Criminology at the University of Cambridge, and Professor of Psychology at the University of Erlangen-Nuremberg, Germany. He has carried out research on juvenile delinquency, prisons, offender treatment, football hooliganism, school bullying, personality disordered offenders, resilience, close relationships, child abuse, family education and evaluation methodology. He is the author or editor of 18 books and over 300 journal articles and book chapters. In recognition of his scientific work, he has received various honours including: the Award for Lifetime Achievement of the European Association of Psychology and Law, the Sellin-Glueck Award of the American Society of Criminology, the Stockholm Prize in Criminology and the German Psychology Prize.

Mary McMurran, is Professor in the University of Nottingham's Institute of Mental Health. She has worked as a clinical and forensic psychologist in

HM Prison Service and in forensic mental health services. Her research interests are centred around the assessment and treatment of alcohol-related aggression and violence, social problem-solving as a model of understanding and treating people with personality disorders, and understanding and enhancing readiness to engage in therapy. She has written over 100 academic articles and book chapters on these topics. She is also a Fellow of the British Psychological Society and was the recipient of the BPS Division of Forensic Psychology's Lifetime Achievement Award in 2005.

Grant Muir spent many years in his family's retail business before he became a mature student in psychology and criminology, obtaining his PhD at St. Andrew's University. He has worked as a researcher on two major criminological projects: first, with Alison Liebling at Cambridge University on an evaluation of the Prison Service's 'Incentives and Earned Privileges' scheme; and second, with Anthony Bottoms and Joanna Shapland at Sheffield University on a study of desistance among young adult recidivist offenders.

Rod Morgan is Professor Emeritus of Criminal Justice at the University of Bristol and Visiting Professor at the Universities Police Science Institute, Cardiff University. From 2004 to 2007, he was Chairman of the Youth Justice Board for England and Wales and, prior to that, was Chief Inspector of Probation (2001 to 2004). He has written widely on aspects of criminal justice, ranging from policing to sentencing and prisoners' rights, and is co-editor of *The Oxford Handbook of Criminology* (5th edition, 2012).

Dame Anne Owers was Chief Inspector of Prisons from 2001 to 2010. Anne led the Inspectorate in developing human rights-based criteria and methodology which could produce robust and independent reports on prisons and other places of detention, to reveal shortcomings and chart progress. She has also been the chair of Clinks and of the Transition to Adulthood Alliance (T2A). In 2000 she was appointed CBE for her work in human rights and was made a Dame in 2009. In April 2012 she was appointed to chair the Independent Police Complaints Commission.

Ineke Pruin is Research Associate at the Department of Criminology at the University of Greifswald. She obtained her PhD in Law (with a thesis on young adults in criminal justice) in 2006 and has taught criminology, juvenile criminal law and prison law at the University of Heidelberg since 2008. Her main research interests lie in juvenile justice and youth criminality, developmental criminology, community sanctions and prison law.

Joanna Shapland is Professor of Criminal Justice and Head of the School of Law at the University of Sheffield. Her research interests span topics such as desistance, restorative justice, probation, the informal economy and victimology. She is currently researching 'quality' in probation one-to-one supervision for the National Offender Management Service and has recently co-published *Restorative Justice in Practice: What Works for Victims and Offenders* (2011) as well as several further articles on the Sheffield Desistance Study, including 'Steps towards desistance among male young adult recidivists', in Farrall *et al.* (eds.), *Escape Routes* (2011).

Foreword

In 2001, as I became Chief Inspector of Prisons, the Labour government entered its second term with a manifesto promise to extend to young adult offenders the focused and specialised attention that it had tried to provide for juveniles during its first term. But this never happened. As a result, they have remained a lost generation, which I described in my last Annual Report as 'a neglected and under-resourced age group'. Time after time, inspection reports would record that young offender institutions (often only notionally distinct from the adult institutions in which they were located) provided far too little activity, high levels of use of force and discipline, and low levels of safety and support.

This volume is therefore both important and timely. It reminds us not just that this is an age-group with high levels of recidivism, but one where there is also the greatest opportunity to divert someone from a criminal career: studies have shown that 18 is also the peak age for desistance from crime. It also reminds us of the obvious fact that blowing out the candles on an 18th birthday cake does not magically transform anyone into a fully functioning and mature adult – even without the life disadvantages many young people in criminal justice have experienced.

The greatest frustration, for those working in the system as well as victims and young offenders, is that we know what does not work, but carry on doing it. Short prison sentences, followed by minimal post-release support, or conventional community sentences with limited engagement from an overworked probation service, cannot be expected to provide the support or challenge that young adults need, as they emerge from the protections – however limited – that they could rely on as juveniles. Many therefore become and remain lost in transition.

Since I left the inspectorate, and became chair of the Transition to Adulthood Alliance (T2A), I have been able to see the difference that can be made in young people's lives if they are able to access the focused, specialised and individual support and approach that matches their age, maturity, needs and strengths. There are no simple equations to turn round already damaged lives – as the papers here make clear, early and focused intervention is the best remedy. But the provision of individualised and focused support and mentoring – walking alongside young people as they try to change the narrative of their lives – does work. Recent evaluations of the T2A pilots have shown that, of 34 young adults tracked, many with prolific offending histories, only three had offended within six months. Even allowing for the halo effect of small, enthusiastically led pilots, these are remarkable findings.

The research and evidence base for a different and specialised approach to those in transition from childhood to adulthood is incontrovertible and well set out in these papers. It is to be hoped that it helps to stimulate a long overdue change in policy and practice: to the benefit of victims and potential victims, as well as young adult offenders themselves.

Dame Anne Owers

1 Introduction

Friedrich Lösel, Anthony Bottoms and
David P. Farrington

In England and Wales, the legal treatment of offenders changes dramatically when they reach their eighteenth birthday. Instead of being dealt with in the youth justice system – which focuses more on rehabilitation – they start being dealt with in the adult criminal justice system – which focuses more on punishment (although rehabilitation programmes are also often provided). Linked to this, sentencing in the adult courts is predominantly focused on the offence, whereas in the youth courts greater attention is paid to the offender and his/her social development.

Some countries soften this kind of dramatic transition by having special provisions for young adult offenders. In England and Wales, however, this is true only to a small extent; offenders aged between 18 and 21, if given a custodial sentence, are normally sent not to a prison but to a Young Offenders Institution and their sentences must be followed by statutory supervision. However, conditions and facilities in Young Offender Institutions are not always very different from those in adult prisons.

When they turn 21, offenders are considered to be fully adult. The changing legal provisions between the ages 17 and 21 can therefore have some interesting consequences when co-offenders are dealt with. For example, if a 17-year-old, a 19-year-old, and a 21-year-old jointly commit an offence with equal responsibility, the 17-year-old might be dealt with by a supervision order supervised by the youth offending team, the 19-year-old might be sent to a Young Offenders Institution, while the 21-year-old might find him/herself entering an adult prison.

What is the justification for these changes, especially the dramatic change at age 18? Is there, at that age, a significant change in offenders' responsibility for their criminal acts? Many justifications have been put forward. It has been argued, for example, that juveniles have less mature judgement, poorer emotion-regulation, poorer self-regulation, poorer decision-making abilities, poorer executive functioning, poorer reasoning capacities, less ability to think abstractly and poorer planning skills. Arguably, juveniles also have poorer impulse control and are more likely to take risks and commit crimes for the sense of excitement rather than according to a rational cost-benefit calculation. In their decision-making, juveniles are thought to be more influenced by immediate desirable consequences than by delayed possible undesirable consequences. Allegedly, they are more susceptible to peer influences, more changeable, more redeemable and less set in their offending habits. Consequently, it can be argued that they are less culpable or blameworthy and are, therefore, less deserving of punishment. Also, they may have lower adjudicative competence and may thus find it hard to communicate with lawyers, make legal decisions, understand and participate in legal procedures, or stand trial.

Do all these abilities change dramatically at age 18? This seems unlikely. Legal age boundaries seem rather arbitrary. For example, 18 is the minimum legal age for voting and for drinking alcohol in England and Wales, but 17 is the minimum age for lawfully driving a car on a public road and 16 is the minimum legal age for heterosexual and homosexual intercourse and for getting married. There are also great variations in legal age boundaries between countries and even between states or provinces within a country, for example in the USA.

There have also been important changes over time. For example, although in the UK the legal age for voting was reduced from 21 to 18 in the second half of the twentieth century, paradoxically it is also true that more young adults aged between 18 and 25 were living independently of their parents in the 1950s than they are now. As Helyar-Cardwell (2009a, p. 11), has pointed out:

> People no longer, if they ever did, reach all of the associated responsibilities and recognised attributes of adulthood by the age of 18. Young adults in the 21st century live at home for longer, and depend on their families financially and emotionally for longer. Undoubtedly, there has been a major social shift over the last century, meaning that today's young adults live in a state of subsidised independence that relies on parental contributions towards their well being and lifestyle. In fact, almost half of 18–25 year-olds still rely on their parents for money as they are unable to meet the daily costs of living.

Building on such insights, Arnett (2000) coined the term 'Emerging Adulthood' to describe the age period from the late-teens to the mid-20s (roughly, the ages 18 to 25). He explained:

> The dominant theory of the life-course in developmental psychology, first proposed by Erikson (1950), postulated that adolescence, lasting from the beginning of puberty until the late teens, was followed by young adulthood, lasting from the late teens to about age 40 when middle adulthood began. This paradigm may have made sense in the middle of the 20th century when most people in industrialised societies married and entered stable full-time work by around age 20 or shortly after. However, by the end of the century, this paradigm no longer fit the normative pattern in industrialised societies. Median ages of marriage had risen into the late 20s, and the early to mid-20s became a time of frequent job changes and, for many people, pursuit of postsecondary education or training. Furthermore, sexual mores had changed dramatically, and premarital sex and cohabitation in the 20s had become widely accepted. Most young people now spent the period from their late teens to their mid-20s not settling into long-term adult roles but trying

out different experiences and gradually making their way toward enduring choices in love and work. The theory of emerging adulthood was proposed as a framework for recognising that the transition to adulthood was now long enough that it constituted not merely a transition but a separate period of the life course.

(Arnett 2007: 68–69)

From a criminological perspective, it is likely that such dramatic changes in the social roles and lifestyles of young people have had an impact on offending. Indeed, recent official crime statistics in various countries show that young adults between the ages of 18 to 21 now have higher prevalence rates in offending than juveniles (see chapter 6 of this volume). This does not necessarily mean that the traditional age–crime curve is no longer valid, but it does suggest that there may be a development towards a broader peak from late adolescence into young adulthood (at least for some types of offending).

Lost in Transition

Due to concerns over the legal treatment of young adult offenders, the Barrow Cadbury Trust established an independent Commission on Young Adults and the Criminal Justice System in 2004, which produced the report *Lost in Transition* in 2005 (Barrow Cadbury Trust 2005). This was the most important report on young adult offenders in England and Wales since the Younger Report of 1974 (Advisory Council on the Penal System 1974). In the Report, the Commission highlighted the fact that every offender aged 18 or over was treated as an adult and that sentencers were under no obligation to take account of the maturity of such offenders. The Commission also argued against using birthdays as indicators of adulthood and instead suggested that, ideally, there should be only one criminal justice system for offenders of all ages that took account of the needs and maturity of offenders of different ages.

More realistically, the Commission argued for special provisions to be made for young adult offenders that took account of their immaturity and malleability. It recommended that Transition to Adulthood (T2A) teams should be established in each local criminal justice area to oversee the treatment of young adult offenders and to ease their transition between the youth and adult justice systems. The Commission also argued that most young adult offenders would naturally desist from crime in their 20s as they matured and claimed that, because predominantly punitive reactions by the criminal justice system allegedly made them more likely to reoffend, there should be presumptions in favour of diversion and against custody for young adult offenders. The Commission also pointed out that nearly 70 per cent of incarcerated 18- to 20-year-olds were reconvicted within two years of their release; (although in the absence of comparative data for similar offenders receiving other sentences this statistic in itself does not necessarily prove that Young Offender Institutions are ineffective or damaging). Finally, the Commission also recommended that sentencers should be required to take account of the emotional

maturity of young adult offenders and that specialists in the National Offender
Management Service should provide an assessment of an offender's maturity in
court.

Criminal careers

According to official records of convictions, the probability of recidivism
decreases from the teenage years to the 20s. In the Cambridge Study in Delinquent Development (Farrington *et al.* 2006) – a prospective longitudinal survey of
411 London males from age 8 to age 50 – 70 per cent of juvenile delinquents (convicted between the ages of 10 and 17) were reconvicted as young adults (age 18
to 25), whereas only 45 per cent of young adult offenders were reconvicted as
older adults (age 26 to 50; see further chapter 4 of this volume). Furthermore, the
median age of the first conviction was 17, whereas the median age of the last conviction was 25, suggesting that many offenders desisted in their 20s. Lastly, in this
sample, the average length of a criminal career was 9 years.

The Cambridge Study also found that 67 per cent of London males who were
convicted between the ages of 10 and 15 were reconvicted between the ages of 16
and 20. By contrast, 40 per cent of males convicted between the ages of 16 and
20 were reconvicted between the ages of 21 and 25 and only 33 per cent of males
convicted between the ages of 21 and 25 were reconvicted between the ages of
26 and 30 (Farrington *et al.* 2006). For a national sample of males born in 1953,
Prime *et al.* (2001) found that the fraction of male offenders who were reconvicted
within five years of their release decreased from 42 per cent at age 17 to 16 per cent
at age 25. For female offenders, the fraction reconvicted in the same time frame
decreased only from 23 per cent at age 17 to 19 per cent at age 25. It is also known
that the decrease in the age–crime curve after the peak period is much steeper for
males than for females. The average criminal career length in this national sample
was 6.2 years for males and 1.8 years for females.

Bowles and Pradiptyo (2005) also analysed the 1953 birth cohort data and found
that – out of about 11,400 offenders in the cohort – about 2,500 desisted between
the ages of 18 and 20, about 1,500 between the ages of 21 and 24, and about 5,000
at age 25 or later. They reported that the peak age of desistance for male offenders
was at age 18, when about 600 males desisted. The age-desistance curve then
declined steadily, with about 400 offenders desisting at age 25 and less than 300
at age 30.

While the prevalence of offending and the probability of recidivism decrease
from the teenage years to the 20s, it does not necessarily follow that the average residual length (in years) of a criminal career (up to the age of desistance)
or the average residual number of offences in a criminal career would decline
similarly. However, Kazemian and Farrington (2006) investigated these quantities
in the Cambridge Study and found that they did decrease steadily with age. For
instance, the average residual career length decreased from 8.8 years for offenders
at age 18 to 6.1 years for offenders at age 25, and the average residual number
of offences decreased from 5.4 at age 18 to 3.8 at age 25. Arguably, these figures

should be taken into account by sentencers and they could be predicted by taking into account the age of the offender, the serial number of the conviction, the time since the last conviction, and the age of onset of offending.

There is also a need for long-term prospective longitudinal studies of more recent age cohorts who have fully experienced the above-mentioned epochal changes of extended youth and 'emerging adulthood'. Such studies should investigate whether the increased prevalence of crime among young adults also leads to changes in the typical patterns of criminal careers and desistance.

Maturity

Prior *et al.* (2011) carried out a very useful literature review for the Barrow Cadbury Trust entitled 'Maturity, Young Adults and Criminal Justice'. They found that physical maturity (the completion of puberty) usually occurred by age 12 or 13, whereas intellectual maturity was usually complete by age 18. However, the higher executive functions of the brain (such as planning, verbal memory and impulse control) may not be fully developed until age 25. As such, they concluded (p. 8) that 'the human brain is not mature until the early to mid-twenties'.

There is also increasing evidence that the brain continues to develop (including on going myelination) during childhood into early adolescence and adulthood, when white matter increases and synapses are pruned. Research also shows that 'the dorsal lateral prefrontal cortex, important for controlling impulses, is among the latest brain regions to mature without reaching adult dimensions until the early twenties' (Giedd 2004, p. 77). The importance of white matter is underscored by the discovery that decreased white matter is significantly more common among boys with psychopathic tendencies (De Brito *et al.* 2009). Biological changes in the prefrontal cortex during adolescence and the early 20s also lead to improvements in executive functioning, including reasoning, abstract thinking, planning, anticipating consequences, and impulse control (Sowell *et al.* 2001).

These findings on brain development, although mostly cross-sectional, are highly congruent with findings that show that reckless acts are still common until early adulthood; this is evident from data on the incidence of car accidents, even when the number of miles travelled is controlled for (Foss 2002). This is widely recognised by insurance companies, whose premiums for car insurance for young drivers (especially males) up to about age 25 are dramatically higher than for older drivers. It is also recognised by car rental companies who either do not rent cars to people under age 25 or levy a surcharge for drivers under that age.

The idea of improved behavioural controls emerging between late adolescence and early adulthood is also evident from psychological research. For example, Steinberg *et al.* (2009) investigated time perspective, planning ahead, and anticipation of consequences among individuals between the ages of 10 and 30. Although this was a cross-sectional study, the results suggest that the ability to plan ahead, along with the anticipation of consequences, improves dramatically between early adolescence and the early 20s, while time perspective improves slightly less in that same period. In general, the research found that psychosocial capacities that improve decision making and risk taking – such as impulse control, emotion regulation, delay of gratification, and resistance to peer influence – continue to mature well into young adulthood (Steinberg 2004).

Basing their work on the research done by Steinberg and Cauffman (1996), Prior *et al.* (2011) divided psychosocial maturity into three categories: responsibility (the ability to act independently, to be self-reliant and to have a clear sense of personal identity); temperance (the ability to limit impulsiveness, to control aggressive responses and risk-taking, and to think before acting); and perspective (the ability to understand and consider the views of others before taking a decision to act). Prior *et al.* (2011) concluded that temperance was especially related to offending. Yet, while responsibility and perspective tended to become relatively settled around age 18, temperance continued to develop up to the mid- to late 20s (Modecki 2008). Prior *et al.* (2011) also discussed the fact that females usually mature earlier than males and referred to the need to distinguish between adolescence-limited and life-course-persistent offenders (see Moffitt 1993). They also advocated the use of instruments to assess maturity in the criminal justice system, highlighting the work of Soderstrom *et al.* (2001) in this respect. In conclusion, their review suggested that extending the age-range for young adult offending up to the age of 25 would be justifiable based on knowledge about physiological and psychological development during maturity.

European perspectives

As Dünkel and Pruin point out in chapter 2 of this volume, the International Association of Penal Law passed a final resolution in 2004 stating that the applicability of the special provisions for offending juveniles could be extended up to the age of 25. Since 1953, young adults in Germany aged between 18 and 21 can be dealt with in the juvenile courts, which are structured so as to allow for the needs of the young adult to be taken into account, and which have an emphasis on educational and rehabilitative measures. Whether the young adult receives a juvenile or adult sanction depends (at least in theory) on whether the moral and psychological development of that young adult is like that of a juvenile and whether the offence committed resembles a typical juvenile crime (e.g. spontaneous, unplanned, and motivated by anger). In this way, Germany has attempted to conform to the 2003 Council of Europe recommendation that young adult offenders under the age of 21 should be treated in a way comparable to juveniles when the judge is of the opinion that they are not as mature or as responsible for their actions as a fully developed adult (see chapter 2 of this volume). In practice, this means that the majority of offenders in Germany aged between 18 and 21 are referred to the juvenile justice system.

Some other European countries, including Sweden and Austria, have separate young adult sentencing options and separate institutions for 18- to 21-year-olds (see Transition to Adulthood Alliance 2010). The Netherlands, the Scandinavian countries, and the countries of the former Yugoslavia also either have special provisions for young adults within the general criminal law framework or provide for the possibility of avoiding the requirements of the adult law. For instance, in Sweden there is 'youth mitigation' up to age 21; while in Finland all those who committed their crime under age 21 are treated by the prison service as juveniles. In Switzerland, young adults can be treated as juveniles until they are aged 25.

Recent developments

In chapter 10 of this book, Rob Allen has reviewed initiatives taken by the Transition to Adulthood Alliance since the publication of *Lost in Transition*. Their two most significant documents were published in 2009: 'A New Start' (Helyar-Cardwell 2009a) and the 'Young Adult Manifesto' (Helyar-Cardwell 2009b). The Manifesto recommended that young adult offenders aged between 18 and 24 should be recognised as a distinct group. Additionally, it advocated that the government should consider how maturity and developmental progress could be taken into consideration in the sentencing of young adults and suggested that they should pilot a maturity assessment instrument for use by the criminal justice system. The Manifesto also recommended that there should be more diversion of young adult offenders away from the courts, increased use of restorative justice, the abolition of short sentences for non-violent offenders, and more support provided in the community to deal with the drug, alcohol, mental health, and employment problems of young adult offenders. An economic analysis of interventions for young adult offenders (Barrow Cadbury Trust 2009) estimated that diversion from adult courts to juvenile courts following a maturity assessment would save £420 per offender, diversion from custody to community orders would save £1,032 per offender, and diversion from community orders to pre-court restorative justice would save £7,050 per offender. On the evidence, we believe that these recommendations are reasonable.

Such differentiated approaches would, we believe, take more adequate account of young adulthood as a particularly important age period for desistance. They would help prevent young adult offenders in custody from having to mix with older adults, who not only differ in many social aspects (Stewart 2008), but also often have more extensive criminal careers. This could exert an undesirable influence on younger offenders and may increase the criminogenic effects of incarceration, as has been suggested by recent research on deterrence (Durlauf and Nagin 2011).

The contribution of this volume

This volume contributes to this developing field of criminological analysis in two main ways. First, it offers some major overviews of the key themes directly relevant to policy choices as regards young adult offenders. In chapter 2, Frieder Dünkel and Ineke Pruin comprehensively survey the very varied legislative and policy approaches to the treatment of young adult offenders in different European countries, and their analysis provides much food for thought as one considers possible future strategies for offenders in this important transitional age-range. As noted above, Rob Allen's contribution in chapter 10 also focuses directly on policy analysis; he describes the little-known policy initiatives for young adult offenders that have been introduced in England and Wales – with special reference to the work of the Transition to Adulthood Alliance – since the publication of *Lost In Transition* in 2005, the third policy overview, provided in chapter 6 by Friedrich Lösel, has a rather different orientation and is chiefly concerned with reviewing the empirical research evidence relating to the success or otherwise of rehabilitative programmes. In this chapter, Lösel shows that – surprisingly, given the important 'transitional' status of this age-group – there is little high-quality evaluative research focusing specifically on the rehabilitation of young adult offenders; accordingly, it is mostly necessary to rely on inferences gleaned from the more general body of research on rehabilitative effectiveness for juveniles and adults. In looking at the empirical evidence on 'what works' and the many relevant factors beyond the programmes, Lösel notes the recent emergence of sometimes polarised debates about the relative merits of what have been called the 'Risk-Need-Responsivity' (RNR), the 'Good Lives', and the 'Desistance' paradigms of rehabilitation. He argues that social scientists should pay less attention to 'controversies about the "right" paradigms' and focus more on developing careful theoretical and empirical knowledge that has the proven potential to reduce reoffending.

The three overview chapters described above all have their origins in a 2007 Cropwood Conference organised by the Cambridge University Institute of Criminology in response to the *Lost in Transition* report – although each has been comprehensively revised and updated in 2011. The other chapters in the volume all have the same origin, but – because of their different character – they have been less fully revised. Between them, however, they have some very important messages to convey, and in the remainder of this Introduction we shall try to highlight some of these messages.

Chapters 3 to 5 focus on three specific aspects of the research literature relating to this age-group. In chapter 3, Mary McMurran reminds us that, although criminologists tend to focus on the young adult age-range because criminality both peaks and begins to decelerate during these years, young adulthood is also an important age-range as this is when drinking alcohol to excess (with its associated aggression) is particularly prevalent. As her chapter makes clear, the research evidence strongly supports adopting a multi-dimensional approach to this issue, although McMurran, who is herself a psychologist, focuses especially on individual-level explanation and treatment.

In chapter 4, David Farrington provides an in-depth analysis of the evidence relating to offending and desistance in young adulthood that can be gleaned from the most important British study of criminal careers, the Cambridge Study in Delinquent Development. This chapter therefore elaborates on some of the points made earlier in this introduction. Because late adolescence and young adulthood coincide with the peak age of conviction, and because many young adult offenders have previous convictions as juveniles, it is not surprising that the number of custodial sentences awarded to young adults is substantial. In chapter 5, therefore, Alison Liebling analyses some of the research evidence relating to the experience of young adults in custodial institutions. She highlights the vulnerability that such offenders sometimes display when in custody – demonstrated, for example, through suicide attempts – but she also draws attention to the more positive effects that 'the moral and social climate of institutions' (including especially, the nature of relationships) can play in influencing offenders' futures.

Chapters 7 and 8 focus especially on research evidence relating to desistance among young adults. In chapter 7, Monica Barry focuses upon the experiences of young women offenders, drawing on her Scottish desistance study which included both males and females, predominantly from the young adult age-range (Barry 2006). Among other things, Barry suggests that 'the women were more concerned [than the men] about their reputations in the wider community [and] their need to be good mothers', all of which helped to generate 'a new sense of responsibility and care' in their lives. There are clearly links here to the psychological literature on maturity, discussed earlier. Chapter 8 by Joanna Shapland, Anthony Bottoms and Grant Muir, emanates from the Sheffield Desistance Study, a longitudinal study of persistent young male offenders first interviewed at (on average) at age 20. In their contribution to this volume the authors focus especially on their subjects' perceptions of the criminal justice system, which were not as positive as one might have hoped: for example, in answer to a general question about how useful probation supervision had been, as many as 45 per cent answered 'not at all useful'. On the basis of their empirical evidence, Shapland and her colleagues argue that, for previously persistent offenders, desistance means 'learning to lead a non-offending life in the community' and they then go on to suggest ways in which the probation service might more actively assist would-be desisters in this quest.

Finally – and returning to the point we made at the start of this introduction – if young adult offenders are to receive the best possible assistance in turning away from crime, it is vital for their experiences of youth justice to have been as constructive as possible, and also that the transition from youth justice to young adult justice should not be experienced as unhelpfully discontinuous. These themes are addressed in chapter 9 by Rod Morgan, originally written when he was still Chair of the Youth Justice Board for England and Wales, and now updated for this volume.

We offer this volume as a contribution to the very important and timely debate currently going on about the treatment of young adult offenders. It is certain that policy is lagging behind research evidence in this field, and we hope that our volume will make a contribution by emphasising the need for special provisions to be made for young adults aged between 18 and 24.

References

Advisory Council on the Penal System (1974). *Young Adult Offenders*. London: HMSO.

Arnett, J. J. (2000). 'Emerging adulthood: A theory of development from the late teens through the twenties'. *American Psychologist*, 55, 469–480.

Arnett, J. J. (2007). 'Emerging adulthood: What is it, and what is it good for?'. *Child Development Perspectives*, 1, 68–73.

Barrow Cadbury Trust (2005). *Lost in Transition*. London: Barrow Cadbury Trust.

Barrow Cadbury Trust (2009). *Economic Analysis of Interventions for Young Adult Offenders.* London: Barrow Cadbury Trust.

Barry, M. (2006). *Youth Offending in Transition: The Search for Social Recognition.* London: Routledge.

Bowles, R. and Pradiptyo, R. (2005). *Young Adults in the Criminal Justice System: Cost and Benefit Considerations.* York: Centre for Criminal Justice Economics and Psychology, University of York.

De Brito, S. A., Mechelli, A., Wilke, M., Laurens, K. R., Jones, A. P., Barker, G. J., Hodgins, S. and Viding, E. (2009). 'Size matters: Increased grey matter in boys with conduct problems and callous–unemotional traits'. *Brain: A Journal of Neurology*, 132, 843–852.

Durlauf, S. N. and Nagin, D. S. (2011). 'Imprisonment and crime: Can both be reduced?'. *Criminology & Public Policy*, 10, 13–54.

Farrington, D. P., Coid, J. W., Harnett, L., Jolliffe, D., Soteriou, N., Turner, R. and West, D. J. (2006). *Criminal Careers up to Age 50 and Life Success up to Age 48: New Findings from the Cambridge Study in Delinquent Development.* London: Home Office (Research Study No. 299).

Foss R. D. (2002). 'Graduated driver licensing to reduce teen fatalities'. *Proceedings from: Translating injury prevention research into action: a strategic workshop.* The David and Lucille Packard Foundation. Dallas, Texas, (February).

Giedd, J. N. (2004). 'Structural magnetic resonance imaging of the adolescent brain'. *Annals of the New York Academy of Sciences*, 1021, 77–85.

Helyar-Cardwell, V. (2009a). *A New Start: Young Adults in the Criminal Justice System.* London: Transition to Adulthood Alliance.

Helyar-Cardwell, V. (2009b). *Young Adult Manifesto.* London: Transition to Adulthood Alliance.

Kazemian, L. and Farrington, D. P. (2006). 'Exploring residual career length and residual number of offences for two generations of repeat offenders'. *Journal of Research in Crime and Delinquency*, 43, 89–113.

Modecki, K. L. (2008). 'Addressing gaps in the maturity judgment literature: Age differences and delinquency'. *Law and Human Behaviour*, 32, 78–91.

Moffitt, T. E. (1993). 'Adolescence-limited and life-course-persistent antisocial behaviour: A developmental taxonomy'. *Psychological Review*, 100, 674–701.

Prime, J., White, S., Liriano, S. and Patel, K. (2001). *Criminal Careers of Those Born Between 1953 and 1978.* London: Home Office (Statistical Bulletin 4/01).

Prior, D., Farrow, K., Hughes, N., Kelly, G., Manders, G., White, S. and Wilkinson, B. (2011). *Maturity, Young Adults and Criminal Justice.* Birmingham: Institute of Applied Social Studies, School of Social Policy, University of Birmingham.

Soderstrom, I. R., Castellano, T. C. and Figaro, H. R. (2001). 'Measuring mature coping skills among adult and juvenile offenders: A psychometric assessment of relevant instruments'. *Criminal Justice and Behaviour*, 28, 300–328.

Sowell, E. R., Delis, D., Stiles, J. and Jernigan, T. L. (2001). 'Improved memory functioning and frontal lobe maturation between childhood and adolescence: A structural MRI study'. *Journal of the International Neuropsychological Society*, 7, 312–322.

Steinberg, L. (2004). 'Risk taking in adolescence: What changes, and why?'. *Annals of the New York Academy of Sciences*, 1021, 51–58.

Steinberg, L., Cauffman, E., Woolard, J., Graham, S. and Banich, M. (2009). 'Are adolescents less mature than adults? Minors' access to abortion, the juvenile death penalty, and the alleged APA "flip-flop"'. *American Psychologist*, 64, 583–594.

Steinberg, L. and Cauffman, E. (1996). 'Maturity of judgment in adolescence: Psychosocial factors in adolescent decision making'. *Law and Human Behaviour*, 20, 249–272.

Stewart, D. (2008). *The Problems and Needs of Newly Sentenced Prisoners: Results from a National Survey.* London: Ministry of Justice (Research Series 16/08).

Transition to Adulthood Alliance (2010). *Young Adults and Criminal Justice: International Norms and Practices.* London: Transition to Adulthood Alliance.

2 Young adult offenders in juvenile and criminal justice systems in Europe

Frieder Dünkel and Ineke Pruin

The question of dealing with young adult offenders is one of the most important areas of juvenile justice reform in Europe. On 24 September 2003, the Committee of Ministers of the Council of Europe passed Recommendation 20 on 'New ways of dealing with juvenile delinquency and the role of juvenile justice'. Rule 11 of this Recommendation states the following:

> Reflecting the extended transition to adulthood, it should be possible for young adults under the age of 21 to be treated in a way comparable to juveniles and to be subject to the same interventions, when the judge is of the opinion that they are not as mature and responsible for their actions as full adults.

In September 2004, the International Association of Penal Law (AIDP) held its World Congress in Beijing, China. The final Resolution of the Congress emphasized 'that the state of adolescence can be prolonged into young adulthood (25 years) and that, as a consequence, legislation needs to be adapted for young adults in a similar way as it is done for minors'. It was recommended that the age of criminal majority should be set at age 18 and, in no circumstances, lower than age 14 (see part number 2 of the Resolution). Part Number 6 of the Resolution also states that: 'concerning crimes committed by persons over 18 years of age, the applicability of the special provisions for minors may be extended up to the age of 25'.

On 5 November 2008, the Committee of Ministers of the Council of Europe passed Recommendation 11 on the European Rules for Juvenile Offenders Subject to Sanctions or Measures (ERJOSSM). One of the basic principles underpinning this document was set out in Rule 17, which states that 'young adult offenders may, where appropriate, be regarded as juveniles and dealt with accordingly'. The commentary to this Rule goes on to explain that:

> It is an evidence-based policy to encourage legislators to extend the scope of juvenile justice to the age group of young adults. Processes of education and integration into social life of adults have been prolonged and more appropriate constructive reactions with regard to the particular developmental problems of young adults can often be found in juvenile justice legislation.
>
> (Council of Europe 2009: 42)

This paper will describe the background to these recommendations, with special emphasis being placed on German legislation and practice which incorporates the most far-reaching extension of the scope of juvenile justice in Europe. This is followed by a comparative overview which demonstrates that more and more countries are following the German approach and that most countries now provide for some special treatment of young adults in their criminal justice system.

Before proceeding, however, we must clarify the formal status of international instruments like the Council of Europe's 2003 Recommendation. Such Recommendations, unless they are formally incorporated into national law, are not binding for national legislators; thus, they are sometimes called 'soft laws'. However, in May 2006 the German Constitutional Court delivered an important decision regarding the persuasive force of such Recommendations:

> It could be an indication that insufficient attention has been paid to the constitutional requirements of taking into account current knowledge and giving appropriate weight to the interests of the inmates if the requirements of international law or of international standards with human rights implications, such as the guidelines or recommendations adopted by the organs of the United Nations or the Council of Europe are not taken into account or if the legislation falls below these requirements.
>
> (BVerfG Neue Juristische Wochenschrift 2006: 2093 ff.;
> a similar statement can be found in a decision of the
> Swiss Federal Constitutional Court in 1992)

Reasons for special legislation for young adults in the criminal justice system

It is one of the major achievements of modern worldwide juvenile criminal policy that minors or juveniles are now supposed to be dealt with differently from adults. This has been recognized by the United Nations Standard Minimum Rules for the Administration of Juvenile Justice (the so-called Beijing Rules of 1985) and by the Council of Europe's Recommendations; such as those on 'Social Reactions to Juvenile Delinquency' of 1987 (Rec [1987] 20) and 'New ways of dealing with juvenile delinquency' (2003: see above).

The empirical criminological base upon which this worldwide standard is based is the evidence that juvenile delinquency is regularly of a petty nature and often ceases to be an issue as young people grow into adulthood. This episodic pattern, therefore, justifies a more tolerant approach to juvenile delinquency. In addition, it is also necessary for the state welfare authorities to provide appropriate support because, as young persons are in a stage of continuous personal development, educational measures are more appropriate than traditional punishments. As a result, in all European countries juvenile legislation provides for special educational measures and sanctions in order not to compromise the developmental process of young persons who are in the transitional stage from youth to adulthood. This also applies for the Scandinavian countries, even though they do not have a separate juvenile justice system.

A further argument for separate juvenile justice systems is based on the idea of '*doli incapax*' (i.e. a diminished criminal capacity). This continental European doctrine – based on early nineteenth-century French law – differentiates two elements of criminal responsibility: first the juvenile or child must be able to recognize the difference between right and wrong, and second, they must have the ability to act according to their own insight. Juvenile systems that emphasize the second of these two elements of 'responsibilization' will generally establish a higher minimum age for criminal responsibility; as in Germany, for example, where the minimum age is 14 years old or in Scandinavia where the age is 15 years old. Children below this age can then be made 'responsible' under civil law or juvenile welfare law; this opens the door for restorative justice and reparation measures to be implemented within an educational approach.

Given this background, then, what were the reasons for the Council of Europe's decision to produce their 2003 proposal to integrate young adults into the juvenile justice system? Section Number 11 of the Recommendation 20 (2003) and Number 17 of the ERJOSSM refer to the 'extended transition to adulthood'. This concept is based on criminological, psychological and sociological research highlighting the changes that have taken place in the living contexts of young adult persons over the last 50 years. We now want to highlight some aspects of these new insights with respect to some German and European data (see Dünkel and Pruin 2010).

Criminological aspects: the age–crime curve and research on developmental aspects of criminal careers

Germany is an appropriate case study for young adult offenders, as the legal framework of German juvenile law allows for the statistical differentiation of this age group. The police statistics, as well as the so-called '*Strafverfolgungsstatistik*' (statistics on court decisions), also provide separate data about 18- to 21-year-old young adult offenders.[1]

From Figure 2.1 we can see the conviction rates per-100,000 of the age group. The data show that during the last few decades, young adults have always had the highest risk of conviction compared to juveniles and adults of over 21.

If we then look more closely at the conviction rates of different age groups, the well-known phenomenon of age and crime distribution gives evidence that crime decreases after a peak between the ages of 21 and 25: this produces the so-called 'age–crime curve' (see Figure 2.2).

Furthermore, during our research we found that the German statistics also show an interesting trend concerning changes in conviction statistics since 1900. Notably, the peak of prevalence rates has altered: in 1886/95 the peak was between the ages of 18 and 21 – a pattern that was maintained even in 1970 and 1980 – but since the 1990s it has increased to age 25. In other words, even though the general shape of the age–crime curve has not changed since the beginning of the

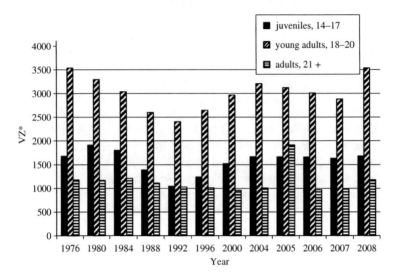

Figure 2.1 Convicted juveniles and young adults in Germany, 1976–2008.

*VZ: Convicted persons per 100,000 of the age group; data 1976–2006: West Germany; 2007–2008: total Germany.

Source: Statistisches Bundesamt (Ed.), Strafverfolgungsstatistik 1976–2008, Table 1.1.

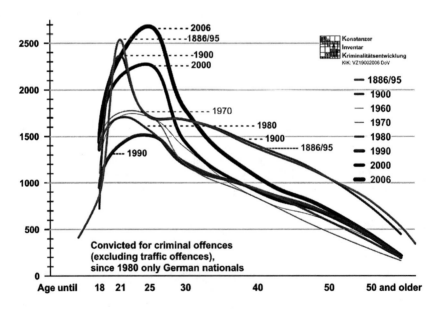

Figure 2.2 Conviction rates according to age groups in Germany, 1886–2006 (per 100,000 of the age group).

Source: *Spieß* 2008, p. 10.

last century, the peak has moved significantly to the right so that it encompasses the age group between 21 and 25 (Spieß 2008: 10).

Looking at the differences between males and females also reveals that the peak for female offenders is earlier than the one for male suspects or convicts (Heinz 2003: 62, Spieß 2008: 15 and Pruin 2007: 115 ff). However, the sharp decrease in the police-registered prevalence rates, as well as in conviction rates, continues for both genders until the age of 30. The age–crime curve is an indicator of the episodic (temporary) nature of 'normal' juvenile crime (Heinz 2003: 74; Bundesministerium des Innern/Bundesministerium der Justiz 2006: 354 ff.) and it can be seen as a universal phenomenon in all countries (Cavadino and Dignan 2002: 285; Junger-Tas *et al.* 2009; Stevens 2009). Nevertheless, as Friedrich Lösel and others have shown, there is still a small group of so-called 'persistent offenders' who continue with criminal activities for longer periods. In most cases, though, even this group discontinues offending in later periods of their lives (Sampson and Laub 1993: 35 f.; 2009).

Over time, the structure of juvenile delinquency has not changed very much in general, although registered violent crime and drug offences have increased in many countries during the last 20 years. This increase is partly due to the increased rate of reporting cases of violence to the police. Furthermore, it has to be emphasized that this increase in registered (violent) crimes and self-reported delinquency during the early 1990s has already levelled-off, and one can actually observe a decline since the early 2000s in many European countries. This has certainly been the case in Eastern Europe, which experienced specific problems after the social changes at the end of the 1980s.[2]

Overall, juveniles and young adults still predominantly commit less serious crimes. Self-reporting and other studies demonstrate that in the transition from juvenile to adult criminality, many persistent offenders discontinue with crime; which is yet another indicator of the episodic nature of juvenile and young adult crime (Heinz 2003: 36 f.; Stelly and Thomas 2001; Farrington, Coid and West 2009).

In the light of the criminological literature, therefore, we can say that the phenomenon of ubiquitous and episodic juvenile crime – which has been the reason behind creating a special juvenile justice system – is also today applicable to young adults.

Psychological and sociological considerations

Changes in the living contexts of young adults have been shown to take place by psychological and sociological research studies. In the field of psychology, it is assumed that the 'transition' from childhood to adulthood takes place through the development of an independent identity. Since the middle of the twentieth century, research in developmental psychology has increasingly focused on sociologically orientated theories of adolescence. These highlight the influence that environmental factors have on a person's development, as well as looking at the specific individuality of stages of development through changing living contexts, specific requirements/demands, increased access to information, and individually-varying life experiences (Fend 2003; Oerter and Montada 2008).

German sociological research shows, however, that the very social environment within which these transitions occur has changed considerably in the last 50 years. These changes occurred particularly in those fields of life that are deemed most significant for a person's integration into adult society and the development of one's own, independent identity (Hurrelmann 2007). For instance, the point in time at which juveniles and young adults enter adult life and become, at least financially, in a position to establish their own identity has been considerably post-poned. In the 1950s, more than 70 per cent of German juveniles finished school at the age of 14 or 15 in order to enter the labour market. Nowadays, German sociologists assume that the age at which a job will provide longer-term financial independence has increased to the age of 25 (Hurrelmann 2007: 39).

On the one hand, this development can be accounted for by changes in the employment market in the last 50 years. Employers have been requiring increasing levels of qualifications from their employees, vocational training and academic degrees are gaining increasing importance, and regular school education has also been prolonged (pupils at high schools generally graduate at the age of 19). On the other hand, the structures of basic schooling as well as vocational education could possibly have been deliberately elongated since the mid-1970s in order to prevent the labour market becoming even further overburdened. This has been, in part, attributed to the pan-European problem of youth unemployment (Hurrelmann 2007: 22; Wahler 2000: 183 ff.).

Furthermore, developments in the economy, intensification of competition, and industrial restructuring have all led to growing demands for increased labour mar-ket flexibility and a reduction of social protection within labour laws (Golsch 2008). This especially affects young people who are in the specific phase of transition between leaving school and entering the labour market known as the 'school-to-work-transition' (see Kurz *et al.* 2008). In many European countries, a substantial increase in temporary or fixed-term jobs can be observed (Bukodi *et al.* 2008; Kurz *et al.* 2008) and there have been significant increases in the length of the search period needed to find a first job (see Buchholz and Kurz 2008; Kurz *et al.* 2008). Labour market entrants aged between 16 and 29 are affected the most by this increase in employment insecurity (Golsch 2008; Blossfeld *et al.* 2005). Furthermore, in many Eastern European countries the processes for enter-ing the labour market also became turbulent after the regime changes at the end of the twentieth century (Kurz *et al.* 2008). Nevertheless, youth unemployment is a European-wide phenomenon (Golsch 2008: Figure 2.1 for data on 10 European countries). To sum up, we can observe from these developments that young adults today increasingly encounter a long period of financial insecurity and a huge degree of dependence, both of which complicate the development of an indepen-dent personality and life structure, which is the most important 'developmental task' in the phase of young adulthood.

Detachment from one's family is regarded as a further important aspect in the development of an individual identity. According to traditional sociological perspectives, this detachment occurs through the founding of one's own family and/or through the establishment of stable bonds to a partner. Yet, according to European data, considerable changes have also occurred in this context (see Figures 2.3 and 2.4).

As can be seen from Figures 2.3 and 2.4, both the average age of mothers at the time of birth of their first child and the average age at which people marry have increased considerably. Moreover, individual life concepts have experienced such a degree of change in the last 50 years that sociologists now point to a change away from the traditional life course towards a 'pluralisation of life concepts' (see Brüderl 2004) in which individual views and decisions can be, and are, acted out.

Another indicator of the emergence of a more prolonged process of transition to adulthood can be seen by looking at the proportion of young adults still living with their parents. A comparative statistic developed by the European Commission shows that throughout Europe, with the exception of Finland, about 50 per cent of 20 to 24 year old young adults (up to almost 90 per cent in Italy and Spain) still live with their parents (see Figure 2.5). Out of those who have left their parental home in the UK, about 20 per cent got married and another 20 per cent found a stable job.

Therefore, we can conclude from the findings of sociological research that, as regards the establishment of an individual personal identity, meaningful and significant roles are now being assumed at comparatively later points in the life course. Furthermore, the sequence of events has also changed. In the past, it could

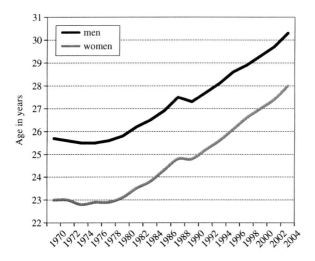

Figure 2.3 Mean age of marriage in Europe, 1970–2004.

Note: The data is taken from Austria, Belgium, Czech Republic, Cyprus, Denmark, England and Wales, Estonia, Finland, Germany, Greece, Spain, France, Hungary, Ireland, Italy, Latvia, Lithuania, Luxembourg, Malta, Netherlands, Poland, Portugal, Slovenia, Slovakia and Sweden.

Source: Office for Official Publications of the European Communities, 2006.

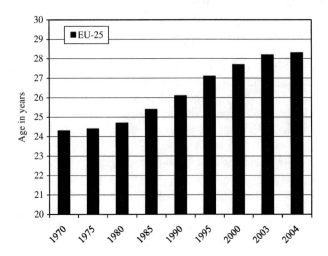

Figure 2.4 Mean age of mothers in years at the time of birth of their first child in Europe, 1970–2004.

Note: The data is from the same countries featured in Figure 2.3.

Source: Office for Official Publications of the European Communities, 2006.

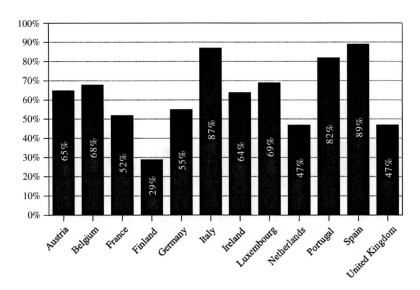

Figure 2.5 European comparison of young adults living with their parents.

Source: European Commission, *Youth in the European Union*, 1997.

be seen as normal for certain events in the life course to occur in a particular order (school graduation, first sexual experiences, moving out from the parents' home several years after the completion of vocational training, the establishment of one's own family, etc.). Nowadays, however, such a 'universal' succession of events in the life course can no longer be assumed. The relatively short 'status passage of adolescence', which had previously been associated with a relatively low degree of autonomy and which was viewed as a phase of introduction into and preparation for adult life, has now been broadened. In addition, a fundamental social tendency towards individualization has apparently reduced the amount of structure and standardization in this phase of life (Grunert and Krüger 2000; Deutsche Shell 2002: 33 ff.).

Implications of the findings for modern criminal policy

The results and findings now presented here, briefly disclose what the Council of Europe Recommendation 20 (2003) aimed to convey with its phrase about the 'extended transition to adulthood'. Nowadays, insecurities regarding the future, as well as dependencies that prevent the establishment of an individual personal identity, endure over a longer biographical period and do not end once the legal age of majority has been attained. What had previously been 'normal' in childhood and adolescence now applies to young adulthood as well. Likewise, the mean age at which episodic criminal behaviour discontinues has also shifted upwards. As such, the arguments and justifications for the special treatment of minors in criminal law therefore now also apply to young adults. Moreover, there are assumed correlations between these results. For example, the relevance of a certain degree of stability in the spheres of employment and personal relationships to desistance from criminal behaviour is particularly emphasized in Sampson and Laub's developmental theory of crime (Laub and Sampson 2003; Sampson and Laub 1993, 2009).[3]

What are the consequences of these social developments for modern criminal policy? It can reasonably be concluded that for young adults – as is the case for juveniles – tentative or cautious penal interventions with flexible, supportive, and rehabilitative provisions are more advisable than predominantly repressive measures with their known disintegrative effects (Pruin 2007: 153 ff.). Such an integrative approach will better promote the development of an individual personal identity as well as the attainment of a certain degree of stability, which will in turn result in desistance from the sort of episodic criminal behaviour that is typical of young people. As a result, the Council of Europe has called for the incorporation of young adults into juvenile criminal law because it is precisely in the sphere of youth justice that such interventions are already provided in many European countries today. The adult criminal justice systems, by contrast, normally adopt more repressive and less re-integrative responses to criminal behaviour.

The German system for dealing with young adult offenders: law and practice

Since a reform of the law in 1953, all young adults in Germany are now transferred to the jurisdiction of juvenile courts. From an international perspective, this decision was remarkable and, coming at such an early stage of European development, it pointed the way towards extending the scope of juvenile courts for young adults between the ages of 18 and 21.

Other European countries subsequently followed Germany's approach (see below). However, in these countries the application of educational measures for young adults remained the exception. By contrast, developments in Germany have been comprehensive and a major reason for this has undoubtedly been the reforms of 1953 which placed all young offenders within the jurisdiction of the juvenile court, independently of whether the sanctions of the Juvenile Justice Act (JJA) or of the general Penal Law (StGB) were to be applied (see § 108 (2) JJA).

The way in which German system works is shown graphically in Figure 2.6.

As can be seen, the application of juvenile criminal law enables the juvenile judge to choose educational measures (such as community service orders) or other restorative measures (like victim–offender mediation) or social training interventions in order to improve social skills, etc. (see Figure 2.7 below). These sanctions can be tailored according to the educational needs of each individual offender. As a last resort, the imposition of a youth prison sentence is possible, which in general will be shorter than for adults as the sentencing frames of the general StGB do not apply (see section 18 Juvenile Justice Act).

The application of adult criminal law, on the other hand, offers little room for constructive sentencing as the German Criminal Law for adults provides only for fines, suspended sentences (probation), and unconditional imprisonment. Moreover, the judge is more-or-less bound to the formal sentencing framework and

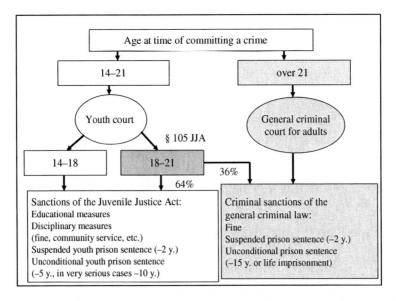

Figure 2.6 German system of dealing with young adult (18–21 year old) offenders.

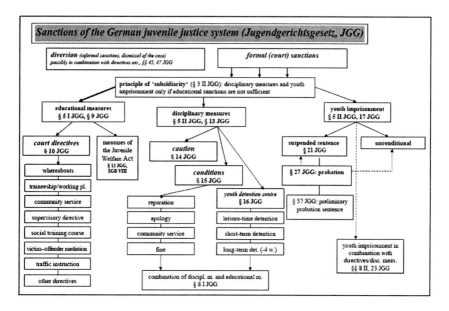

Figure 2.7 The German juvenile sanctions system.

Source: Dünkel 2006: 259.

there is less room for individualized sentencing. By contrast, the procedural regulations of juvenile law provide greater possibilities for mitigation by diversionary measures compared to the criminal procedure for adults (Pruin 2007: 35 ff.).

Section 105 (1) No. 1 of the JJA allows for the application of juvenile law to a young adult if 'a global examination of the offender's personality and of his social environment indicates that at the time of committing the crime the young adult in his moral and psychological development was like a juvenile' ('Reifeentwicklung'). Furthermore, it is also stated that juvenile law has to be applied if it appears that the motives and the circumstances of the offence are similar to those of a typical juvenile crime ('Jugendverfehlung', see § 105 (1) No. 2 JJA).

The Federal Supreme Court (the '*Bundesgerichtshof*' or 'BGH') stipulates that a young adult has the maturity of a juvenile if 'elements demonstrate that a considerable development of the personality is still to be seen' ('Entwicklungskräfte noch in größerem Umfang wirksam sind', BGHSt 12, 116; 36, 38). This tends to be the case with the majority of young adult offenders. Thus, the court does not rely upon an imagined prototype of a juvenile personality, but upon aspects of each individual's personal development. As early as the beginning of the 1960s, the BGH was basing its definitions upon sociological and psychological empirical evidence based on changes in the living contexts of young adults. There is no doubt that these arguments could also permit a further extension of the juvenile court's jurisdiction, for example for 21- to 24-year-old adults.

The interpretation of a 'typical juvenile crime', which is extensively used in Germany, follows a similar logic. As mentioned above, the second alternative in section 105 of the JJA allows for the application of sanctions from the juvenile law if it appears that the motives and the circumstances for the offence are those of a typical juvenile crime ('*Jugendverfehlung*', see § 105 (1) No. 2 JJA). The BGH (BGHSt 8, 90) has also declared that typical juvenile crimes are 'spontaneous acts resulting from the developmental forces of juvenile age' ('*aus den Antriebskräften der Entwicklung entspringende Entgleisungen*'). Examples of such 'typical juvenile crimes' include: spontaneous and anger-motivated behaviour, aggressive acts with slight reason behind them, vandalism, or hooliganism.[4] The jurisprudence of youth courts is not restricted to minor crimes only, but also includes serious crimes. For example, the BGH accepted applying sanctions (typically, youth prison) from the JJA in one case where a 21-year-old young adult killed his three-month-old baby because he was angered by the baby's crying (BGH NStZ 1986: 549).

As can be seen in Figure 2.8, the German juvenile courts have gradually become convinced of the value of the application of juvenile law to young adults. For example, in 1965 only 38 per cent of young adults were sentenced under the JJA, but by 1990 this had nearly doubled to 64 per cent. In 1995 the proportion decreased slightly to 60 per cent, but it then increased again to 64 per cent in 2006 and 66 per cent in 2008 (see Dünkel 2002; 2010: 588 ff.). This trend clearly indicates that the full integration of young adults into the juvenile justice system has been accepted in practice. The regulations mentioned above have also been

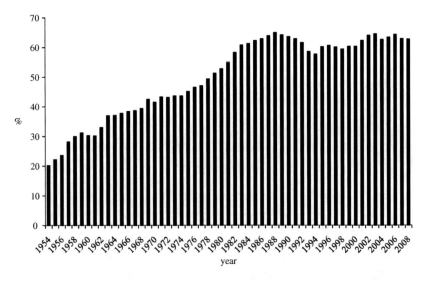

Figure 2.8 Proportion of young adults sentenced according to juvenile law in West Germany, 1954–2006, and in the whole of Germany, 2007–2008.

Source: *Statistisches Bundesamt* (ed.): Strafverfolgungsstatistik 1955–2008, own calculations.

widely interpreted by the courts to allow for the application of juvenile law in all cases where there are doubts about the maturity of the young offender (BGHSt, 12: 116; BGH Strafverteidiger 1989: 311; Eisenberg 2010, notes 7 ff. to § 105). These developments can largely be attributed to the greater flexibility of the juvenile justice law in comparison to the limited sanctioning options of the general criminal law (Pruin 2007: 98 ff.; Dünkel 2010: 587 ff.).

The application of the juvenile justice law differs slightly for young adult men and young adult women (see Figure 2.9). In 2008 65 per cent of young adult men and 52 per cent of young adult women were sentenced to a sanction taken from the JJA, while the remaining convicted young adults were dealt with according to the general criminal law (StGB). This, however, does not indicate the existence of a harsher sentencing practice towards female offenders. Rather, it indicates that they are more involved in less serious crimes (such as theft, fraud, and minor drug or traffic offences) that can be, and in some Federal States regularly are, punished by summary fines according to the general criminal law (Heinz 2003: 63; Bundesministerium des Innern und Bundesministerium der Justiz 2006: 552 ff.). Furthermore, in practice there are considerable differences with respect to specific crimes and their treatment in different regions.

For the most serious crimes, such as murder, rape, or robbery, nearly all (more than 90 per cent) young adult offenders are sentenced in terms of the relatively milder juvenile law (see Figure 2.10). The reason is that the higher minimum and maximum sentences provided by the 'ordinary' criminal law do not apply in the

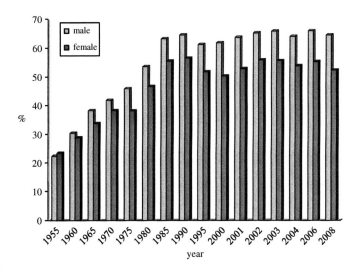

Figure 2.9 Proportion of male and female young adults sentenced according to juvenile law in West Germany, 1955–2006, and in the whole of Germany, 2008.

Source: Statistisches Bundesamt (ed.): Strafverfolgungsstatistik 1955–2008, own calculations.

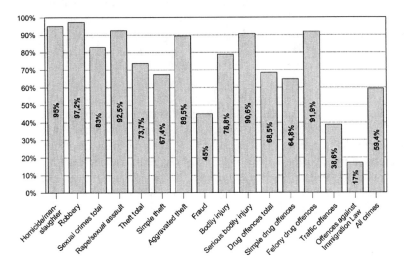

Figure 2.10 Sentencing of young adults according to juvenile law for different crimes, 2008.

Source: Statistisches Bundesamt (ed.): Strafverfolgungsstatistik 2008, own calculations.

juvenile law (see § 18 (1) JJA). Juvenile court judges, therefore, are not bound by the otherwise obligatory life sentence for murder or the minimum of five years of imprisonment in the case of armed robbery (see further: Dünkel 1993: 157; Kröplin 2001: 162; Pruin 2007: 98 f). In this respect, German legal practice seems to be contrary to the so-called 'waiver decisions' of the USA, where the most serious young offenders are transferred to the 'ordinary' criminal justice system (Stump 2003).

Interestingly, it is in the case of traffic offences that the majority (61 per cent in 2008) of young adult offenders in Germany are sentenced in accordance with the criminal law for adults. This is because, in these cases, there is the procedural possibility of imposing fines without an oral hearing through the use of '*Strafbefehlsverfahren*': a summary procedure, using only a written file in cases of less severe offences (particularly traffic and property offences), which is excluded from the juvenile penal law (Dünkel 2003: 20; 2006: 247 ff.; Kröplin 2001: 326). Young adult foreigners committing an offence against the immigration law are also usually dealt with as adults: 83 per cent were sentenced according to the general criminal law in 2008 (see Figure 2.10). In this case, it is not clear whether the reason for applying the general criminal law is to apply summary fines or to impose a more severe punishment of imprisonment.

There are, however, reservations among some German commentators about the regional inequalities that have emerged in the application of these laws. According to a study of the 1980s, for example, within North Rhine-Westphalia convictions in accordance with the terms of the juvenile law ranged, in the different areas, between 27 per cent and 91 per cent of all convicted juveniles (Dünkel 1990: 92). When the old Federal States are compared, the 2008 figures ranged from 47 per cent in Baden-Württemberg and 54 per cent in Berlin, to 80 per cent in Hamburg and 89 per cent in Schleswig-Holstein (see Figure 2.11). It appears, therefore, that juvenile court judges have different conceptions of the 'typical' personality of the juvenile offender and of the 'typical' nature of juvenile delinquency. Overall, there seems to be a north-south divide, with the Federal States in the north increasingly applying juvenile criminal law, whereas in the south the juvenile court judges rely to a greater extent on the criminal law for adults. The relatively low application of sanctions according to the JJA in Berlin (54 per cent) might be a result of an over-representation of foreigners or juveniles with a migrant background who could more often be deemed to be mature, particularly if they are more independent from their parents or family.

Regarding the new Federal States of the former East Germany, we can see that practice varies, but in general they are more reluctant to apply juvenile law than is the case in the average West German Federal State (see Figure 2.11). In 2008, for example, the proportion of young adults sentenced according to the JJA was only 46 per cent in Mecklenburg-Western Pomerania, 50 per cent in Saxony, 53 per cent in Brandenburg, 55 per cent in Thuringia and 56 per cent in Saxony-Anhalt (see for earlier data Heinz 2001: 79 ff.). In 2001 the figure was 55 per cent in Mecklenburg-Western Pomerania; it has therefore decreased slightly. The low rates in Brandenburg (53 per cent; increased from only 35 per cent in 2006) and

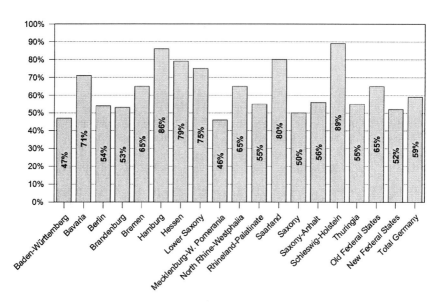

Figure 2.11 Percentage of young adult offenders sentenced under juvenile criminal law according in different federal states, 2008.

Source: Statistisches Bundesamt (ed.): Strafverfolgungsstatistik 2008, own calculations.

Saxony (50 per cent; increased from only 34 per cent in 2006) are, however, not due to the distrust of juvenile court judges towards the JJA. Rather, they are the result of a specific bureaucratic routine in the application of the '*Strafbefehlsverfahren*' (see Kröplin 2001; Dünkel 2010: 590). Nevertheless, the marked increase in these States since 2006 is interesting and important.

In relation to policy discussions about young adult offenders, two main areas of debate can be identified. On the one hand, there is a 'rhetorical' debate in the field of criminal policy, focussed upon the critique by conservative parties of over-lenient (or hyphenate when split over the line) sanctioning through the application of JJA sanctions instead of the provisions of general criminal law.[5] These conservative politicians argue that young adults should be made to assume increased 'responsibility', thereby allowing for more severe punishment to be imposed. On the other hand, the practitioners 'on the ground' have different problems. They want to eschew the application of the general criminal law in order to avoid the imposition of more severe punishment, but would like to be able to impose fines in a summary procedure (without an oral hearing), which, up until now, is not provided by the JJA ('*Strafbefehlsverfahren*'; Eisenberg 2010, note 5 to § 105, notes 18 f. to § 109; Dünkel 1990: 90). This procedure is very economical and time-saving and, as indicated above, is used particularly for traffic offences such as drink-driving.

In cases where the juvenile court decides not to invoke the 'maturity' provisions, the young adult offender is sentenced according to the general criminal law. In these cases, however, the young adult still has the benefit of a special rule mitigating the sentence of the adult criminal law. According to section 106 of the JJA, instead of a life sentence, a young adult offender may receive a determinate prison sentence of up to 15 years. Although the wording of section 106 of the JJA is restricted to life sentences (which should be avoided), the section is generally understood to be a mitigating rule for the sentencing of young adults. Therefore, any sentence on a young adult should be, and regularly will be, mitigated compared to older adults over the age of 21.

Germany, therefore, fulfils the requirements of the Recommendations of the Council of Europe and of the other international organisations mentioned in the introduction to this paper. The German legislation can, however, be criticized because of the vague concept of 'maturity' and the consequent regional disparities in the application of sanctions of the juvenile law. Therefore, reform proposals by German scholars to apply juvenile law more generally should be supported (see Dünkel 2003, 2006; Deutsche Vereinigung für Jugendgerichte und Jugendgerichtshilfen 2002; Ostendorf 2002; Schöch 2001: 132 ff.; Sonnen 2002; Walter 2001). However, only a few members of the conservative Christian Democratic Union (CDU/CSU) are pressing for further restrictions in applying juvenile law, although these conservative political demands have no chance of being successful in parliamentary debates in the near future.

The weakness of the German legislation, by its inclusion of the concept of 'maturity', was discussed in the Committee on Crime Problems of the Council of Europe when they were drafting the ERJOSSM. The result was that the term 'maturity' was not used in the document. Therefore, difficulties of interpretation have been avoided in the final version of the ERJOSSM by simply stating that juvenile law may be applied for young adults 'where appropriate' (see Basic Principle No. 17 of the ERJOSSM; see Council of Europe 2009: 42). This opens the floor for an even wider application of the juvenile law sanctions to young adults than is the case in Germany.

Young adult offenders in other European countries

In European civil law there is a uniform age of legal majority, but that is not the case as regards criminal law (see Pruin 2010; Doob and Tonry 2004; Cipriani 2009). However, young adults are still seen almost everywhere as a special age group and are treated differently from older adults either within the general criminal law or within the juvenile law. Regulations in the juvenile law also often provide for the application of specific educational sanctions for young adults, while regulations for adults within the criminal law frequently provide for mitigations of the normal sentences for young adults.

Table 2.1 gives an overview on the age of criminal responsibility in general and dealing with young adults in Europe in particular.

As can be seen, the age of criminal responsibility varies between the age of 10 in England, Wales, Cyprus and Switzerland to ages 18 or 16, depending on the nature of the crimes, in Belgium and some Middle European and Eastern European countries.[6] Cyprus and Switzerland only provide educational measures for those aged from 10 to 14 or 15. Similar restrictions can be seen in other countries as well and, in the majority of countries, criminal responsibility starts at the age of 14 or 15 (see in detail Pruin 2010: 1535 ff.; Dünkel *et al.* 2010: 1820 ff.).

As for the treatment of young adults, one can differentiate three models:

- Countries with special regulations within the (juvenile) law which make educational, procedural, or correctional measures applicable also for young adults (e.g. Germany)
- Countries with special regulations in the general criminal law that mitigate the sentences imposed on young adults (e.g. the Scandinavian countries)
- Countries with very few special rules for young adults (e.g. England and Wales)[7]

The criminal laws of most European countries provide for special arrangements to be made when dealing with young adults either in criminal or in juvenile law. Many countries – including Belgium, Croatia, Denmark, France, Germany, Greece, Italy, and the Ukraine – allow for the possibility of prolonging juvenile measures or sanctions which had been started before the offender's eighteenth birthday to a higher age. What is more interesting – especially with respect to the European Council's 2003 Recommendations – is how countries deal with young adults who have committed an offence after they have turned 18. Overall, the provisions for this age category vary greatly. In many European countries there

Table 2.1 Comparison of the age of criminal responsibility in Europe

Country	Diminished criminal responsibility (juvenile criminal law)	Criminal responsibility (adult criminal law can/must be applied)	Legal majority
Austria	14	18/21	18
Belgium	16[b]/18	16[b]/18	18
Belarus	14[c]/16	14/16	18
Bulgaria	14	18	18
Croatia	14/16[a]	18/21	18
Cyprus	10/14[a]	16/18/21	16–18
Czech Republic	15	18/18+ (mitigated sentences)	18
Denmark[d]	14	14/18/21	18
England/Wales	10/12/15[a]	18	18
Estonia	14	18	18
Finland[d]	15	15/18	18
France	10[f]/13	18	18
Germany	14	18/21	18
Greece	8[f]/15	18/21	18
Hungary	14	18	18
Ireland	10/12/16[a]	18	18
Italy	14	18/21	18
Latvia	14	18	18
Lithuania	14[c]/16	14/16	18
Macedonia	14[c]/16	14/16	18
Moldova	14[c]/16	14/16	18
Montenegro	14/16[a]	18/21	18
Netherlands	12	16/18/21	18
Northern Ireland	10	17/18/21	18
Norway[d]	15	18	18
Poland	13[e]	15/17/18	18
Portugal	12[e]/16	16/21	18
Romania	14/16	18/(20)	18
Russia	14[c]/16	18/21	18
Scotland	12[e]/16	16/21	18
Serbia	14/16[a]	18/21	18
Slovakia	14/15	18/21	18
Slovenia	14/16[a]	18/21	18
Spain	14	18	18
Sweden[d]	15	15/18/21	18
Switzerland	10[f]/15[a]	18/18[g]	18
Turkey	12	15/18	18
Ukraine	14[c]/16	18	18

Notes:

a Criminal majority concerning juvenile detention (youth imprisonment etc.)

b Only for road offences and exceptionally for very serious offences

c Only for serious offences

d Only mitigation of sentencing without separate juvenile justice legislation

e No criminal responsibility *strictusensu*, but application of the Juvenile (Welfare) Law

f Only educational sanctions (including closed residential care) and measures

g Youth custody for offenders aged 18–25, a special sanction of the general Penal Code, executed in special young adult offender institutions (until the age of 30) are special measures that can be imposed on young adults that are not applicable to adult offenders (see Table 2.2 below).[8] These measures place a particular emphasis on re-socialization and are normally part of the sanctioning catalogue of the juvenile laws. However, whereas the imposition of these special sanctions is obligatory for juveniles, their application for young adult offenders is optional in most cases.

The 2003 Recommendation of the Council of Europe goes beyond such measures. Indeed, the Council demands that the member countries of Europe should consider the possibility of sentencing young adults under provisions that normally apply to juveniles. This would require a certain number of applicable measures to be made available, and it is here that the systems in Europe differ greatly. In Croatia, the Czech Republic, Germany, Lithuania, the Netherlands, Portugal, Slovenia, Switzerland and Russia the law does allow for the application of numerous educational measures stemming from juvenile criminal law.[9] On the other hand, the number of such special sanctions is very limited in England, Wales, Finland, France, the Republic of Ireland, Northern Ireland and Sweden.

Normally, the different national laws at least prescribe that custodial sentences are to be administered in a particularly educational manner for this age category or they stipulate that imprisonment has to be served in youth prisons until a certain age (even – under special conditions – up to the age of 27 in Austria) (Dünkel and Stańdo-Kawecka 2010). In the Republic of Ireland, Northern Ireland, Scotland and England and Wales young adults are normally sent to special institutions for young (adult) offenders.[10] Similarly, in 2002 the Netherlands created a separate regime for young adults in the prison system that was aimed at offering extra protection and perspectives for young adult detainees between the ages of 18 and 24. Switzerland too has specific institutions for young adult offenders that place particular emphasis upon schooling and vocational training in order to promote societal reintegration. Turkey likewise provides for special (closed and open) institutions for young adults. However, the Swiss regulation for 18- to 25-year-old young adult offenders is part of the general criminal law for adults, not part of the juvenile justice legislation.

Nevertheless, it should be noted that the existence of such legal provisions gives no indication of how they are actually applied in practice. Currently, there is little comparative data available on the actual practice of applying educational measures from juvenile law to young adults. As we have seen, in Germany such practice is the rule, at least in the vast majority of the Federal States (see Dünkel (2003; 2006), Eisenberg (2010), notes 4 ff. to §105). By contrast, in the Netherlands (see in detail Pruin 2007), Lithuania, Slovenia, and Russia courts seem to be much more reluctant to use the juvenile law for young adults. The reasons for such restricted application can be manifold. For example, in Lithuania and Russia it is reported that the judges refer to the absence of clear legal criteria for the application of juvenile law.[11] In Slovenia the reluctance to apply juvenile law to young adults could stem from the fact that this age group is not dealt with by juvenile courts. Instead, young adults are adjudicated on by judges in adult courts who are not specialists in this field and who are, therefore, often insecure about the forms and procedures of the educational measures used for juveniles.

By contrast, in Germany – as mentioned above – the specialized juvenile judge or court is always competent enough to sentence young adult offenders. This can clearly be seen as advantageous for the application of juvenile law to young adults because the juvenile judge is familiar with the kind of juvenile measures and sanctions available. Also, due to their specialization in educational and developmental issues, they can better judge the appropriateness of educational measures in each individual case. Therefore, the decision of the German Legislator in 1953 to extend the competence of juvenile courts to young adults was the basis for a successful implementation of the rules to young adults.

Another reason for a reluctant application of juvenile law to young adults might be that in some countries, and in contrast to Germany, flexible responses to criminal behaviour can be found within the adult criminal law, with a wide range of community sanctions available to judges. Consequently, in such countries (e.g. the Netherlands), applying juvenile law to young adults is not necessarily always more advantageous or appropriate. This stands in stark contrast to the situation in Germany, where the adult criminal law is very limited with respect to sentencing flexibility or in terms of the range of community sanctions that are available.

Furthermore, it is also interesting to compare the differences between different national laws in writing and the ways in which they are practiced. For example, in Greece there is legally no way to apply juvenile law to young adults. However, according to Pitsela (2010), judges in Greece nevertheless still sometimes issue juvenile measures in young adult cases. Other discrepancies are reported from Germany. In this case, only the general criminal law provides a summary procedure for imposing fines on traffic offenders (without an oral hearing). Juvenile prosecutors, particularly in some Federal States, tend, therefore, to apply the general criminal law in cases of traffic offences that are usually sanctioned with fines. Another apparent anomaly is that in Germany, more than 90 per cent of the most serious crimes committed by young adults (such as murder, robbery, rape etc.) are sentenced according to juvenile law, thus avoiding the increased minimum and maximum sentences of the general criminal law which would not be proportionate for young adults. As mentioned previously, this practice is contrary to the widespread practice found in other countries whereby perpetrators of the most serious crimes are transferred to adult courts (see Stump 2003; Bishop 2009; Weijers, Nuytiens and Christiaens 2009).

If one interprets the intention of the Council of Europe's 2003 Recommendation as being the development and establishment of a flexible range of alternative and educational sanctions for young adult offenders, then an effective implementation of this demand would not necessarily need to be measured by the number of available juvenile justice measures. For instance, the sanctioning systems of Sweden and the Netherlands show that flexible responses to criminal behaviour can also exist within adult criminal law. Indeed, these countries have a comparatively high degree of flexibility in the applicability of 'rehabilitative' sanctions and measures for adults. Nevertheless, in most European countries it is still the juvenile justice system that provides such educational/rehabilitative sanctions or measures (Pruin 2007: 231 ff.).

As a rule, then, we can conclude that, in most European countries, the provisions of the respective juvenile justice systems are more appropriate and suitable for dealing with young adults who are still 'developing'. Furthermore, it is important to ascertain whether young adults are sentenced by criminal judges who are responsible for adult offenders or by judges who are experienced in the fields of youth and youth crime and, therefore, have more insight into the interests and needs of the age group in question.

A number of countries – including Croatia, Germany, Kosovo, Lithuania, the Netherlands, Slovenia and Switzerland – have now, depending on the existence of specific preconditions, introduced the optional possibility of applying special measures from juvenile criminal law to young adults. For instance, a predictive assessment of the effectiveness of the applicable sanctions is often required in order to determine whether adult or juvenile criminal law is to be applied. In Germany special criteria with regard to the psychosocial development of the offender have also to be considered. In some countries, the judges may have difficulties in deciding whether the criteria for classification as a 'young adult' have been met in a single case because the criteria can often be vaguely formulated and/or because the court lacks background information about the psychosocial development of the young adult offender (see Shchedrin 2010). Such information is typically provided by social inquiry reports drafted by the welfare services, who sometimes even bring in psychological or psychiatric experts for advice and assistance. If these services are not approached or if the regulations are too vague, then the judge may be more reluctant to use juvenile measures (see Sakalauskas 2010).

Instead of, or alongside, the special measures described above, there are in Austria, Croatia, Cyprus, the Czech Republic, Denmark, England and Wales, Finland, France, Germany, Greece, Hungary, Italy, Poland, Portugal, Romania, Slovakia, Sweden, and Switzerland also provisions for mitigating the sentences that young adult offenders receive. While this mitigation is mandatory in Austria, the Czech Republic, and Slovakia, it is optional in the other countries mentioned above. The legal wording regarding this issue is very particular in the Czech Republic. Instead of defining fixed legal age limits and categories, their law allows for the possibility of mitigating sentences for persons who are of an age that is 'close to adolescence'. It has also been reported that the age of an offender is taken into consideration when sentencing in countries such as the Republic of Ireland, England, and Wales, despite the absence of explicit respective legal provisions. In Hungary, meanwhile, there are sentencing guidelines from the Supreme Court which state that being between the ages of 18 and 21 (and thus close to the age of a juvenile) at the time the offence was committed is an important mitigating factor. By contrast, in Serbia, Slovenia, and other states of the former Yugoslavia, the applicability of special regulations is in accordance with the age of the offender at the time of the proceedings and not their age at the time of the offence. This approach bears the risk that delays in the proceedings are ultimately at the expense of the young adult.

By comparison, the 2007 amendment to the juvenile law in Switzerland provides an interesting approach to this area. In this case, where criminal proceedings are instituted against a juvenile who has committed further crimes after the age of 18, the procedural provisions of the juvenile law still, formally, apply for all offences, and the youth court can choose between measures from the juvenile or the adult criminal law.[12] In some countries, however, resorting to the special provisions of juvenile criminal law is, in practice, ruled out in cases of especially serious criminal offences (although German law and jurisdiction does explicitly open the provisions of juvenile criminal law to all types of offenders and offences).

Particularly in the light of current European juvenile criminal law reforms in Austria, the Czech Republic, Kosovo, Lithuania, Serbia, and Slovenia, one can speak of a European trend towards broadening the possibilities for applying the special provisions open to juveniles to young adults as well. This trend has predominantly emerged in the Eastern European countries that were (and sometimes still are) in a phase of transformation away from 'Soviet' legal traditions towards the modern Continental European model of juvenile justice. Furthermore, there have been reports from Austria, the Czech Republic, Hungary, the Netherlands, and Spain that recent draft laws have contained proposals calling for a wider incorporation of young adults into juvenile procedures, but that these were later amended. Therefore, one may conclude that the experts who are regularly responsible for drafting laws in their respective countries are convinced of the necessity to integrate young adults in the juvenile justice system despite the fact that this notion has not (yet?) achieved acceptance from politicians in the legislatures. In light of these trends, it will be interesting to see how other current reform proposals, for example in Hungary (see Csuri 2008; Váradi-Csema 2010), develop in the future.

The different models for dealing with young adult offenders in Europe are summarized in Table 2.2.

As can be seen, 20 out of the 35 countries (57 per cent) provide for either the application of educational measures from juvenile law or have special rules concerning specific sanctions for young adults in the general penal law. Furthermore, 18 out of the 35 countries (51 per cent) have special rules in their adult criminal law concerning the mitigation of penalties for young adults. On top of this, 9 out of the 35 countries (26 per cent) provide for both the mitigation of sanctions according to the general criminal law *and* the application of sanctions from the juvenile law. It is, therefore, quite exceptional when special rules for young adult offenders are not provided at all and, as far as we are aware, there are only seven such countries in Europe that fit this bill: Belgium, Bulgaria, Estonia, Latvia, Spain, Turkey, and the Ukraine.[13]

Conclusion and future prospects

To summarise, then, the recent findings of research into the living situations of young people are supportive of maintaining and/or establishing flexible possibilities for the sanctioning of young adult offenders. This is also in line with the requirements of the Council of Europe's 2003 Recommendations. The review

Table 2.2 Young adults in European (juvenile) criminal law

Country	Special rules for young adults providing the application of sanctions specific (juvenile law)	Special rules for young adults concerning mitigating sentences	Age range for youth detention/ custody or similar forms of deprivation of liberty
Austria	X	X	14–27
Belgium	(X)[a]	–	Only welfare institutions
Bulgaria	–	–	14–21
Croatia	X	X	14–21
Cyprus	–	X	14–21
Czech Republic	X[b]	X	15–19[c]
Denmark	X[d]	X	15–23
England/Wales	X[e]	X	10/15–21[f]
Estonia	–	–	14–21
Finland	X[g]	X	15–21
France	(X)[h]	X	13–18 + 6 m./23
Germany	X	X	14–24
Greece	(–)[i]	X	13–21/25
Hungary	–	X	14–24
Ireland	X[j]	–	10/12/16–18/21
Italy	X	X	14–21
Kosovo	X	–	14/16–23
Latvia	–	–	14–21
Lithuania	X	–	14–21
Montenegro	X	–	14/16–23
Netherlands	X	–	12–21
Northern Ireland	X[k]	–	10–16/17–21
Poland	–	X	13–18/15–21
Portugal	X	X	12/16–21
Romania	–	X[l]	14–21
Russia	X	–	14–21
Scotland	X[m]	–	16–21
Serbia	X	–	14/16–23
Slovakia	–	X	14–18
Slovenia	X	–	14–23
Spain	–	–	14–21
Sweden	X[n]	X	15–21
Switzerland	(X)[o]	X[p]	10–22
Turkey	–	–	12–18/21[q]
Ukraine	–	–	14–22

Notes:

(a) If the offence was committed before the age of 18 juvenile welfare measures can be prolonged until the age of 23.

(b) Application of educational measures and mitigation of sentences if the young adult is at an age 'close to a juvenile'. According to the jurisprudence this is the case until the age of 21 is reached.

(c) Obligatory: until the age of 19 in youth prison.

Notes:

(d) No special juvenile law. Special regulations with respect to early release can be applied to young adults. Furthermore, young adults can be placed in alternative institutions, see Corrections Act, sect. 78 (formerly Criminal Code, sect. 49, subsection 2).

(e) Detention in a YOI instead of imprisonment; attendance centre order can be applied.

(f) The English YOIs are differentiated to institutions holding 15–17 year olds, 18–21 year olds and institutions holding both age groups. 10–12 year old persistent offenders and 12–14 year olds can in exceptional cases be sent to secure training facilities.

(g) No special juvenile law. The application of suspended sentences (conditional imprisonment) is extended and combined with supervision. Young adult offenders under the age of 21 can be released on parole earlier (after one third or half of the sentence) than adults over 21.

(h) The educational measure of judicial protection (*'protection judiciaire'*) can be prolonged beyond the age of 18.

(i) If the offence was committed before the age of 18, educational or therapeutic measures can be prolonged until the age of 21. Furthermore, according to the Greek report (see Pitsela 2010), in practice the judges apply in some cases educational measures on offenders who were 18 or older at the time of the offence.

(j) A young male offender between 17–21 can be sentenced to detention in St. Patrick's Institution.

(k) Young offenders (age 17–21) are usually sentenced to the young offenders centre.

(l) The law does not define the age as a mitigating factor, but in practice the judges impose less harsh sentences on young adults.

(m) Juveniles and young adults between 16–21 can be sentenced to detention in a YOI.

(n) No special juvenile law but special procedures and measures such as the transfer to the Social Services. The imposition of custodial sanctions is particularly restricted (see Dünkel/Stańdo-Kawecka, 2010).

(o) Special educational measures can be applied if a further offence was committed after the age of 18, but criminal proceedings had been instituted before.

(p) The general Criminal Law (Art. 61 Swiss PC) provides for special institutions for 18–25 year old offenders.

(q) Special open and closed institutions for young adults.

of the 35 legal systems presented in the present paper also shows that this idea is already widely shared across Europe. Moreover, even if the implementation of these goals is not always satisfying, there is in fact a clear trend towards expanding and broadening the scope of juvenile justice so as allow for the inclusion of young adults. This is in accordance with current criminological, psychological, and sociological research which shows that the most appropriate way of dealing with young adult offenders is to incorporate them fully into juvenile justice systems. As such, there are many good reasons for following the European Council's approach of giving special concern to the young adult age group (see the Council of Europe Recommendation [2003] 20, Rule 11 and [2008] 11, Rule 17) and there are good reasons as well to generally treat young adults as juveniles.

However, in order to prevent the possibility of young adults becoming 'lost in transition' (Barrow Cadbury Commission 2005), there is a need for some countries to change their legislation. This is especially true in Bulgaria, Estonia, Latvia, Spain, and Turkey. On top of this, many European countries should also adapt their legal practice so that young adult offenders are able to more frequently receive alternative and rehabilitative sanctions. One appropriate approach could be to fully integrate young adults into juvenile justice systems (where they are available) and to ensure that specialized judges and prosecutors deal with this age group in court.

Notes

1 The German sentencing statistics ('Strafverfolgungsstatistik') comprise all defendants and convicts whose criminal proceedings have been completed by a conviction, after either an oral hearing or a written summary decision ('Strafbefehl'), or when the proceedings have been discontinued by the court.

2 See Estrada (2001); Kivivuori (2007); van Dijk, Manchin and van Kesteren (2007); Steketee *et al.* (2008); Junger-Tas and Dünkel (2009: 215 ff.); and Stevens (2009).

3 It is however interesting in the present context to note that Sampson and Laub's theory was developed with special reference to the Gluecks' (1950) sample of juvenile delinquents, who grew into adulthood before the recent social changes.

4 Other examples mentioned include crimes committed in groups or under the influence of a group and very violent crimes that have arisen in a specific situation (possibly in combination with alcohol abuse); see Eisenberg (2010: notes 34 ff. to § 105)

5 These arguments do not consider that sometimes the application of sanctions of the JJA may be a disadvantage rather than a benefit, as can be shown by the fact that in the juvenile justice system the minimum prison sentence is six months, in the general criminal law only one month (see Dünkel 1990; Pfeiffer 1991).

6 Until recently, the lowest age was provided by Irish law where 7-year-old children could still be made criminally responsible. The Children Act of 2001 changed the minimum age to 12 years, but this was not implemented until 2006.

7 In England and Wales, the sentence of imprisonment is not available to the courts for persons aged under 21 at the time of sentence. Instead, a court wishing to pass a custodial sentence on an offender aged 18–21 must pass a sentence of 'Detention in a Young Offenders Institution'. An Act of 2000 contained a provision abolishing this separate sentence; the purpose of this was to give the prison authorities greater flexibility in the use of custodial accommodation (because at present only young adults can be held in designated YOIs). The enactment of 2000 remains on the statute book, but it has not been brought into force. The only other special sentencing provision for young adult offenders in England and Wales is the 'attendance centre order' (a kind of day training centre). This is mainly available to juvenile courts, but there also exist a limited number of 'senior attendance centres' for offenders aged 18–21. However, this disposal is now of little practical importance: in 2009, only 206 offenders aged 18–20 were sentenced to an attendance centre order in the whole country.

8 Until recently, Spain also belonged to these nations (see de la Cuesta and Blanco 2006: 7).

9 In the Czech Republic it used to be the case that educational measures could only be imposed in combination with a suspended sentence; since 1 January 2010, however, they may be used in combination with any other sanction for adult offenders. In Switzerland, this procedure applies only if a further offence was committed after the offender had turned 18, but criminal proceedings had been instituted beforehand.

10 In the Republic of Ireland young male offenders aged 17–21 can be sent to detention in St. Patrick's Institution. In Scotland, there are five YOIs for young people aged 16–21. Similarly in Northern Ireland young adults aged 17–21 are usually sentenced to the Young Offenders Centre (see Dignan, Walsh, Burman *et al.* and the chapter by O'Mahony in Dünkel *et al.* 2010).

11 Lithuanian law provides for the application of juvenile sanctions if the young adult, according to his 'social maturity', is closer to a juvenile than to an adult over 21.

12 This concerns only educational measures; criminal sanctions have to be applied according to the adult criminal law.

13 However, even these countries provide that young adults are accommodated in juvenile prisons or special institutions or units for young adults (separated from adults aged over 21).

References

Barrow Cadbury Commission (2005). *Lost in Transition: a report of the Barrow Cadbury Commission on Young Adults and the Criminal Justice System.* London: Barrow Cadbury Trust.

Bishop, D. (2009). 'Juvenile transfer in the United States'. In J. Junger-Tas and F. Dünkel (eds), *Reforming Juvenile Justice.* Dordrecht: Springer.

Blossfeld, H.-P., Klijzing, E., Mills, M. and Kurz, K. (2005). *Globalization, Uncertainty and Youth in Society.* London and New York: Routledge.

Brüderl, J. (2004). 'Die Pluralisierung partnerschaftlicher Lebenslagen in Westdeutschland und Europa'. *Aus Politik und Zeitgeschichte* 19: 3–10.

Bundesministerium des Innern, Bundesministerium der Justiz (eds.) (2006). *Zweiter Periodischer Sicherheitsbericht.* Berlin.

Cavadino, M. and Dignan, J. (2002). *The Penal System: an introduction* (4th edition). London: Sage.

Cipriani, D. (2009). *Children's Rights and the Minimum Age of Criminal Responsibility. A Global Perspective.* Farnham: Ashgate.

Council of Europe (2003). *New Ways of Dealing with Juvenile Delinquency and the Role of Juvenile Justice.* Strasbourg: Council of Europe.

Council of Europe (2009). *European Rules for Juvenile Offenders Subject to Sanctions or Measures.* Strasbourg: Council of Europe.

de la Cuesta, J. L. and Blanco, I. (2007). 'El enjuiciamiento de menores y jóvenes infractores en Espana'. *Revista electrónica de la Asociación Internacional de Derecho Penal* 1–24.

Csuri, A. (2008). 'Der Lebensabschnitt der "jungen Erwachsenen" als neue Alterskategorie im ungarischen Strafrecht – Kritische Überlegungen rechtsdogmatischer Natur'. *Zeitschrift für Jugendkriminalrecht und Jugendhilfe* 19: 167–171.

Doob, A. N. and Tonry, M. (2004). 'Varieties of youth justice'. In M. Tonry and A. N. Doob (eds.). *Youth Crime and Justice* 31: 1–20. London: University of Chicago Press.

Deutsche Vereinigung für Jugendgerichte und Jugendgerichtshilfen (2002). *Abschlussbericht der 2. Jugendstrafrechtsreform-Kommission'*, *DVJJ Extra* Nr. 5.

Deutsche Shell (ed.) (2002). *Jugend 2002: Zwischen pragmatischem Idealismus und robustem Materialismus.* Frankfurt am Main.

Dünkel, F. (1990). *Freiheitsentzug für junge Rechtsbrecher.* Bonn: Forum Verlag Bad Godesberg.

Dünkel, F. (1993). 'Heranwachsende im (Jugend)-Kriminalrecht'. *ZStW* 105:137–165.

Dünkel, F. (2002). 'Heranwachsende im Jugendstrafrecht-Erfahrungen in Deutschland und aktuelle Entwicklungen im europäischen Vergleich'. In R. Moos *et al.* (eds.). *Festschrift für Udo Jesionek.* Wien, Graz: Nbeuer Wissenschaftlicher Verlag.

Dünkel, F. (2003). 'Youth violence and juvenile justice in Germany'. In F. Dünkel and K. Drenkhahn (eds.). *Youth Violence: new patterns and local responses – experiences in East and West.* Mönchengladbach: Forum Verlag Bad Godesberg.

Dünkel, F. (2006). 'Juvenile Justice in Germany: between welfare and justice'. In J. Junger-Tas and S. H. Decker (eds.). *International Handbook of Juvenile Justice.* Berlin, New York: Springer.

Dünkel, F. (2010). 'Germany'. In F. Dünkel, J. Grzywa, P. Horsfield and I. Pruin (eds.). *Juvenile Justice Systems in Europe: current situation and reform developments. Vol. 2.* Mönchengladbach: Forum Verlag Godesberg.

Dünkel, F., Grzywa, J., Horsfield, P. and Pruin, I. (eds.) (2010). *Juvenile Justice Systems in Europe: current situation and reform developments.* Mönchengladbach: Forum Verlag Godesberg.

Dünkel, F. and Pruin, I. (2010). 'Young adult offenders in the criminal justice systems of European countries'. In F. Dünkel, J. Grzywa, J., P. Horsfield, and I. Pruin (eds.). *Juvenile Justice Systems in Europe: current situation and reform developments. Vol. 4.* Mönchengladbach: Forum Verlag Godesberg.

Dünkel, F. and Stańdo-Kawecka, B. (2010). 'Juvenile imprisonment and placement in institutions for deprivation of liberty'. In F. Dünkel, J. Grzywa, P. Horsfield and I. Pruin (eds.). *Juvenile Justice Systems in Europe: current situation and reform developments. Vol. 4.* Mönchengladbach: Forum Verlag Godesberg.

Eisenberg, U. (2010). *Jugendgerichtsgesetz* (14th edition). Munich: C. H. Beck.

Estrada, F. (2001). 'Juvenile violence as a social problem: trends, media attention and societal response'. *British Journal of Sociology* 41: 225–262.

European Commission (1997). *Youth in the European Union.* Brussels.

Farrington, D. P., Coid, J. W. and West, D. J. (2009). 'The development of offending from age 8 to age 50: recent results from the Cambridge Study in Delinquent Development'. *MschrKrim* 92:160–173.

Fend, H. (2003). *Entwicklungspsychologie des Jugendalters* (3rd edition). Opladen: Westdeutscher Verlag.

Glueck, S. and Glueck, E. (1950). *Unraveling Juvenile Delinquency.* Cambridge, Mass.: Harvard University Press.

Golsch, K. (2008). 'Youth unemployment in Western Europe: the effects of individual market, and institutional factors'. In H.-P. Blossfeld, S. Buchholz, E. Bukodi and K. Kurz (eds.). *Young Workers, Globalization and the Labor Market.* Cheltenham: Edward Elgar.

Grunert, C. and Krüger, H.-H. (2000). 'Zum wandel von jugendbiographien im 20. jahrhundert'. In U. Sander and R. Vollbrecht (eds.). *Jugend im 20. Jahrhundert.* Neuwied, Kriftel, Berlin: Luchterhand.

Heinz, W. (2001). 'Die jugendstrafrechtliche Sanktionierungspraxis im Ländervergleich'. In D. Dölling (ed.). *Das Jugendstrafrecht an der Wende zum 21. Jahrhundert.* Berlin, New York: de Gruyter.

Heinz, W. (2003). *Jugendkriminalität in Deutschland.* [pdf] www.uni-konstanz.de/rtf/kik/Jugendkriminalitaet-2003–7-e.pdf.

Heinz, W. (2004). *Kriminalität in Deutschland unter besonderer Berücksichtigung der Jugend- und Gewaltkriminalität.* [pdf] www.uni-konstanz.de/rtf/kik/Heinz_Kriminalitaet_in_Deutschland.htm.

Heinz, W. (2005). *Das strafrechtliche Sanktionensystem und die Sanktionierungspraxis in Deutschland 1882–2003 (version: 2/2005).* [pdf] www.uni-konstanz.de/rtf/kis/sanks03.pdf.

Hurrelmann, K. (2007). *Lebensphase Jugend* (8th edition). Weinheim, München: Beltz.

Junger-Tas, J. and Dünkel, F. (2009). 'Reforming Juvenile Justice: European Perspectives'. In J. Junger-Tas and F. Dünkel (eds.). *Reforming Juvenile Justice.* Dordrecht: Springer.

Junger-Tas, J., Haen Marshall, I., Enzmann, D., Killias, M., Steketee, M. and Gruszczynska, B. (eds.) (2009). *Juvenile Delinquency in Europe and Beyond: results of the Second International Self-Report Delinquency Study.* Berlin, New York: Springer.

Kivivuori, J. (2007). *Delinquent Behaviour in Nordic Capital Cities.* Helsinki: Hakapainooy.

Kröplin, M. (2001). *Die Sanktionspraxis im Jugendstrafrecht in Deutschland im Jahr 1997.* Mönchengladbach: Forum Verlag Bad Godesberg.

Kurz, K., Buchholz, S., Schmelzer, P. and Blossfeld, H.-P. (2008). 'Young people's employment chances in flexible labor markets: a comparison of changes in eleven modern societies'. In H.-P. Blossfeld, S. Buchholz, E. Bukodi, and K. Kurz (eds.). *Young Workers, Globalization and the Labor Market.* Cheltenham: Edward Elgar.

Laub, J. H. and Sampson, R. H. (2003). *Shared Beginnings, Divergent Lives.* Cambridge, Mass.: Harvard University Press.

Meier, B.-D., Rössner, D. and Schöch, H. (2003). *Jugendstrafrecht.* München: C. H. Beck.

Oerter, R. and Montada, L. (2008). *Entwicklungspsychologie* (5th edition). Weinheim: Beltz.

Office for Official Publications of the European Communities (2006). *Population Statistics.* Luxembourg: European Union publications.

Ostendorf, H. (2002). 'Weiterführung der Reform des Jugendstrafrechts'. *Strafverteidiger* 22: 436–445.

Pitsela, A. (2010). 'Greece'. In F. Dünkel, J. Grzywa, P. Horsfield, and I. Pruin (eds.). *Juvenile Justice Systems in Europe: current situation and reform developments.* Mönchengladbach: Forum Verlag Godesberg.

Pruin, I. (2007). *Die Heranwachsendenregelung im deutschen Jugendstrafrecht und ihre Anwendungspraxis im europäischen Vergleich.* Mönchengladbach: Forum Verlag Godesberg.

Pruin, I. (2010). 'The scope of juvenile justice systems in Europe'. In F. Dünkel, J. Grzywa, P. Horsfield, and I. Pruin (eds.). *Juvenile Justice Systems in Europe: current situation and reform developments. Vol. 4.* Mönchengladbach: Forum Verlag Godesberg.

Pfeiffer, C. (1991). 'Wird nach Jugendstrafrecht härter gestraft?'. *Strafverteidiger* 11: 363–370.

Sakalauskas, G. (2010). 'Lithuania'. In F. Dünkel, J. Grzywa, P. Horsfield and I. Pruin (eds.). *Juvenile Justice Systems in Europe: current situation and reform developments. Vol. 2.* Mönchengladbach: Forum Verlag Godesberg.

Sampson, R. and Laub, J. (1993). *Crime in the Making: pathways and turning-points through life.* Cambridge, Mass.: Harvard University Press.

Sampson, R. J. and Laub, J. H. (2009). 'A life course theory and long term project on trajectories of crime'. *MschrKrim,* 92: 226–239.

Schöch, H. (2001). 'Wie soll die Justiz auf Jugendkriminalität reagieren?'. In D. Dölling (ed.). *Das Jugendstrafrecht an der Wende zum 21. Jahrhundert.* Berlin, New York: de Gruyter.

Shchedrin, N. (2010). 'Russia'. In F. Dünkel, J. Grzywa, P. Horsfield and I. Pruin (eds.). *Juvenile Justice Systems in Europe: current situation and reform developments. Vol. 3.* Mönchengladbach: Forum Verlag Godesberg.

Sonnen, B.-R. (2002). 'Ist das deutsche Jugendstrafrecht noch zeitgemäß?'. *DVJJ-Journal* 13: 115–122.

Spieß, G. (2008). '*Jugendkriminalität in Deutschland – zwischen Fakten und Dramatisierung. Kriminalstatistische und kriminologische Befunde'*. [pdf] http://www.uni-konstanz.de/rtf/gs/Spiess-Jugendkriminalitaet-in-Deutschland-2008.pdf.

Steketee, M. *et al.* (2008). *Juvenile Delinquency in Six New EU Member States.* Utrecht: Verwey – Jonker Institute.

Stelly, W. and Thomas, J. (2001). *Einmal Verbrecher – immer Verbrecher?'* Wiesbaden: Westdeutscher Verlag.

Stevens, A. (2009). 'Trends in youth offending in Europe'. In J. Junger-Tas, and F. Dünkel (eds.). *Reforming Juvenile Justice,* Dordrecht: Springer.

Stump, B. (2003). *Adult Time for Adult Crime – Jugendliche zwischen Jugend-und Erwachsenenstrafrecht.* Mönchengladbach: Forum Verlag Godesberg.

Van Dijk, J. J. M., Manchin, R. and van Kesteren, J. N. (2007). *The Burden of Crime in the EU: A comparative analysis of the European Survey of Crime and Safety (EUICS) 2005.* Brussels: Gallup-Europe.

Váradi-Csema, E. (2010). 'Hungary'. In F. Dünkel, J. Grzywa, P. Horsfield and I. Pruin (eds.). *Juvenile Justice Systems in Europe: current situation and reform developments. Vol. 2.* Mönchengladbach: Forum Verlag Godesberg.

Wahler, P. (2000). 'Jugend in Berufsausbildung und Arbeit'. In U. Sander and R. Vollbrecht (eds.). *Jugend im 20. Jahrhundert.* Neuwied, Kriftel, Berlin: Luchterhand.

Walter, M. (2001). 'Die Krise der Jugend und die Antwort des Strafrechts'. *ZStW* 113: 743–773.

Weijers, I., Nuytiens, A. and Christiaens, J. (2009). 'Transfer of minors to the criminal court in Europe: Belgium and the Netherlands'. In J. Junger-Tas and F. Dünkel (eds.). *Reforming Juvenile Justice.* Dordrecht: Springer.

3 Youth, alcohol and aggression

Mary McMurran

There is little controversial in the assertion that drunken violence by young adults is a source of much concern in the UK today. At night, and especially at weekends, city centres are temporarily taken over by intoxicated young people and those charged with trying to control them. This scenario is replicated all over the country. The consequences for some individuals are severe in terms of injuries or criminal justice sanctions, and society bears the burden of the resultant healthcare and criminal justice costs.

Yet, rather than vilify the young for their drunken misbehaviour, a comprehensive understanding of where the risks for drunken violence lie can enable more focused and potentially more effective efforts to be made towards prevention and control. In the first part of this chapter, a brief overview of risk factors for alcohol-related aggression is presented, along with a commentary on the implications this has for prevention. In the second part of the chapter, individual-level mechanisms whereby alcohol leads to aggression and violence are examined; this is then followed by a description of what tactics might be effective in treatment. Pertinent to this volume, the focus throughout this chapter is on risk factors that have specific relevance to young adults, who are typically more vulnerable to alcohol-related aggression than older people because they drink more, get drunk more frequently, drink in higher-risk social venues, and drink for different reasons.

A multi-level approach

The risk of alcohol-related aggression depends on who is drinking, what sort of drink they are drinking, in what quantity and manner, in what place and whether or not that person encounters a provocation. This complex set of factors is represented in Figure 3.1, to which is added one additional level of risk; namely, culture (and subculture). In understanding risk, the constituent parts of this complex picture apply to all drinkers, yet differences in the specifics of each part deliver the flexibility needed to understand variability by age, gender, culture, context, and so on.

Within the UK, there are different cultures and subcultures with different rules and attitudes towards drinking. Alcohol-related aggression and violence is most typically associated with young white males who drink to a point of intoxication

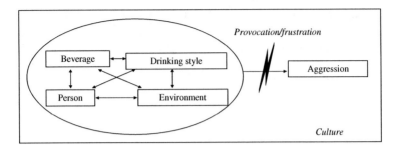

Figure 3.1 Factors explaining the alcohol–aggression relationship.

(Richardson and Budd 2003; Singleton, Farrell and Meltzer 1999). By contrast, although young women are drinking more than they used to (Goddard 2006), they are unlikely to be violent (Richardson and Budd 2003). Heavy drinking and violence among young white men is a longstanding issue, and the problem is not diminished by a culture that appears to promote heavy drinking.

Hobbs (2002: 58) has observed that many UK cities are 're-inventing themselves as sites of consumption and leisure', with high concentrations of superpubs, fun-pubs, disco bars, and night clubs, many of which have extended opening hours, giving rise to a lucrative 'night time economy'. Not only has the drinking context changed, but a wider choice of drinks is also available; this is particularly true at the high-alcohol end of the range, with strong lagers, white ciders, and 'designer' drinks such as alcopops and jelly shots commonly available. Moreover, many city centre drinking establishments also lend themselves to drinking quickly and drinking to get drunk by, for instance, having standing room only and through promotional offers. These tactics are ones that appeal primarily to younger people.

In settings where patrons are predominantly young and drunk, the likelihood of aggression and violence is increased. This is exacerbated where there is a high probability of meeting with provocation, which is more likely in bars or clubs that are rowdy, where disorder is tolerated, and where customers are poorly monitored by staff (Graham *et al.* 2006). Moreover, drinkers who are too young or too impoverished to drink in bars may instead do so in groups in parks or other public areas (Honess, Seymour and Webster 2000), where there is no supervision at all.

Although successive governments purport to want to encourage a culture-shift towards a more civilised and convivial drinking culture, more like those of our Southern European neighbours, the evidence suggests that in recent years young people's drinking has not become more restrained; rather, it suggests that the police have been doing a good job of controlling drunken disorder in city centres (Sivarajasingam, Moore and Shepherd 2007). Additionally, broader police-led prevention projects have the potential to reduce crime by licensing and training door staff, promoting harm-reduction practices among licensees and targeting trouble hot-spots (e.g. Maguire and Nettleton 2003). As well as policing bars, there is evidence for the effectiveness of training bar staff in responsible beverage service and developing house policies to reduce risk by reducing levels of intoxication and aggression (Graham 2000). While efforts to make cities and bars safer are essential, tackling the problem of alcohol-related aggression by discouraging heavy drinking and intoxication may require unpopular measures such as raising the legal drinking age (Gerard 2007), increasing alcohol prices (Matthews, Shepherd and Sivarajasingam 2006), and/or exercising greater controls on the alcohol industry.

Individual-level explanations for alcohol-related aggression

The intake of alcohol increases the risk of aggression in four main ways (Pihl and Hoaken 2002). First, alcohol activates the cue for reward system. Since alcohol is associated with positive outcomes, it increases psychomotor activity, which in turn increases an organism's approach behaviour, and, in the course of this increased activity (particularly in certain contexts), the likelihood of provoking aggression is increased. Second, alcohol affects the cue for punishment system. Alcohol's pharmacological effect is to reduce anxiety, which protects against punishment by inhibiting behaviour in the presence of novel or threatening stimuli; hence, it increases the likelihood of risk-taking behaviour, including aggression. Third, alcohol affects the pain system in two ways. With low doses, pain sensitivity is increased, which may serve to increase the significance of threats and may, therefore, lead to pre-emptive action to remove the threat. With high doses, however, pain sensitivity decreases, which may serve to increase risk-taking or may be a condition actively sought by those who intend to act violently. Fourth, alcohol interferes with the cognitive control system. Primarily, it does this by disrupting executive cognitive functioning, which include higher-order cerebral activities such as attention, abstracting relevant information, reasoning, problem-solving, planning, and self-regulation. When intoxicated, people make poorer decisions, including responding more aggressively to perceived threats. In this chapter, three topics relevant to cognitive control will be addressed separately: restricted attention, social problem-solving, and outcome expectancies.

Restricted attention

Acute intoxication impairs problem-solving abilities by restricting the range of cues perceived and attended to in any situation (Steele and Josephs 1990). In short, the more intoxicated a person becomes, the more they will focus on salient, immediate, and instigatory cues and less on distal and inhibitory cues. Furthermore, intoxication leaves few resources to access complex cognitive strategies that could help defend against threat (Josephs and Steele 1990). Clearly, avoiding intoxication in situations where provocation is likely is desirable.

Social problem-solving

Poor executive cognitive functioning is associated with aggressiveness, impulsive violent crime, and antisocial personality disorder (Giancola 2000; Hoaken,

Shaughnnessy and Pihl 2003). Therefore, further impairment of this functioning by means of alcohol intoxication may potentially heighten the risk of violence. The relationship between poor executive cognitive functioning and aggression appears to be an inability to cope with the range of response options, a failure to access socially appropriate responses, and a likelihood of making default aggressive responses when provoked (Hoaken *et al.* 2003); in short, poor social problem-solving.

Longitudinal research with young men by Welte and Wieczorek (1999) has showed that both drinking and IQ predicted violence, with a combination of heavy drinking and low verbal IQ being the strongest predictor of all. They concluded that, if alcohol causes violence by reducing intellectual functioning and promoting misunderstandings, then those with low IQ – particularly low verbal IQ – are more vulnerable to the negative consequences of alcohol. Conversely, studies of student samples have found no relationship between self-reported drinking and aggression and it is possible that students' good social problem-solving skills protect against aggression even when intoxicated (McMurran, Blair and Egan 2002; Ramadan and McMurran 2005).

Furthermore, Howard (2006) has suggested that drinking heavily during adolescence is likely to cause permanent impairment to frontal lobe functioning which, in youngsters with disinhibitory psychopathology, increases the likelihood of aggression continuing into adulthood. This suggests that parents and carers of children need to set rules regarding alcohol consumption and children's behaviour needs to be monitored. Additionally, the prohibition of alcohol sales to under-age youth in licensed premises and off-licences needs to be enforced.

Alcohol outcome expectancies

Alcohol outcome expectancies are the effects one expects to experience as a result of drinking (Goldman, Del Boca and Darkes 1999). Expectancies develop not only through experience, but also through instruction and observation. Put simply, expectancies may be construed as cognitive representations of an 'if-then' relationship ('If I drink, then . . .'), with the outcome varying for different people and for any one person across different situations. Expectancies may be positive, such as enhancing social and sexual functioning, or negative, such as a loss of self-control or feelings of depression (Jones, Corbin and Fromme 2001; Leigh and Stacy 2004). Because of this, it is clear that society has a responsibility to control the messages it conveys to young people about alcohol in advertising, in the media, in sport, and by example.

Expectancies of alcohol-related aggression

Some studies have shown that the belief that alcohol leads to aggression is correlated with alcohol-related violence in young men (McMurran *et al.* 2006; Quigley, Corbett and Tedeschi 2002; Zhang, Welte and Wieczorek 2002). However, Giancola (2006) tested the alcohol–aggression outcome expectancy on aggressive responding in a laboratory task and found that alcohol–aggression expectancies significantly predicted aggression for men, but not women; however, this relationship disappeared when dispositional aggressiveness was taken into account. Giancola (2006) therefore concluded that intoxicated aggression, at least in men, is mainly the result of the pharmacological properties of alcohol in conjunction with an aggressive disposition. This clearly points to the need to reduce intoxication if there is to be a reduction in alcohol-related aggression, particularly in inherently aggressive men. While it is important to minimise alcohol intoxication, this may not always (or even often) be the most successful tactic to adopt; particularly, in respect of young men for whom drinking to intoxication is a cultural norm. In this situation, protecting against aggression while intoxicated may be partially accomplished by targeting alcohol-related aggression outcome expectancies as one component in interventions to tackle alcohol-related aggression.

Expectancies of increased confidence

Alcohol-related aggression expectancies are not the only expectancies associated with aggression. There is also evidence that alcohol-related violence in young offenders is associated with expectancies of positive changes in social behaviour after drinking (McMurran 1997). In a study with male prisoners, McMurran (2007) measured the relationship between proneness to alcohol-related aggression, as measured by the Alcohol-Related Aggression Questionnaire (McMurran *et al.* 2006), and alcohol-related violence that was mediated by the expectancy that drinking would increase confidence, as measured by the Drinking Expectancy Questionnaire (DEQ) (Young and Oei 1996). The 'increased confidence' scale (Lee *et al.* 2003) contains factors such as the ability of alcohol to enable the expression of feelings, to encourage increased friendliness, and to enable one to be less concerned about one's behaviour. This confirms McMurran's (1997) earlier findings, where expectancies of positive social change after drinking were associated with alcohol-related violence in young offenders. The DEQ 'increased confidence' scale also predicted hazardous drinking in young adults. Thus, heavy drinking to increase confidence in social situations appears to be an important facet of young men's drinking, and is one that is associated with violence.

Young men are also likely to drink to increase their confidence in venues where confidence is relevant, for instance, in places where there is competition to find a sexual partner (Egan and Hamilton 2006). As such, aggression and violence are more likely in drinking venues where intoxicated and confident (perhaps overconfident) young men meet others like themselves in noisy, crowded drinking venues (Lang *et al.* 1995).

McMurran (2007) also found evidence that – for male prisoners at least – expectancies about alcohol increasing tension, irritability, and aggressiveness actually predicted hazardous drinking, suggesting either that this group views these as positive rather than negative consequences, or that other benefits, such as increased confidence, outweighed these negatives in the cost-benefit balance. This paradoxical finding may explain in part why alcohol education has a poor track record in changing young people's behaviour (Foxcroft *et al.* 2003), as appealing to young people to drink less to avoid the negative effects of intoxication either does not accord with their personal logic or fails to take into account the greater value of some of the positive effects.

Treatment

At present, few treatment programmes aimed specifically at alcohol-related violence exist, even though there has been a long-acknowledged need for interventions that 'not only employ standard treatment techniques (e.g. anger management), but also use knowledge of the effects of alcohol and the process of aggression in treating violent individuals' (Graham *et al.* 1998: 670). One structured cognitive-behavioural treatment programme for alcohol-related violence, informed by the evidence presented in this chapter, is Control of Violence for Angry Impulsive Drinkers (COVAID) (McMurran and Cusens 2003).

Central to COVAID is Robins and Novaco's (1999) 'angry-aggression system', in which anger provocations are appraised in the light of hostile beliefs, leading to angry arousal and then to aggression or violence. Alcohol intoxication is understood to exacerbate this system at all points because: certain drinking contexts increases the likelihood of experiencing anger provocations; alcohol impairs the perception and cognitive processing of social information and activates the alcohol–aggression outcome expectancy; the anxiolytic and analgesic effects of alcohol reduce violence inhibitions; and alcohol intoxication reduces the accessibility of more complex alternatives to aggression as a response to provocation. The COVAID intervention teaches participants to address all parts of the 'angry-aggression system', alongside avoiding drinking to intoxication, with the aim of reducing aggression and violence.

Over ten sessions, COVAID covers the following components:

1 Explaining drunken aggression
2 Crime harm reduction
3 Managing stress and arousal
4 Modifying drinking
5 Altering triggers
6 Weakening beliefs about the effects of alcohol
7 Identifying and coping with high risk situations
8 Enhancing problem-solving skills
9 Lifestyle change

Two main themes run through COVAID, both of which make the programme particularly suited to young people. The first is that participants are taught to become 'personal scientists' by learning the skills for analysing problem behaviours and experimenting with change. Encouraging these skills avoids the trap of telling young people what they ought to do. Second, COVAID enhances self-efficacy by identifying methods that participants already use to control aggression. This builds young peoples' confidence in their ability to succeed.

In one study, six COVAID participants showed improvements on psychometric measures of the treatment targets; namely, anger, impulsiveness, and alcohol-related aggression. Short-term reconviction data favoured COVAID over a group of ten who either did not start or did not complete COVAID (McMurran and Cusens 2003). In a second study, change scores on psychometric questionnaires were examined for nine participants by calculating clinical significance and reliability of change (McCulloch and McMurran 2007). All participants improved on the Alcohol-Related Aggression Questionnaire (ARAQ) (McMurran *et al.* 2006), with five showing both clinically significant and reliable change. On top of this, all the participants improved on both subscales of the Controlled Drinking Self-Efficacy Scale (CDSES) (Sitharthan *et al.* 2003), with six showing clinically significant improvement on at least one scale. Six participants also reported a reduction in alcohol consumption from the first to the second half of the programme and, at a mean of 29 weeks post-treatment, none of the participants had been reconvicted for a violent offence. Additionally, participants reported finding COVAID useful and interesting. Overall, then, these results are supportive of the possibility that COVAID may assist in reducing alcohol-related aggression and violent offending and a larger-scale evaluation is now underway.

Conclusion

As with most social problems, there is no single or simple cure for alcohol-related aggression. Instead, alcohol-related aggression must be targeted comprehensively at the levels of legislation, media, the drinks industry, point of sale, policing, community, family, and the individual. It is also worth emphasizing that young people who drink and become disorderly ought not to be vilified. Young people may be heavy drinkers, but so too are many middle-aged adults (Goddard 2006), many of whom would have been troublesome in their youth. Their drinking may no longer lead to the same degree of aggression and disorder because they are less inclined to drink to increase their social confidence, have lost their competitive edge, and get drunk in safer social environments. While young people must accept responsibility for their own behaviour, they also need to be provided with an environment that minimises risks to health and safety. Unfortunately, in the UK we still appear to care very little about protecting our young from the risks of drinking.

References

Egan, V. and Hamilton, E. (2008). 'Personality, mating effort and alcohol-related violence expectancies', *Addiction Research & Theory*, 16: 369–381.

Foxcroft, D., Ireland, D., Lister-Sharp, D. J. and Breen, R. (2003). 'Longer-term primary prevention for alcohol misuse in young people: a systematic review', *Addiction*, 98: 397–411.

Gerard, J. (2007). 'Should we raise the age of legal drinking?' *Public Policy Research*, March–May, 31–35.

Giancola, P. R. (2000). 'Executive functioning: a conceptual framework for alcohol-related aggression', *Experimental and Clinical Psychopharmacology*, 8: 576–597.

— (2006). 'Influence of subjective intoxication, breath alcohol concentration, and expectancies on the alcohol–aggression relationship', *Alcoholism: Clinical and Experimental Research*, 30: 844–850.

Goddard, E. (2006). *Smoking and Drinking Among Adults, 2005*. London: Office for National Statistics.

Goldman M. S., Del Boca, F. K. and Darkes, J. (1999). 'Alcohol expectancy theory: the application of cognitive neuroscience'. In K. E. Leonard and H. T. Blane (eds). *Psychological Theories of Drinking and Alcoholism, 2nd Ed*. New York: Guilford.

Graham, K. (2000). 'Preventive interventions for on-premise drinking: a promising but under-researched area of prevention', *Contemporary Drug Problems*, 27: 593–668.

Graham, K., Bernards, S., Osgood, D. W. and Wells, S. (2006). 'Bad nights or bad bars? multi-level analysis of environmental predictors of aggression in late-night large-capacity bars and clubs', *Addiction*, 101: 1569–1580.

Graham, K., Leonard, K. E., Room, R., Wild, T. C., Pihl, R. O., Bois, C. and Single, E. (1998). 'Current directions in research on understanding and preventing intoxicated aggression', *Addiction*, 93: 659–676.

Hoaken, P. N. S., Shaughnessy, V. K. and Pihl, R. O. (2003). 'Executive cognitive function and aggression: is it an issue of impulsivity?', *Aggressive Behavior*, 29: 15–30.

Hobbs, D. (2002). 'The night time economy'. In Alcohol Concern (ed). *100% Proof: Research for Action on Alcohol*. London: Alcohol Concern.

Honess, T., Seymour, L. and Webster, R. (2000). *The Social Context of Underage Drinking, Research, Development and Statistics Directorate*. London: Home Office.

Howard, R. (2006). 'How is personality disorder linked to dangerousness? A putative role for early-onset alcohol abuse', *Medical Hypotheses*, 67: 702–708.

Jones, B. T., Corbin, W. and Fromme, K. (2001). 'A review of expectancy theory and alcohol consumption', *Addiction*, 96: 57–72.

Josephs, R. A. and Steele, C. M. (1990). 'The two faces of alcohol myopia: attentional mediation of psychological stress', *Journal of Abnormal Psychology*, 99: 115–126.

Lang, E., Stockwell, T., Rydon, P. and Lockwood, A. (1995). 'Drinking settings and problems of intoxication', *Addiction Research*, 3: 141–149.

Lee, N. K., Oei, T. P. S., Greeley, J. D. and Baglioni, A. J. (2003). 'Psychometric properties of the Drinking Expectancies Questionnaire: a review of the factor structure and a proposed new scoring method', *Journal of Studies on Alcohol*, 64: 432–436.

Leigh, B. C. and Stacy, A. W. (2004). 'Alcohol expectancies and drinking in different age groups', *Addiction*, 99: 215–227.

Maguire, M. and Nettleton, H. (2003). *Reducing Alcohol-Related Violence and Disorder: An Evaluation of the 'TASC' Project, Home Office Research Study No. 265*. London: Home Office.

Matthews, K., Shepherd, J. and Sivarajasingam, V. (2006). 'Violence-related injury and the price of beer in England and Wales', *Applied Economics*, 38: 661–670.

McCulloch, A. and McMurran, M. (2008). 'Evaluation of a treatment programme for alcohol-related aggression', *Criminal Behaviour and Mental Health*, 18: 224–231.

McMurran, M. (1997). 'Outcome expectancies: an important link between substance use and crime?'. In S. Redondo, V. Garrido, J. Pérez, and R. Barbaret (eds.), *Advances in Psychology and Law*. Berlin: De Gruyter, 312–321.

— (2007). 'The relationships between alcohol–aggression proneness, general alcohol expectancies, drinking, and alcohol-related violence in adult male prisoners', *Psychology, Crime and Law*, 13: 275–284.

McMurran, M. and Cusens, B. (2003). 'Controlling alcohol-related violence: a treatment programme', *Criminal Behaviour and Mental Health*, 13: 59–76.

McMurran, M., Blair, M. and Egan, V. (2002). 'An investigation of the correlations between aggression, impulsiveness, social problem-solving, and alcohol use', *Aggressive Behavior*, 28: 439–445.

McMurran, M., Egan, V., Cusens, B., van den Bree, M., Austin, E. and Charlesworth, P. (2006). 'The Alcohol-Related Aggression Questionnaire', *Addiction Research and Theory*, 14: 323–343.

Pihl, R. O. and Hoaken, P. N. S. (2002). 'Biological bases of addiction and aggression in close relationships'. In C. Wekerle and A.-M. Wall (eds). *The Violence and Addiction Equation*. New York: Brunner-Routledge.

Quigley, B. M., Corbett, A. B. and Tedeschi, J. T. (2002). 'Desired image of power, alcohol expectancies, and alcohol-related aggression', *Psychology of Addictive Behavior*, 16: 318–324.

Ramadan, R. and McMurran, M. (2005). 'Alcohol and aggression: gender differences in their relationships with impulsiveness, sensation seeking and social problem solving', *Journal of Substance Use*, 10: 215–224.

Richardson, A. and Budd, T. (2003). *Alcohol, Crime and Disorder: A Study of Young Adults, Home Office Research Study No. 263*. London: Home Office.

Robins, S. and Novaco, R. (1999). 'Systems conceptualization and treatment of anger', *Journal of Clinical Psychology*, 55: 325–337.

Singleton, N., Farrell, M. and Meltzer, H. (1999). *Substance Misuse among Prisoners in England and Wales*. London: Office for National Statistics.

Sitharthan, T., Job, R. F. S., Kavanagh, D. J., Sitharthan, G. and Hough, M. (2003). 'Development of a controlled drinking self-efficacy scale and appraising its relation to alcohol dependence', *Journal of Clinical Psychology*, 59: 351–362.

Sivarajasingam, V., Moore, S. and Shepherd, J. P. (2007). *Violence in England and Wales 2006: An Accident and Emergency Perspective*. Cardiff: Cardiff University.

Steele, C. M. and Josephs, R. A. (1990). 'Alcohol myopia: its prized and dangerous effects', *American Psychologist*, 45: 921–933.

Welte, J. W. and Wieczorek, W. F. (1999). 'Alcohol, intelligence, and violent crime in young males', *Journal of Substance Abuse*, 10: 309–319.

Young, R. McD. and Oei, T. P. S. (1996). *Drinking Expectancy Profile: Test Manual*. Brisbane, Australia: University of Queensland.

Zhang, L., Welte, J. W. and Wieczorek, W. W. (2002). 'The role of aggression-related alcohol expectancies in explaining the link between alcohol and violent behavior', *Substance Use and Misuse*, 37: 457–471.

4 Childhood risk factors for young adult offending

Onset and persistence

David P. Farrington

In England and Wales (and many other countries), persons legally become adults in the criminal justice system at age 18. The treatment of offenders aged 18 or over is very different from the treatment of offenders aged 17 or less. In 2005, the Barrow Cadbury Commission on Young Adults and the Criminal Justice System recommended that young adults (those aged between 18 and some unspecified age between 21 and 25) should be treated differently from older adults because they are less mature and because they are likely to desist from offending in their early 20s. The Commission argued that adult criminal justice treatment in the early 20s could impede this desistance and that special treatment was, therefore, needed for young adults.

The main aim of this chapter is to provide information about young adult offenders (defined as those aged between 18 and 25) using the data from a prospective longitudinal study – the Cambridge Study in Delinquent Development – of males from age 10 to age 50. Various issues will be addressed in this chapter. What kinds of children become young adult offenders? To what extent can they be predicted? What kinds of lives do they lead in adulthood? To what extent is there continuity in offending over time? What proportion of young adult offenders persist in offending later in life and what subsequently happens to persisters and desisters?

Some information relevant to young adult offending has been provided in previous publications from the Cambridge Study. West and Farrington (1977) reported childhood predictors of convictions that later took place between the ages of 17 and 20, and lifestyle correlations at age 18 for convicted youths; the so-called 'delinquent way of life'. Farrington (1979) also documented predictors of juvenile and young adult (those between the ages of 17 and 20) convictions and self-reported delinquency. In a later study (1986b) that looked at stepping-stones to adult criminal careers, he reported predictors of convictions at ages 10 to 13, 14 to 16, 17 to 20 and 21 to 24. Even more recently (2000), Farrington has studied childhood predictors of adult convictions between the ages of 21 and 40. Zara and Farrington (2009) have also documented childhood, adolescent and adult predictors of onset adult offending (between the ages of 21 and 50). Finally, criminal career information about onset, desistance, duration and continuity of offending over time has been provided by Farrington (1992), Farrington *et al.* (1998) and Piquero *et al.* (2007).

In this chapter, the specific questions that will be addressed are as follows:

- What are the most usual ages for the onset of and desistance from offending (measured by convictions for criminal offences)?
- What proportion of young adult offenders persist in offending at older ages?
- What are the most important childhood risk factors that encourage young adult offending?
- What risk factors predict which young adult offenders will persist in offending and which will desist?
- What are the later life (between the ages of 32 and 48) outcomes for persisters and desisters?

The Cambridge Study in Delinquent Development

The Cambridge Study in Delinquent Development is a prospective longitudinal survey of the development of offending and antisocial behaviour in 411 males. When they were first contacted in 1961–62, these boys were all living in a working-class inner-city area of South London. The sample was chosen by taking all the boys who were then aged between 8 and 9 and on the registers of six state primary schools within a one-mile radius of a research office that had been established. Therefore, the most common year of birth for these males was 1953.

In nearly all cases (94 per cent), the family breadwinner at that time (usually the father) had a working-class occupation (skilled, semi-skilled or unskilled manual worker) and most of the males (87 per cent) were white and of British origin. The majority of the boys were living in conventional two-parent families with both a father and a mother figure: at age 8 to 9, only 6 per cent of the boys had no operative father and only 1 per cent had no operative mother. Overwhelmingly, then, this was a traditional white, urban, working class sample of British origin.

The study was originally directed by Donald J. West and, since 1982, it has been directed by myself (my work with the project stretches back to 1969). The major results of the study can be found in books by West (1969, 1982) and by West and Farrington (1973, 1977) and in summary papers by Farrington and West (1981, 1990) and Farrington (1995, 2003). The most recent report (Farrington *et al.* 2006) lists 145 publications from the study. These publications should be consulted for more details about the predictor variables measured in this chapter. We are also very grateful to the Home Office and to the Department of Health for funding the study.

The original aims of the study were: to describe the development of delinquent and criminal behaviour in inner-city males; to investigate how far it could be predicted in advance; to explain why juvenile delinquency began; to explain why it did or did not continue into adult crime; and to explain why adult crime usually ended as men reached their 20s. Throughout we focused on continuity or discontinuity in behavioural development, the effects of life events on development, and the prediction of future behaviour. The study was not designed to test any one particular theory about delinquency, but was instead meant to test many different hypotheses about the causes and correlates of offending. One reason for casting the net so wide at the start and measuring many different variables was the idea that, because theoretical fashions tend to change over time, it was important to try to measure as many variables as possible in which future researchers might be interested. Another reason for measuring a wide range of variables was the fact that long-term longitudinal surveys were very uncommon and that the value of this particular one would be enhanced if it yielded information of use, not only to delinquency researchers, but also to those interested in alcohol and drug use, educational difficulties, poverty, poor housing, unemployment, sexual behaviour, aggression, other social problems and general human development.

Data collection

The males were interviewed and tested in their schools by psychologists when they were aged about 8, 10 and 14. They were then interviewed by young social science graduates in a research office when they were aged about 16, 18 and 21. After this, they were then interviewed by young social science graduates in their homes when they were aged about 25, 32 and 48. At all ages, except 21 and 25, the aim was to interview the whole sample, and it was always possible to trace and interview a high proportion: 389 were interviewed out of 410 still alive at age 18 (95 per cent), 378 out of 403 still alive at age 32 (94 per cent) and 365 out of 394 still alive at age 48 (93 per cent). The tests carried out in the schools measured individual characteristics such as intelligence, attainment, personality and psychomotor impulsivity, while information was collected in the interviews about such topics as living circumstances, employment histories, relationships with females, illnesses and injuries, leisure activities (such as drinking, fighting and drug use) and offending behaviour.

Tremendous efforts were made to secure interviews based on our belief (based in part on previous results obtained in this study) that the most interesting persons in any research on offending tend to be the hardest to locate and/or the most unco-operative (Farrington *et al.* 1990). Moreover, surveys in which less than 75 per cent of the target sample is interviewed may also produce results that seriously underestimate the true level of criminal behaviour. Generally, an increase in the percentage interviewed from 75 per cent to 95 per cent leads to a disproportionate increase in the validity of the results. At age 18, for example, 36 per cent of the one-sixth of the sample who were the most difficult to interview had been convicted, compared with only 22 per cent of the majority who were interviewed more easily; a statistically significant difference (West and Farrington 1977).

In addition to interviews and tests with the boys, interviews with the parents were carried out by female social workers who visited their homes. These took place about once a year from when the boy in question was about age 8 until he was aged 14 to 15 (which was the last year of compulsory education). The primary informant was the mother, although many fathers were also seen. The parents provided details about such matters as the boy's daring or nervousness, the family income and the family size as well as detailing their own employment histories, their child-rearing practices (including attitudes, discipline levels and parental conflict), their histories of psychiatric treatment, the degree to which they supervised the boy and any temporary or permanent separations he may have had from them.

Teachers also completed questionnaires when the boys were aged about 8, 10, 12 and 14. These provided us with data about troublesome and aggressive school behaviour, hyperactivity or poor concentration, frequent lying, anxiety, school achievement and truancy. Ratings were also obtained about such topics as the boys' daring, dishonesty, troublesomeness and popularity from their peers when they were in primary school.

For the present analyses, each variable was dichotomized, as far as possible, into the 'worst' quarter of males (i.e. the quarter with the lowest income or lowest intelligence) versus the remainder. This was done in order to compare the importance of different variables and also to permit a 'risk factor' approach (Farrington and Loeber 2000). Because most variables were originally classified into a small number of categories, and because fine distinctions between categories could not be made very accurately, this dichotomizing did not usually involve a great loss of information. The one-quarter/three-quarters split was chosen so as to match the prior expectation that about one-quarter of the sample would be convicted as juveniles. Variables were not included in the analysis if more than about 10 per cent of the sample had not provided results for them (for lists of key risk factors at different ages see Farrington 2006a).

Criminal records

Searches were also carried out in the Central Criminal Record Office (CRO), the National Identification Service (NIS) and later, on the Police National Computer (PNC) to try to locate findings of guilt for the males, their parents, their brothers and sisters, and their wives and female partners (Farrington *et al.* 1996). These repeated searches over a 40-year period were essential to the study, as the medium for data storage changed from paper to microfiche to computers and many records were deleted or not transferred during these changeovers. The minimum age of criminal responsibility in England is 10 and the CRO/NIS/PNC contains records of all relatively serious offences committed in Great Britain or Ireland. In the case of eighteen males who had emigrated outside the jurisdictions of Great Britain and Ireland by age 32, we made applications to search their criminal records in the eight countries where they had settled and searches were actually carried out in five of these countries. However, since most males did not emigrate until their 20s, and since these emigrants had rarely been convicted in England, it is likely that hardly any convicted males were not recorded. The latest search of conviction records in NIS and PNC took place in December 2004, when most of the males were aged 50. Altogether, 167 males (41 per cent) had been convicted up to this age (Farrington *et al.* 2006).

In this chapter, the recorded age of offending is the age at which an offence was committed, not the age upon conviction. This choice was made because there can be delays of several months, or even more than a year, between offences and convictions, making conviction ages different from offending ages. Offences are defined as acts leading to convictions, and only offences committed on different days were counted. Where two or more offences were committed on the same day, only the most serious one was counted. Most court appearances arose from only one offending day. Convictions were only counted if they were for offences normally recorded in the CRO/NIS/PNC. All motoring offences were excluded, along with other minor crimes such as common assault and drunkenness. The most usual offences included were thefts, burglaries and the unauthorized taking of vehicles, although there were also quite a few cases of violence, vandalism, fraud and drug abuse (see Farrington *et al.* 2006). Official cautions were nationally recorded from 1995 and a few were included after that date. In order not to rely completely on official records for information about delinquency and crime, self-reports of offending were also obtained from the males at every age from 14 onwards (Farrington 1989).

To sum up, then the Cambridge Study in Delinquent Development has a unique combination of features:

- Nine personal interviews with the males have been completed over a period of 40 years, from age 8 to age 48.
- The main focus of interest is on offending, which has been studied from age 10 to age 50 in official records and self-reports.
- The sample size of about 400 is large enough for many statistical analyses, but small enough to permit detailed case histories of the males and their families.
- There has been a very low attrition rate, since 93 per cent of the males still alive were interviewed at age 48.
- Information has been obtained from multiple sources: the males, their parents, teachers, peers and official records.
- Information has been obtained about a wide variety of factors, including biological, individual, family, peer and school measures.

Criminal career features

Seven males were considered not to be at risk of a recorded conviction because they had emigrated permanently before the age of 21, had not been convicted and had not been searched abroad. No unconvicted male died before age 21. Of the 404 males at risk, 167 (41 per cent) were convicted of criminal offences up to age 50. Table 4.1 shows that the median age of the first conviction was 17 (interquartile range 14.3–20.8), while the median age of the last conviction was 25.2 (interquartile range 18.8–36.9). Because the age-crime curve is skewed (Farrington 1986a), the average ages of onset (19.1) and desistance (28.2) were higher than the median ages. The average criminal career duration was 9.1 years. Excluding the 49 offenders with only one conviction (and, hence a career duration of zero years), the average career duration was 12.8 years.

Up to the age of 17, three emigrated males were considered to be not at risk of a conviction. Of the remaining 408, 103 (25 per cent) were convicted between the ages of 10 to 17 (referred to here as juvenile delinquents). Between the ages of 18

Table 4.1 Onset, desistance and career duration

Percentile	Age at First Conviction	Age at Last Conviction	Career Duration (1)	Career Duration (2)
25	14.3	18.8	0	3.3
50	17.0	25.2	3.9	9.9
75	20.8	36.9	14.9	21.1
Average	19.1	28.2	9.1	12.8

Note: 'Career Duration (1)' includes 49 one-time offenders (in years)
'Career Duration (2)' excludes 49 one-time offenders (in years).

and 25, seven males who emigrated and two males who died before the age of 21 were considered to be not at risk. Of the remaining 402, 109 (27 per cent) were convicted as young adults (from age 18 to 25). Between the ages of 26 and 50, 14 males who emigrated and eight males who died before age 35 were considered to be not at risk. Of the remaining 389, 78 (20 per cent) were convicted as adults (from age 26 to 50).

There was considerable continuity in offending over time. Of the 101 juvenile delinquents (convicted at age 10 to 17), 71 (70 per cent) were convicted as young adults (from age 18 to 25), compared with only 38 (13 per cent) of the 301 males who were not convicted as juveniles. Of the 107 young adult offenders, 48 (45 per cent) were convicted as adults (from age 26 to 50), compared with only 30 (11 per cent) of the 282 males who were not convicted as young adults.

The main measure used in this chapter to establish the strength of relationships is the Odds Ratio (OR), which roughly indicates the increase in risk associated with a risk factor. An OR of 2 or greater signifies a strong relationship (Cohen 1996), compared with the chance value of 1. An OR of 0.5 signifies a similarly strong but negative relationship. For juvenile versus young adult offending, OR = 16.4 ($p < .05$). For young adult versus adult offending, OR = 6.8 ($p < .05$).

The likelihood of a young adult offender becoming an adult offender was greater if the male had also been a juvenile delinquent (54 per cent) than if he had not (29 per cent; OR = 2.8, $p < .05$). However, the likelihood of a male who was not convicted between the ages of 18 and 25 being convicted as an adult was not significantly greater if he had been a juvenile delinquent (15 per cent) than if he had not (10 per cent; OR = 1.5, not significant or ns). Therefore, the influence of past convictions decreased after a number of conviction-free years.

Table 4.2 shows the degree to which age of onset (10–17, 18–25 or 26–50) predicted criminal career features. Of those first convicted as juveniles, 84 per cent were reconvicted, and they accrued 6.5 convictions on average. Of those first convicted as young adults, 53 per cent were reconvicted, and they accrued 2.3 convictions on average. Of these first convicted as adults, 42 per cent were reconvicted, and they accrued 2 convictions on average. The average criminal

Table 4.2 Age of onset vs. criminal career features

	Age of Onset			Total
	10–17	*18–25*	*26–50*	
Number	103	38	26	167
% Reconvicted	84	53	42	71
No. of Convictions	6.5	2.3	2.0	4.8
Age at first conviction	14.8	20.8	33.7	19.1
Age at last conviction	26.3	27.5	36.6	28.2
Career duration (1)	11.5	6.6	2.9	9.1
Career duration (2)	13.6	12.6	6.8	12.8

Note: 'Career duration (1)' includes 49 one-time offenders (in years)
       'Career duration (2)' excludes 49 one-time offenders (in years)

career duration was 11.5 years after juvenile onset, 6.6 years after young adult onset and 2.9 years after adult onset.

Childhood risk factors

Table 4.3 shows the degree to which childhood risk factors (measured at age 8 to 10) predicted young adult offending. For example, 41 per cent of boys from low income families at age 8 were convicted as young adults, compared with 23 per cent of those from higher income families; a significant difference ($OR = 2.4$, $p < .05$). For comparison, the ORs for predicting juvenile (2.7) and adult (1.3) offending are also shown. Low family income at 8 was a slightly stronger predictor of juvenile delinquency than of young adult offending, and it did not significantly predict adult offending. Since 65 per cent of young adult offenders had been juvenile delinquents, predictors of juvenile delinquency were likely to be quite similar to predictors of young adult offending.

Out of 29 key childhood risk factors (specified in Table 4.3), 21 significantly predicted young adult offending. The strongest predictors (all significant) were: a convicted parent ($OR = 3.8$); troublesomeness rated by teachers and peers ($OR = 3.6$); low junior school attainment ($OR = 3.1$); a delinquent sibling ($OR = 3.0$); poor parental supervision ($OR = 2.7$); large family size (i.e. five or more children in the family; $OR = 2.6$); dishonesty rated by peers ($OR = 2.6$); a disrupted family (i.e. the loss of a biological parent, usually the father; $OR = 2.5$); hyperactivity (i.e. lacks concentration or restless in class, rated by teachers; $OR = 2.5$); and low family income ($OR = 2.4$). Nervous-withdrawal ($OR = 0.6$) and a lack of friends ($OR = 0.4$) were negatively related to young adult offending. The 'antisocial' factor was a combined measure of antisocial personality traits, including: troublesome behaviour, dishonest behaviour, conduct problems, being difficult to discipline, a past record of stealing, a liability to get angry, daring behaviour, hyperactivity, impulsivity and truancy (Farrington 1991). Significantly, the more antisocial boys at age 8 to 10 tended to become young adult offenders.

Table 4.3 Childhood risk factors for young adult convictions

Age 8–10 Risk Factor	% Convicted		Odds Ratio		
	Absent	Present	18–25	10–17	26–50
Socio-economic					
Low family income	23	41	2.4*	2.7*	1.3
Poor housing	22	36	2.0*	2.0*	1.6
Large family size	22	43	2.6*	3.0*	2.2*
Delinquent school	24	41	2.2*	3.0*	1.3
Family					
Convicted parent	19	48	3.8*	4.4*	2.7*
Delinquent sibling	24	49	3.0*	3.5*	1.6
Young mother	24	37	1.8*	2.0*	1.9*
Depressed mother	22	35	1.9*	1.5	1.1
Poor supervision	22	44	2.7*	2.5*	2.3*
Disrupted family	23	42	2.5*	2.3*	2.7*
Parental conflict	22	39	2.3*	2.1*	1.3
Individual					
Low non-verbal IQ	24	38	2.0*	2.2*	1.9*
Low verbal IQ	24	37	1.9*	1.7*	1.8*
Low attainment	21	45	3.1*	2.8*	1.8*
High daring	22	39	2.2*	3.9*	2.3*
Hyperactive	23	43	2.5*	2.3*	2.5*
Nervous-withdrawn	29	18	0.6*	0.7	1.9*
Few friends	28	13	0.4*	0.5	0.9
Behavioural					
Troublesome	21	49	3.6*	4.7*	2.0*
Dishonest	22	42	2.6*	3.3*	3.1*
Antisocial	21	48	3.5*	4.9*	3.0*

Note: 'Absent' means risk factor absent; 'Present' means risk factor present.
* $p < 0.05$ Not significantly predictive of young adult convictions: low socio-economic status, depressed father, harsh discipline, psychomotor impulsivity, unpopular, high extraversion, high neuroticism, small boy.

In many cases, these childhood risk factors predicted juvenile delinquency more strongly than adult convictions. This is only to be expected, since predictive efficiency is likely to decrease with the time interval between the predictor and the outcome. For example, the ORs for troublesomeness were 4.7 in predicting juvenile delinquency, 3.6 in predicting young adult offending, and 2.0 in predicting adult offending. The greatest discrepancy concerned high daring or risk-taking, which was a much stronger predictor of juvenile delinquency (OR = 3.9) than of young adult offending (OR = 2.2). The strongest childhood predictors of adult offending were dishonesty (OR = 3.1), a convicted parent (OR = 2.7), a disrupted family (OR = 2.7) and hyperactivity (OR = 2.5). Nervous-withdrawal was a positive predictor of adult offending (OR = 1.9), whereas it had been a negative predictor of young adult offending (OR = 0.6).

Logistic regression analyses were carried out to investigate the independent predictors of juvenile delinquency, young adult offending and adult offending

Table 4.4 Logistic regression analyses predicting convictions

Age 8–10 Risk Factor	LRCS Change	p	Partial OR	p
Age 18–25 Convictions				
Convicted parent	31.54	.0001	2.9	.0003
Large family size	9.53	.002	2.3	.007
Few friends (−)	10.57	.001	0.2	.005
Disrupted family	6.12	.013	2.1	.014
Low attainment	5.09	.024	2.2	.012
Nervous-withdrawn (−)	4.95	.026	0.5	.033
Age 10–17 Convictions				
Convicted parent	35.68	.0001	3.8	.0001
High daring	27.11	.0001	4.0	.0001
Low attainment	10.09	.002	2.2	.010
Delinquent sibling	5.83	.016	2.6	.015
Age 26–50 Convictions				
Disrupted family	13.40	.0003	2.6	.002
High daring	10.83	.001	3.2	.0001
Unpopular	11.27	.0008	2.8	.0007
Nervous-withdrawn	5.41	.020	2.2	.018
Onset at age 18–25				
Depressed mother	7.15	.008	3.0	.006
Nervous-withdrawn (−)	10.75	.001	0.1	.009
Disrupted family	4.97	.026	2.6	.033
Low attainment	4.06	.044	2.5	.038
Persistence after age 10–17				
Convicted parent	7.51	.006	4.3	.007
Small (−)	5.32	.021	0.2	.009
Low attainment	5.66	.017	3.8	.026

Note: 'LRCS' (Likelihood Ratio Chi Squared); 'OR' (Odds Ratio)

(Table 4.4). Measures of childhood antisocial behaviour (troublesomeness and dishonesty) were not included as predictors, so that this analysis might reveal factors that were possibly explanatory. The strongest predictors of young adult offending were a convicted parent, large family size, few friends (negative), a disrupted family, low school attainment and nervous-withdrawal (negative). The strongest predictors of juvenile delinquency were a convicted parent, high daring, low school attainment and a delinquent sibling. The strongest predictors of adult offending were a disrupted family, high daring, unpopularity and nervous-withdrawal (positively).

Nervous-withdrawn boys were unlikely to become juvenile delinquents: 19 per cent of nervous-withdrawn boys compared with 26 per cent of the remainder (OR = 0.7, ns). Similarly, nervous-withdrawn boys were unlikely to become young adult offenders: 18 per cent of nervous-withdrawn boys compared with 29 per cent of the remainder (OR = 0.5, $p < .05$). However, nervous-withdrawn boys were significantly more likely to become adult offenders: 28 per cent of nervous-withdrawn boys compared with 17 per cent of the remainder (OR = 1.9, $p < .05$). Not surprisingly, young adult offenders who had been nervous-withdrawn boys were more likely to persist into adult offending than other young adult offenders: 65 per cent compared with 39 per cent of the remainder (OR = 2.9, not quite significant). Similarly, males who were not convicted between the ages of 18 to 25 were more likely to subsequently be convicted if they had been nervous-withdrawn boys: 19 per cent compared with 7 per cent (OR = 3.1, $p < .05$).

As mentioned, because of the considerable overlap between juvenile delinquents and young adult offenders, many of the childhood risk factors were similar for both. It is, therefore, useful to disentangle juvenile and young adult offending by investigating the predictors of the 38 (out of 301) young adult offenders who were not convicted as juveniles. In this case, the strongest predictors were: a disrupted family (OR = 2.7, $p < .05$); poor parental supervision (OR = 2.6, $p < .05$); an anxious-depressed mother (OR = 2.4, $p < .05$); low school attainment (OR = 2.2, ns); and poor housing (OR = 2.0, $p < .05$), together with the negative predictor of a nervous-withdrawal (OR = 0.3, $p < .05$). Table 4.4 shows that the independently important predictors of onset between the ages of 18 and 25 were an anxious-depressed mother, nervous-withdrawal (negative), a disrupted family and low school attainment.

It is also useful to investigate the predictors for the 71 young adult offenders among the 101 juvenile delinquents. In this instance, the strongest predictors were: peer-rated dishonesty (OR = 3.8, $p < .05$); a convicted parent (OR = 2.9, $p < .05$); low school attainment (OR = 2.9, $p < .05$); hyperactivity (OR = 2.9, not quite significant); low social class (OR = 2.9, ns); and an anxious-depressed father (OR = 2.9, ns), together with the negative predictor of small stature (low height: OR = 0.5, ns). Table 4.4 shows that the independently important predictors of persistence after the ages 10 to 17 were a convicted parent, small stature (negative) and low school attainment.

Small stature (low height) also predicted juvenile delinquency: 38 per cent of relatively small boys became delinquents, compared with 22 per cent of the remainder (OR = 2.1, $p < .05$). However, juvenile delinquents who were small boys were less likely to persist into young adult offending than other delinquents: 59 per cent compared to 75 per cent of the remainder (OR = 0.5, ns). Interestingly, young adult offenders who were relatively tall boys were more likely to persist into adult offending than the remainder: 63 per cent compared with 37 per cent of the remainder (OR = 2.8, $p < .05$).

Risk factors for persistence

Table 4.5 shows risk factors for persistence after young adult offending. All ORs of 2.0 or more or 0.5 or less are shown. The 48 males who persisted in adult offending were compared with the 59 males who were not convicted after age 25. The strongest predictors at age 8 to 10 were harsh parental attitude and discipline (OR = 3.0), nervous-withdrawn boy (OR = 2.9 but not quite significant because

Table 4.5 Risk factors for persistence after young adult offending

Risk Factor	% Convicted 26–50		Odds Ratio
	Absent	*Present*	
Age 8–10			
Poor housing	54	36	0.5
Delinquent school	49	32	0.5
Convicted parent	36	54	2.0
Harsh discipline	34	61	3.0*
Disrupted family	38	58	2.3*
High daring	38	54	2.0
Tall	37	63	2.8*
Nervous-withdrawn	39	65	2.9
Unpopular	37	59	2.5*
Dishonest	36	61	2.8*
Antisocial	37	56	2.1
Age 12–14			
Low social class	48	33	0.5
Early school leaving	21	51	3.8*
Hyperactive	36	56	2.3*
Frequent liar	32	59	3.0*
Anxious/Nervous	38	58	2.3*
Aggressive	36	53	2.0
Hostile to police	36	59	2.5*
Delinquent friends	36	55	2.2
High SR violence	37	55	2.1
High SR delinquency	34	59	2.7*
Antisocial	31	61	3.5*
Age 16–18			
Low take-home pay	49	33	0.5
No examinations	33	51	2.1
High extraversion	39	56	2.0
Tattooed	42	63	2.3
Small	49	33	0.5
Hostile to police	37	55	2.1
Sexually promiscuous	37	55	2.1
Heavy drinker	34	62	3.2*
Drunk driver	40	59	2.1
Motoring offender	41	60	2.2
Injured	50	25	0.3*
Antisocial	31	69	2.2

Note: 'Absent' means risk factor absent; 'Present' means risk factor present. *$p < 0.05$ 'SR' (Self-reported).

of small numbers), tall stature (OR = 2.8), dishonesty (OR = 2.8), unpopularity (OR = 2.5), and a disrupted family (OR = 2.3).

The strongest predictors at age 12 to 14 were early school leaving (OR = 3.8), frequent lying according to teachers (OR = 3.0), high self-reported delinquency (OR = 2.7), hostility to the police according to an attitude questionnaire

Table 4.6 Logistic regression analyses predicting persistence

Risk Factor	LRCS Change	P	Partial OR	P
Age 8–10				
Harsh discipline	7.73	.005	3.7	.010
Unpopular	5.22	.022	3.5	.011
Tall	5.94	.015	3.5	.018
Age 8–18				
Heavy drinker 18	11.45	.0007	5.4	.003
Harsh discipline 8	5.56	.018	5.3	.009
Injured 18(−)	6.91	.009	0.14	.012
Tall 8–10	5.04	.025	4.7	.016
Unpopular 8–10	5.59	.018	3.7	.022

Note: 'LRCS' Likelihood Ratio Chi-Squared; 'OR' (Odds Ratio).

(OR = 2.5), hyperactivity according to teachers (OR = 2.3) and anxiousness according to teachers or nervousness-according to parents (OR = 2.3). Only two variables at age 16 to 18 significantly predicted persistence: heavy drinking (40 units of alcohol or more per week: OR = 3.0) and hospital treatment due to injury (a negative relationship, OR = 0.3). Injuries were usually incurred in assaults, motorcycle accidents, at home, in industrial premises or in sport. Injured males significantly tended to be convicted between the ages of 15 and 18 (Shepherd *et al.* 2002). The combined antisocial personality measure predicted persistence at all ages.

Table 4.6 shows the independent predictors of persistence found in logistic regression analyses. The most important childhood predictors were harsh parental attitude and discipline, unpopularity and tall stature. The most important predictors at all ages were heavy drinking at age 18 and harsh discipline at age 8.

Life success or failure

Analysing the Cambridge Study sample in adulthood, Farrington *et al.* (2006) identified nine criteria for life success or failure in the previous five years:

1 Accommodation (e.g. home owner, poor home conditions, frequent moves).
2 Cohabitation (e.g. living with female partner, divorced in last five years, gets on well with female partner).
3 Employment (e.g. currently unemployed, low social class job, low take-home pay).
4 Involved in fights in the last five years.
5 Alcohol use (e.g. driven after drinking 10 units or more in the last five years, heavy drinker of 40 units or more per week, CAGE score 2 or more to detect alcoholism: see Mayfield *et al.* 1974).

Table 4.7 Unsuccessful life at ages 32 and 48

Failure Criteria	Age 32			Age 48		
	% of Unconv. (222)	% of Des. (57)	% of Pers. (43)	% of Unconv. (216)	% of Des. (53)	% of Pers (42)
Accommodation	28	38	49*	16	17	43*
Cohabitation	21	22	37*	25	15	29
Employment	18	21	56*	13	13	43*
Fights	27	47*	77*	10	17	40*
Alcohol use	26	53*	77*	15	28*	38*
Drug use	11	21	53*	10	13	50*
SR Offending	4	14*	44*	2	4	10*
GHQ 5 or more	20	26	33	16	14	18
Not convicted	0	0	67*	0	0	53*
Unsuccessful life	10	26*	70*	5	4	50*

Note: 'Unconv.'(Unconvicted)
    'Des.' (Desisters: convicted at 18–25, but not at 26–50)
    'Pers.' (Persisters: convicted at 18–25 and at 26–50)
    *Significantly ($p < .05$) different from unconvicted
    'SR' (Self-reported); 'GHQ' (General Health Questionnaire)
    Failure criteria usually referred to the previous five years.

6 Drug use (taken marijuana or other drugs in the last five years).
7 Self-reported offending in the last five years (e.g. burglary, theft of vehicle, theft from vehicle, shoplifting, theft from machine, vandalism).
8 Anxiety-depression (score of 5 or more on the General Health Questionnaire: see Goldberg 1978).
9 Convicted in the last five years.
   These exact criteria were measured at ages 32 and 48.

Table 4.7 shows the percentages of males considered to be unsuccessful in the 9 criteria at each age. Males who failed on four or more of the criteria were considered to be leading unsuccessful lives. At age 32, for example, 26 per cent of unconvicted males were unsuccessful on alcohol use, compared with 47 per cent of desisters after young adult offending and 77 per cent of persisters. The percentages of persisters and desisters who were unsuccessful were significantly greater than the percentage of unconvicted males.

At age 32, persisters were significantly less successful than unconvicted males on all criteria except anxiety/depression, while desisters were significantly worse on fighting, drinking and self-reported offending. At age 48, persisters were significantly less successful than unconvicted males on all criteria except cohabitation and anxiety/depression, while desisters were significantly worse only on drinking.

The life success of all categories of males improved between the ages of 32 and 48. For example, whereas 70 per cent of persisters were considered to be leading unsuccessful lives at age 32, only 50 per cent were at age 48. Most notably, the desisters were worse than the unconvicted males at age 32 (26 per cent unsuccessful compared with 10 per cent), but barely different at age 48 (4 per cent unsuccessful compared with 5 per cent). This suggests that, 20 years after desisting, ex-offenders were equivalent to non-offenders in their life success.

Conclusion

The Cambridge Study has many unique strengths, but as with all other projects, it also has some limitations. For instance, because the results come from white, urban, working-class samples of males of British origin born in the 1950s, it is unclear how far they can be generalized more widely. However, similar findings were obtained from later samples of males born in London in 1960 (Farrington & Maughan 1999), male working-class boys born in Stockholm in 1953 (Farrington & Wikström 1994), males and females born in Finland in about 1960 (Pulkkinen 1988) and for inner-city boys born in Pittsburgh between 1974 and 1980 (Farrington and Loeber 1999). Moreover, most reviews of childhood risk factors for offending find that results obtained in different longitudinal projects are, to a large extent, similar (Farrington 2007; Farrington and Welsh 2007). Another major limitation of the Cambridge Study is that, due to the difficulty of obtaining funding, the measurements were less frequent than we would have liked.

Past research on the Cambridge Study has found that the most important childhood predictors of offending tend to fall into six independently important categories:

1 antisocial child behaviour (troublesomeness, dishonesty)
2 criminality in the family (a convicted parent, a delinquent sibling)
3 school failure (low IQ, low school attainment)
4 poor parenting (harsh discipline, poor supervision, a disrupted family)
5 impulsiveness (daring or risk-taking, restlessness or poor concentration)
6 economic deprivation (low income, poor housing, large family size)

Farrington (2005) has proposed a developmental theory of offending that includes all of these constructs.

The most important predictors of young adult offending included: troublesomeness, a convicted parent, large family size, a disrupted family, and low school attainment. However, daring behaviour was less important as a predictor of young adult offending than as a predictor of juvenile delinquency.

Being nervous-withdrawn and having few friends seemed to be protective factors against young adult offending. Farrington *et al.* (1988) earlier noted that the best predictor of unconvicted boys from criminogenic backgrounds was having few or no friends, possibly because most juvenile offences were committed with others (Reiss and Farrington 1991). However, nervousness was a significant predictor of adult offending, and Zara and Farrington (2009) have found that nervousness predicted the onset of adult offending. As the importance of co-offending decreased with age, the relationship between nervous-withdrawn behaviour and offending changed from negative to positive. Similarly, the relationship between height and offending changed from negative for juvenile delinquency, to positive for adult offending.

In general, there was continuity in offending over time. Continuity from juvenile delinquency to young adult offending was predicted by the usual childhood risk factors; namely, dishonesty, a convicted parent, low school attainment and hyperactivity. However, low social class was a more important predictor of persistence than it had been of juvenile delinquency. Continuity from young adult offending to adult offending was predicted by harsh discipline, nervous-withdrawal, tall stature, dishonesty, unpopularity and a disrupted family. Heavy drinking at age 18 and frequent lying between the ages of 12 to 14 were also important predictors of persistence after young adult offending. Farrington and Hawkins (1991) also found that almost 90 per cent of offenders who were unemployed and heavy drinkers at age 18 were reconvicted between the ages of 21 and 32. The onset of young adult offending among previously unconvicted boys was predicted by an anxious-depressed mother (which was more important in predicting psychopathy than offending: see Farrington 2006b), low nervousness, a disrupted family, low school attainment and poor parental supervision. These results pose challenges to existing criminological theories.

While there was generally continuity in offending over time, offenders who desisted tended to have good outcomes. Among those who were not young adult offenders, a previous history of juvenile delinquency did not predict a significantly increased risk of adult offending. The young adult offenders who then desisted were similar to unconvicted males in all aspects of life success except heavy drinking. The message, then is a positive one. Just as ex-smokers become similar to non-smokers after at least 10 years of abstinence (The Times 2007), so ex-offenders go on lead lives as successful as non-offenders after 20 years of abstinence (and possibly even after 10 years, but the infrequency of our data collection made it impossible to establish this for certain).

Overall, the main policy implications from the study are that efforts should be made to prevent both onset and persistence by targeting key risk factors. Effective interventions include: home visiting programmes with pregnant women; parent management training; pre-school intellectual enrichment programmes; cognitive-behavioural skills training programmes; treatment foster care; and multi-systems therapy (Farrington 2007; Farrington and Welsh 2007). In all of this work, the motto should be 'never too early, never too late' (Loeber and Farrington 1998). Nevertheless, more research is needed on criminal careers and on the childhood, adolescent and adult lives of young adult offenders. This is needed both to prevent the development of 'the delinquent way of life' and to encourage it to end as soon as possible.

References

Barrow Cadbury Commission (2005) *Lost in Transition: A Report of the Barrow Cadbury Commission on Young Adults and the Criminal Justice System*. London: Barrow Cadbury Trust.

Cohen, P. (1996) 'Childhood risks for young adult symptoms of personality disorder: method and substance', *Multivariate Behavioural Research*, 31: 121–148.

Farrington, D. P. (1979) 'Environmental stress, delinquent behavior and convictions', in I. G. Sarason and C. D. Spielberger (eds), *Stress and Anxiety, vol. 6*. Washington, D.C.: Hemisphere: 93–107.

— (1986a) 'Age and crime', in M. Tonry and N. Morris (eds), *Crime and Justice, vol. 7*, Chicago: University of Chicago Press: 189–250.

— (1986b) 'Stepping stones to adult criminal careers', in D. Olweus, J. Block and M. R. Yarrow (eds), *Development of Antisocial and Prosocial Behavior: Research, Theories and Issues*. New York: Academic Press.

— (1989) 'Self-reported and official offending from adolescence to adulthood', in M. W. Klein (ed), *Cross-National Research in Self-Reported Crime and Delinquency*. Dordrecht, Netherlands: Kluwer.

— (1991) 'Antisocial personality from childhood to adulthood', *The Psychologist*, 4: 389–394.

— (1992) 'Criminal career research in the United Kingdom', *British Journal of Criminology*, 32: 521–536.

— (1995) 'The development of offending and antisocial behaviour from childhood: Key findings from the Cambridge Study in Delinquent Development', *Journal of Child Psychology and Psychiatry*, 36: 929–964.

— (2000) 'Psychosocial predictors of adult antisocial personality and adult convictions', *Behavioral Sciences and the Law*, 18: 605–622.

— (2003) 'Key results from the first 40 years of the Cambridge Study in Delinquent Development', in T. P. Thornberry and M. D. Krohn (eds), *Taking Stock of Delinquency: An Overview of Findings from Contemporary Longitudinal Studies*. New York: Kluwer/Plenum.

— (2005) 'The Integrated Cognitive Antisocial Potential (ICAP) theory', in D. P. Farrington (ed.) *Integrated Developmental and Life-Course Theories of Offending*. New Brunswick, N. J.: Transaction.

— (2006a) 'Comparing football hooligans and violent offenders: Childhood, adolescent, teenage and adult features', *Monatsschrift fur Kriminologie und Strafrechtsreform*, (*Journal of Criminology and Penal Reform*), 89: 193–205.

— (2006b) 'Family background and psychopathy', in C. J. Patrick (ed.) *Handbook of Psychopathy*. New York: Guilford Press.

— (2007) 'Childhood risk factors and risk-focussed prevention', in M. Maguire, R. Morgan and R. Reiner (eds), *The Oxford Handbook of Criminology, 4th edn*. Oxford: Oxford University Press.

Farrington, D. P. and Hawkins, J. D. (1991) 'Predicting participation, early onset, and later persistence in officially recorded offending', *Criminal Behaviour and Mental Health*, 1: 1–33.

Farrington, D. P. and Loeber, R. (1999) 'Transatlantic replicability of risk factors in the development of delinquency', in P. Cohen, C. Slomkowski and L. N. Robins (eds), *Historical and Geographical Influences on Psychopathology*. Mahwah, N. J.: Lawrence Erlbaum.

— (2000) 'Some benefits of dichotomization in psychiatric and criminological research', *Criminal Behaviour and Mental Health*, 10: 100–122.

Farrington, D. P. and Maughan, B. (1999) 'Criminal careers of two London cohorts', *Criminal Behaviour and Mental Health*, 9: 91–106.

Farrington, D. P. and Welsh, B. C. (2007) *Saving Children from a Life of Crime: Early Risk Factors and Effective Interventions*. Oxford: Oxford University Press.

Farrington, D. P. and West, D. J. (1981) 'The Cambridge Study in Delinquent Development (United Kingdom)', in S. A. Mednick and A. E. Baert (eds), *Prospective Longitudinal Research*. Oxford: Oxford University Press.

— (1990) 'The Cambridge Study in Delinquent Development: A long-term follow-up of 411 London males', in H.-J. Kerner and G. Kaiser (eds), *Kriminalitat: Personlichkeit, Lebensgeschichte und Verhalten (Criminality: Personality, Behaviour and Life History)*. Berlin: Springer-Verlag.

Farrington, D. P. and Wikström, P.-O. H. (1994) 'Criminal careers in London and Stockholm: A cross-national comparative study', in E. G. M. Weltekamp and H.-J. Kerner (eds), *Cross-National Longitudinal Research on Human Development and Criminal Behaviour*. Dordrecht, Netherlands: Kluwer.

Farrington, D. P., Gallagher, B., Morley, L., St. Ledger, R. J. and West, D. J. (1988) 'Are there any successful men from criminogenic backgrounds?', *Psychiatry*, 51: 116–130.

— (1990) 'Minimizing attrition in longitudinal research: Methods of tracing and securing cooperation in a 24-year follow-up study', in D. Magnusson and L. Bergman (eds), *Data Quality in Longitudinal Research*. Cambridge: Cambridge University Press.

Farrington, D. P., Barnes, G. and Lambert, S. (1996) 'The concentration of offending in families', *Legal and Criminological Psychology*, 1: 47–63.

Farrington, D. P., Lambert, S. and West, D. J. (1998) 'Criminal careers of two generations of family members in the Cambridge Study in Delinquent Development', *Studies on Crime and Crime Prevention*, 7: 85–106.

Farrington, D. P., Coid, J. W., Harnett, L. M., Jolliffe, D., Soteriou, N., Turner, R. E. and West, D. J. (2006) *Criminal Careers Up to Age 50 and Life Success Up to Age 48: New Findings from the Cambridge Study in Delinquent Development, Research Study No. 299*. London: Home Office.

Goldberg, D. (1978) *Manual of the General Health Questionnaire*. Windsor, Berks: NFER-Nelson.

Loeber, R. and Farrington, D. P. (1998) 'Never too early, never too late: Risk factors and successful interventions for serious and violent juvenile offenders', *Studies on Crime and Crime Prevention*, 7: 7–30.

Mayfield, D., McLeod, G. and Hall, P. (1974) 'The CAGE questionnaire: Validation of a new alcoholism screening instrument', *American Journal of Psychiatry*, 131: 1121–1123.

'New medical research' (2007) *The Times (Times 2)*, 27 March, 2.

Piquero, A. R., Farrington, D. P. and Blumstein, A. (2007) *Key Issues in Criminal Career Research: New Analyses of the Cambridge Study in Delinquent Development*. Cambridge: Cambridge University Press.

Pulkkinen, L. (1988) 'Delinquent development: theoretical and empirical considerations', in M. Rutter (ed.), *Studies of Psychosocial, Risk*. Cambridge: Cambridge University Press.

Reiss, A. J. and Farrington, D. P. (1991) 'Advancing knowledge about co-offending: results from a prospective longitudinal survey of London males', *Journal of Criminal Law and Criminology*, 82: 360–395.

Shepherd, J. P., Farrington, D. P. and Potts, A. J. C. (2002) 'Relations between offending, injury and illness', *Journal of the Royal Society of Medicine*, 95: 539–544.

West, D. J. (1969) *Present Conduct and Future Delinquency*. London: Heinemann.

— (1982) *Delinquency: Its Roots, Careers and Prospects*. London: Heinemann.

West, D. J. and Farrington, D. P. (1973) *Who Becomes Delinquent?* London: Heinemann.

— (1977) *The Delinquent Way of Life*. London: Heinemann.

Zara, G. and Farrington, D. P. (2006) 'Later criminal careers: psychological influences', in J. Obergfell-Fuchs and M. Brandenstein (eds), *Nationale und Internationale Entwicklungen in der Kriminologie (National and International Developments in Criminology)*. Frankfurt: Verlag fur Polizeiwissenschaft.

5 Young adult offenders in custodial institutions

Vulnerability, relationships and risks

Alison Liebling

Much of the history of criminology has been shaped by the study of juvenile delinquency (see, e.g. Matza 1964; West and Farrington 1973; Rutter and Giller 1983). We know a great deal about this age group, including the short-term nature of their beliefs, rules and goals, their individualistic and hedonistic motivation, the fragility of their identities, their low self-control, their reluctance to trust those in authority, their use of avoidant coping strategies, poor health behaviour and the façade of gesture and language which often masks a lack of confidence and faith in attachment (see, e.g. Hollin and Howells 1996). Troubled adolescents often 'protest self-sufficiency, while feeling completely un-self-sufficient' (Toch 1977/1992: 107).

My research life began with young offenders in custody. In 1986 I was employed at Hull University on a Home Office funded project on the concept of young offender throughcare. This project explored the then new unified 'Youth Custody system' in a former detention centre, a former borstal, and a former YP prison, as they were previously known. We interviewed 150 young offenders in custody and 70 prison and probation officers, and we examined the files of a further 150 recently released young offenders. Our main findings were that young people in custody had troubled histories and complex unmet needs. Shared working between the prison and probation services was patchy at best and hampered by very different cultures and working practices in the two services concerned (McAllister *et al.* 1992). Promising elements of throughcare work were poorly integrated with other elements, and interventions rarely went deep enough to address the origins of offending behaviour or have a lasting impact. The creation of the National Offender Management Service (NOMS) in 2004 suggests that there is still much work to be done in this area, but that in England and Wales, we are now engaged in another, rather more concerted, attempt to make integration work. This is a particularly important development given the very high reconviction rates of young offenders released from custody (Howard League 2006), and – as I will argue – the links between these dismal offending histories and the shaky hold some young people have on life.

In the Hull study, personal officers working in prisons, and probation officers working from the outside, were seen at their best as 'someone you could go to with your problems'. Most young offenders wanted more help, more contact, and earlier contact with their outside probation officers whilst in custody. Probation officers, on the other hand, tended to prioritise offenders in the community, and to wait until their released clients reappeared in their areas before meeting in person. This was partly a question of resources, but it was also a matter of different perceptions about how useful a visit might be whilst a young offender was in custody. In terms of building a relationship, on which the effectiveness of other types of work might depend, contact during custody was an important investment. Young offenders compared notes on how good or poor their probation officers were in this respect, one or two waving letters about to demonstrate to others that their probation officer was coming to see them and that they were, therefore, a person of value. Poor contact throughout custody has been found to justify poor cooperation on release (Foad 1984: 31). It has also been found that those clients with the greatest needs and the most intractable problems are often those least likely to receive support during a custodial sentence (McAllister *et al.* 1992: 108).

During the fieldwork for the young offender through-care project, I became a specialist prisons researcher. What drew me in was the charm and vulnerability of young people in prison, the dedication and imagination of many of those working with them in secure settings, including probation officers, physical education instructors, education officers and prison officers, and yet the tragic distance that existed between what went on in institutions designed to help reduce reoffending with this age group, and the nature and extent of their problems and needs. My subsequent PhD on suicides and suicide attempts in four young offenders institutions expanded on these early concerns. I shall shortly return to those findings. I shall then consider, in the final part of the chapter, a more recent development of that study carried out by one of my recent PhD students. I will also refer selectively to other relevant research conducted over the years between. My overall argument is that in becoming preoccupied with risk, we can forget need; that young adulthood is a significant age at which intervention matters; that families constitute a major issue for this age group (close relationships are often fragile and unreliable and threats to these relationships often precipitate a crisis); that young offenders are emotionally vulnerable when imprisoned (they have a very strong need for social contact and support, and for activity); and that relationships with staff often mirror relationships with family: (they can be fragile, explosive, ambivalent and demanding) (Liebling 1992). Additionally, one in ten young *women* in custody are mothers, so that we have a population of young people for whom parenting is by no means over, but who are shortly to embark on their own parenting careers. In this sense their own lives, and the lives of future generations, depend on addressing the many problems they have, as well as pose. For all of these reasons, my view is that whatever the immediate practical arguments (which are principally about finding spaces in overcrowded prisons) there are overwhelming strategic arguments in favour of retaining the specialness of the 18–20 year old age group and for emphasising the needs of this population in penal policy.

Suicides and attempted suicides in custodial settings

I will illustrate these points by focusing on suicide and suicide risk in particular. It has been a concern for many years that, nationally, the suicide rate amongst young men from lower socio-economic classes has increased, and remains high despite a significant drop in suicide rates among other populations. The rate doubled in the last 30 years of the twentieth century, reaching a peak in 1998 when it accounted for one fifth of all young adult male deaths (Oliver and Storey 2006; and on women, see Liebling 1994). Unemployment, homelessness, drug and alcohol problems, poor educational history, confusing role models and lack of social ties are thought to account for some of this increase. Suicides among young prisoners also occur disproportionately, and in certain establishments these deaths have been linked to bullying, hostile sub-cultures, and lack of ability or resources to cope with life in prison. Around ten young people aged between 18 and 20 take their own lives in prison in England and Wales each year. Around a thousand a year injure themselves intentionally, sometimes requiring resuscitation. Clusters of deaths are somewhat more common amongst young prisoners, in particular establishments or sometimes in specific wings. Situational factors are often highly significant in precipitating suicidal feelings with this young age group. Their level of predisposition is also high, however. Their offences are often acquisitive – or not very serious – and they are unlikely to have a psychiatric diagnosis. My study of this age group (Liebling 1992) compared a group of 50 suicide attempters with a group of non suicidal young prisoners and found many significant differences.

Considering first their criminal justice histories, the suicide attempt group were more likely to have pessimistic social inquiry reports (now known as pre-sentence reports) as they were then known. That is, their probation officers were fairly pessimistic about their chances of receiving a community penalty at the time of sentence, partly due to their social and domestic circumstances. The suicide attempt group also had higher numbers of previous convictions, and were less likely to have stayed outside of prison between sentences for long (many had managed less than three months of liberty). In terms of their backgrounds, suicide attempters were even less likely than the comparison group to have qualifications from school. They were more likely to have been bullied at school, to have been placed in local authority care, to have had previous psychiatric treatment, to report major problems with drink or drugs, to have witnessed parental violence and to have injured themselves before. It was instructive, however, that so many young prisoners had such difficult backgrounds that in order to differentiate between suicide attempters and the comparison group, questions about the severity of parental violence have to be used to differentiate between the populations. So for example, if I asked, 'and did anyone have to go to hospital as a result of this violence?' the suicide attempt group were significantly more likely to say 'yes' to this question. In fact, generally on background differences, it was a matter of degree: looking simply for the presence or absence of certain factors in their histories was insufficiently precise to distinguish the highly vulnerable from the rest. As one psychologist said, all young prisoners could be classed as vulnerable, some are simply at the extreme end of the continuum.

Turning to their experience in custody, suicide attempters preferred to share a cell, and they disliked physical education (often as a result of, for example, lack of confidence, poor coordination, or a susceptibility to bullying). They reported not being able to think of anything to do when locked in their cells, and yet they spent more time there. They reported feeling bored, and not being able to find ways of relieving boredom. They made few friends in custody, and met the only mates they did know in custody. They therefore stuck by themselves, reported experiencing difficulties with other prisoners, appeared as disciplinary problems in the prison, and felt the disciplinary system was less fair. They spent more time in segregation, were frequently referred to the doctor or psychiatrist, and they reported many current problems. In other words, they did not adapt easily to the prison experience and stood out, normally as management or disciplinary problems. We have found in subsequent research that there is a disproportionate tendency for such prisoners to find themselves on the 'basic' level of privileges in the so-called Incentives and Earned Privileges Scheme, and therefore in the most restricted circumstances in prison (Liebling *et al.* 1997). Coping difficulties for prisoners can easily become 'discipline problems' for staff in busy, complex prisons.

As regards family and outside support, suicide attempters received fewer visits, wrote fewer letters, missed family members more and received less contact from the probation service. They found thinking about outside more difficult. In their own accounts of their states of mind and coping behaviour, suicide attemptees were more likely to want to change something about themselves, and more likely to daydream. They were less hopeful about their release, had major problems sleeping, found being locked up more difficult, scored much higher on a hopelessness scale and reported more frequent and serious thoughts of suicide. They were more likely to see others' suicide attempts as serious and to think that 'not being able to handle the sentence' was a major cause of suicidal thinking in prison.

What all this adds up to is a kind of emptiness and lack of stability, or what might be described as 'resourcelessness' among certain young prisoners. It links their offending behaviour outside prison to a lack of ability to handle the sentence once inside. As mentioned earlier, this pattern was not unusual and could be seen as the extreme end of a continuum. All the young offenders in this study shared some of these characteristics; indeed, around 20 per cent of the comparison group reported having thought about suicide at some stage. Yet since young people often express their feelings in their behaviour rather than in speech, they were often impulsive and impatient, and regarded by prison staff as troublesome rather than vulnerable (Liebling 1992, 1995, 1999).

In a more recent evaluation of a major suicide prevention strategy in ten high-risk establishments including two Young Offenders Institutions (YOI), we found that distress was often lower where offenders were engaged in offending behaviour programmes, as well as where they were generally occupied and in well organised, predictable establishments in which 'association' (free time on the wings) was infrequently cancelled. The most important predictor of distress was a feeling of lack of safety in establishments, and this in turn was related to three main areas of life in the prison: the quality of relationships with and treatment by prison staff, levels of care for individuals at risk, and the control of drugs (Liebling *et al.* 2005a; Liebling 2007; Liebling and Tait 2007). Prisoners in the two YOIs in the study felt less safe than adult prisoners did. They were slightly more likely than prisoners in adult prisons to be in prison for the first time. At Feltham YOI, where significant progress was made in the implementation of the new strategy and in culture change, prisoners still experienced quite high (albeit lower) levels of distress at the outcomes stage of the study, but they reported feeling quite well supported, particularly on entry into custody, by enthusiastic multi-disciplinary teams including prison officers (Liebling *et al.* 2005a). Prisoners said throughout the project that 'the way staff talk to you' could make a difference between feeling motivated to 'go on' and giving up in despair. Two of our more troubling findings, however, were first, that no matter how positive the culture, there were limits as to how far serious distress could be alleviated, and second, that prisons could get worse over time as well as better, despite the apparent implementation of ameliorative programmes costing considerable amounts of money. By way of illustration, Table 5.1 shows some of the responses from young adults to the questions asked at Feltham and Glen Parva YOIs at the before and after stages of the evaluation. The data in this Table show that even after considerable improvement to buildings, practices and attitudes, only 37 per cent of young people felt 'looked after' when they first came into prison. Indeed, unfortunately, prisoners are often regarded as 'attention seeking' when they self-harm, despite the known links between self-harm and future suicide risk (Liebling 1999).

At an organisational level, it is clear that the values of senior managers and staff, the culture of staff in general, and day to day practices in relation to individuals at risk, make a difference to the experience of imprisonment (see Liebling *et al.* 2005b; Liebling and Tait 2007). But it should be remembered that there are limits to how positive or constructive an experience of imprisonment can be. At an individual psychological level, there is scope for clearer thinking about the burgeoning concepts of well-being or 'good lives' in relation to both reducing re-offending and reducing suicide risk among young people (Ward and Mann 2003), and for closer integration between criminal justice work with this population and the promising mental health promotion initiatives taking place in the community (see for example, National Institute for Mental Health in England 2005).

Adaptation to imprisonment

In his study of *Young Men in Prison* Joel Harvey (2007) studied in detail the transition to imprisonment and first month in custody of 70 young male offenders received into Feltham Young Offenders Institution. He found them to be preoccupied with fear and safety, and to avoid looking others in the eyes, or being defensive in their behaviour towards other prisoners and staff unless they could be reassured that things were not as bad as they expected them to be. Even time spent in specially devised first night centres and deliberately attentive induction

Table 5.1 Perceptions of key activities and processes in two young offenders institutions, 2002 and 2004

Item/Statement	Feltham %	Glen Parva %
'When I first came to this prison I felt looked after.'	37	29
'This prison is good at providing care for those who are at risk of suicide.'	51	34
'This prison is good at improving the well-being of prisoners who have drug problems.'	40	43
'Wing staff take an interest in helping to sort out my health care needs.'	48	29
'The induction process in this prison helped me to know what to expect in the daily regime and when it would happen.'	43	33
'Anyone with a drug problem coming into this prison gets the help they need to detox safely.'	34	34
'Anyone who harms themselves is considered by staff to be more of an attention seeker than someone who needs care and help.'	28	28

units led to anxieties about what the prison would 'really be like' once they were moved onto a main wing. Prisoners familiar with Feltham worried about the mix of prisoners and staff, or being transferred from the juvenile to the young adult side, changes in rules and regulations, as well as the outcome of their own court case or their release date. These worries were in addition to the serious anxieties they had about family and loved ones: 'do they know where I am?', 'will this mean they will finally throw me out?', 'will my girlfriend end the relationship now?' And so on. They knew or felt that they had 'thrown everything away' (Harvey 2007: 42), but it was too late to turn the clock back:

> You get to prison and it feels like there is a big abyss in your life. You're standing at the end of this abyss and you know you can see something on the other side, but you don't know how to get there ... it's like society doesn't want you'.
>
> (Prisoner, in Harvey 2007: 42)

Organising and getting phone numbers cleared so that contact could be established with family was harder in this era of mobile phones, in which we enter phone numbers into our mobiles and find we don't know them if asked.

Whilst most prisoners reported finding this initial part of the custodial experience distressing, those young prisoners who scored lowest on a measure of internal locus of control experienced significantly higher levels of distress during these early weeks. They felt less safe, and were less likely to be able to seek out resources in the environment, create niches, or actively 'glean' from their experience of custody (Harvey 2007: 48–9). They did not see themselves as good adapters, and they felt less able to regulate their thoughts and emotions. Harvey's work shows how if young prisoners cannot adapt emotionally to the prison setting, then they are unable to adapt socially and practically. Such adaptation is necessary to active survival.

At the end of a one month period, some young offenders had successfully adapted to custody, others remained in what Harvey called a 'liminal zone', failing to settle, remaining on induction units, thinking excessively about their circumstances, plagued by feelings of separation and loss, and not moving into education or work. They felt unable to trust others, and had not come to terms with their situation. Many of these individuals had psychiatric histories, had self-harmed in the past, or were withdrawing painfully from serious drug use. These prisoners sometimes found themselves in segregation units or in health care centres, unassimilated and unable to understand what the regime required. They were out of their depth in custody, and if they were on ordinary locations, were treated as if they had adapted. Staff did not have the time to interrupt the flow of normal prison life in order to cater for their needs. Being bullied, or shouted at by staff, could set the clock back to zero. Adapting to custody required social and psychological resources that some simply did not have. Whilst staff were often very supportive, highly vulnerable young prisoners were often least likely to seek support from staff and were easily overlooked.

Conclusion

The research reported in this paper illustrates that custody can be a negative and damaging experience for many, and that adapting to it requires considerable skill, or support. Any assumption that so-called positive regimes can assist generally in the process of reducing re-offending needs to take account of these kinds of hurdles, the realities of prison life, and the vulnerability and attachment difficulties of some young offenders in particular. Individuals who adapted successfully found ways of embedding themselves socially (with staff and fellow prisoners) and psychologically, orienting themselves positively towards the regime, finding out what was on offer and taking control of their circumstances. They submitted applications for prized jobs, attended education, and became involved in the gym, in football or in playing pool. This could increase their social confidence and kick-start a reciprocal relationship between their behaviour and a kind of reinforcement that came back to them from the environment. The prison world seemed like a safer, more manageable place. Self-efficacy was an important skill for these young people to develop, as others have noted before (Lösel 1996).

To end on a more positive note, adolescence is a turbulent stage of life, which often involves some delinquency, yet many make the transition to adulthood successfully. As Little (1990: 47) put it:

> Adolescence is an extremely important time of life which sees amongst other things, the development of moral conceptions and ego-identity. Adolescents

form groups consisting of three to six others. It is a time of experimentation and usually involves some delinquency.

Within this time of experimentation, young adults are influenced by their experiences, and by the adults they encounter. That means that the moral and social climate of the institutions we devise, which in turn means the competence and calibre of staff working with this age group, as well as certain promising programmes and interventions, have a crucial role in their futures:

> It is generally accepted that young people are more easily influenced than adults. Their personalities are not yet fully formed, and their attitude and outlook on life can change rapidly. They are also at a time of life when opportunities taken or missed, and habits formed, can have a lasting effect on the rest of their lives. Young people who are sentenced to be detained in a Young Offender Institution are bound to be influenced by their experience, and it is *vital to ensure that the good influences outweigh the bad*. Positive relationships with members of staff can be one of the most powerful good influences the establishment offers.
>
> (Home Office, in Lyon *et al.* 1994, emphasis added)

As the Prisons Inspectorate said in the Preface to their 1997 *Thematic Review of Young Prisoners*:

> Changing the attitudes and behaviour of many of the young criminals who end up in custody requires tough, challenging regimes run by very skilled staff. But unless they receive individual attention and opportunities to change, their time in custody will make them worse rather than better'.
>
> (HMCIP 1997: Preface)

References

Foad, K. (1984) *A review of the development of throughcare practice*, unpublished MSc dissertation, University of East Anglia.

Harvey, J. (2007) *Young Men in Prison: surviving and adapting to life inside.* Cullompton, Devon: Willan.

HM Chief Inspector of Prisons (1997) *Thematic Review of Young Prisoners*. London: Home Office.

Hollin, C. R. and Howells, K. (eds.) (1996) *Clinical Approaches to Working with Young Offenders*. Chichester: John Wiley.

Howard League (2006) *Out for Good: the resettlement needs of young men in prison.* London: Howard League for Penal Reform.

Liebling, A. (1992) *Suicides in Prison.* London: Routledge.

— (1994) 'Suicides amongst women prisoners'. *Howard Journal of Criminal Justice*, 33: 1–9.

— (1995) 'Vulnerability and prison suicide'. *British Journal of Criminology*, 35: 173–187.

— (1999) 'Prison suicide and prisoner coping', in M. Tonry and J. Petersilia (eds), *Prisons, Crime and Justice: an annual review of research, 26.* chicago: University of Chicago Press.

— (2007) 'Prison suicide and its prevention', in Y. Jewkes (ed.), *The Prisons Handbook.* Cullompton, Devon: Willan.

Liebling, A. and Tait, S. (2006) 'Improving staff-prisoner relationships', in G. E. Dear (ed.), *Preventing Suicide and Other Self-Harm in Prison.* London: Palgrave-Macmillan.

Liebling, A., Muir, G., Rose, G. and Bottoms, A. E. (1997) 'An evaluation of Incentives and Earned Privileges: final report to the Prison Service', unpublished report, in the library of the Institute of Criminology, University of Cambridge.

Liebling, A., Durie, L., Stiles, A. and Tait, S. (2005a) 'Revisiting prison suicide: the role of fairness and distress', in A. Liebling, and S. Maruna (eds), *The Effects of Imprisonment.* Cullompton, Devon: Willan.

Liebling, A., Tait, S., Stiles, A., Durie, L. and Harvey, J., assisted by Rose, G. (2005b) 'An evaluation of the Safer Locals Programme': unpublished final report to the Home Office, unpublished report.

Little, M. (1990) *Young Men in Prison: criminal identity explored through the rules of behaviour.* Aldershot: Dartmouth.

Lösel, F. (1996) 'Working with young offenders: the impact of meta-analyses', in C. R. Hollin and K. Howells (eds), *Clinical Approaches to Working with Young Offenders.* Chichester: John Wiley.

Lyon, J., Lowe, K., Wilson, A., Coleman, J., McLellan, S. and Davies, C. (1994) *The Nature of Adolescence: understanding and working with young men in custody,* 3rd edition. Brighton: Trust for the Study of Adolescence.

MacAllister, D., Bottomley, A. K. and Liebling, A. (1992) *From Custody to Community: throughcare for young offenders.* Aldershot: Avebury.

Matza, D. (1964) *Delinquency and Drift.* New York: Wiley.

National Institute for Mental Health in England (2005) *National Suicide Prevention Strategy for England.* Annual Report on Progress. Leeds: NIMHE.

Oliver, C. and Storey, P. (2006) *Evaluation of Mental Health Promotion Pilots to Reduce Suicide Amongst Young Men: final report.* London: Thomas Coram Research Unit, Institute of Education.

Rutter, M. and Giller, H. (1983) *Juvenile Delinquency: trends and perspectives.* Harmondsworth: Penguin Books.

Toch, H. (1977/1992) *Living in Prison: the ecology of survival.* New York: Free Press.

Ward, T. and Mann, R. (2003) 'Good lives and the rehabilitation of sex offenders: a positive approach to treatment', in P. A. Linley and S. Joseph (eds), *Positive Psychology in Practice.* Chichester: John Wiley.

West, D. J. and Farrington, D. P. (1973) *Who Becomes Delinquent?* London: Heinemann Educational.

6 What works in correctional treatment and rehabilitation for young adults?

Friedrich Lösel

Criminal law and the criminal justice system need clear terms and categories to ensure fair procedures and decisions. Accordingly, there are fixed age thresholds of criminal responsibility and specific regulations for child, juvenile and adult offenders. However, these thresholds have often been questioned. In England and Wales, for example, the debate over the low threshold of age 10 for criminal responsibility has been revitalized by the Bulger Case and other recent spectacular child offences (e.g. Commission on Families and the Wellbeing of Children 2005). In Europe this threshold varies from age 10 in England and Wales and Switzerland, to age 12 in the Netherlands, age 13 in France and Poland, age 14 in Austria, Germany, Italy and Russia, age 15 in the Czech Republic and the Scandinavian countries, age 16 in Portugal and Spain and up to age 18 years for specific crimes in countries such as Belgium and Romania. These international differences are based more on different legal traditions than on scientific evidence. Although there is some research favouring an age of criminal responsibility between 12–15 (see Lösel and Bliesener 1997), the key question is whether the respective age regulations are accompanied by effective interventions from the criminal justice or social welfare system.

The same issues are mirrored at the upper threshold of the youth category. Although nearly all European countries give full civil rights to people at age 18 (Switzerland: 20), they vary substantially in the age at which their criminal law treats young offenders as 'adults'. Some countries have a relatively low threshold of age 16 (e.g. Latvia, Lithuania and Russia), whereas others have a higher one of age 18 (e.g. Belgium, Bulgaria, the Czech Republic, Estonia, Finland, France, Hungary, Ireland, Norway, Slovakia and Switzerland). Many nations have introduced some flexibility into the system by using different age thresholds at which the young offender can (as opposed to must) be treated as an 'adult' within the criminal justice system. In some countries this applies to the period between the ages 15–18, but others have specific legal regulations for young offenders up to age 21 (e.g. Croatia, Germany, Italy, the Netherlands, Portugal, Romania and Sweden). In England and Wales offenders aged 18–20 are treated as adults, although if they receive a custodial sentence they are partially separated in Young Offender Institutions (YOIs). Depending on the needs of offenders (e.g. education, professional training and/or treatment programmes), there can be some overlap in the regimes of prisons and YOIs, but at age 21 offenders are generally accommodated in prisons for adults. In Germany, by comparison, the criminal justice system can deal with and treat offenders aged 18–20 as 'youth' if their intellectual or moral development is still that of typical youth or if their index offences are typical of a youth. In cases of custody, a majority of offenders at this age go to prisons for juveniles and many even remain there beyond age 21 until their sentence terminates.

Although young adult offending is a topical issue in many countries, current discussions are driven more by a punitive climate than by empirical questions. However, criminal justice must always ask how best to balance the penal aims of compensation, protection of the public, general deterrence and retribution with the rehabilitative aim of preventing reoffending. Moreover, as Cesare Beccaria and Franz von Liszt emphasized in the eighteenth and nineteenth centuries, a future-oriented penal system should give particular weight to the latter aim. Accordingly, one should ask whether current practice fits the needs of young adult offenders and whether it effectively reduces their reoffending. These are not new questions (e.g. Hood 1974). However, research still tends to concentrate on either juvenile or adult offenders, not paying the young adult group much attention. Indeed, in most publications and practical approaches young adults are simply incorporated into the very heterogeneous population of 'adults.' The present chapter will tackle this oversight by addressing the question of correctional rehabilitation of young adults (roughly defined as being aged 18–25).

First, some basic characteristics of this offender group are discussed. Second, I will, in the main part of the chapter, review the core issues of the 'what works' literature on offender rehabilitation with a specific focus on young adult offenders. Throughout, the emphasis will be on empirical evidence, but recent controversies about the 'right' paradigm for rehabilitation (Brayford *et al.* 2011; Ward and Maruna 2007) will also be addressed briefly. The chapter then ends with conclusions and recommendations for future research, policy and practice. As the topic is relevant for many countries, the aim of the discussion is international. This may help to avoid national blind spots that sometimes occur even in otherwise excellent reviews that do not recognize that there is a world beyond North America (e.g. Cullen 2005).

Young adult offenders

In modern societies the development of young people has changed considerably over recent decades. On the one hand, physical acceleration and more liberal parenting have led to an earlier start of youth-typical behaviours (e.g. going out at night, drinking, smoking, sexual relations, etc.). On the other hand, coping with important developmental tasks is extended far beyond youth (e.g. secondary education, regular work and income, independence from parents, founding of their own family, etc.). Research has shown that the offending of young people is related to developmental transitions and coping (Moffitt 1993) and young adulthood may contain similar risks and problems. This view is supported by analyses showing

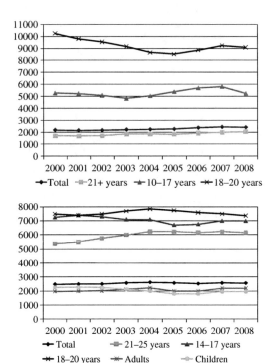

Figure 6.1 Persons arrested for offences in England and Wales (top) and Germany (bottom) by age group per 100,000 of the respective population.

Sources: Police Crime Statistics (only data on offenders with German nationality is provided in the bottom graph).

that young adults are at a particularly high risk of social exclusion (Toynbee 2003; Webster *et al.* 2004). Bearing this in mind, the typical age–crime curve, with its decline in late adolescence, can be seen to tell only one part of the story. And, indeed, data suggest that crime problems in young adulthood are not less prevalent than in youth.

For example, Figure 6.1 shows that for young adult offenders (aged 18–20) the rate of arrests per 100,000 in England and Wales is much higher than for juvenile offenders (aged 10–17). This is partially due to the relatively low crime rates in early adolescence. However, police data from Germany – a country where the lower age threshold for youth crime is age 14 – reveal a similar tendency; since 2000, the curve for arrested young adults aged 18–20 is above that of juvenile offenders, and the respective rate figures for young adults aged 21–25 are not much lower.

Although public discussion and research is much more focussed on youth crime, the crimes of young adults are no less serious. For example, data from the 2005

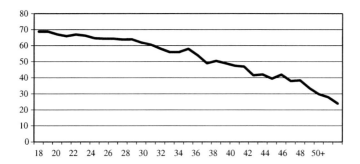

Figure 6.2 Reoffending rates by age in the two-year period following release from prison or commencement of a community sentence.

Source: Home Office Statistical Bulletin 25/2005.

British Crime Survey show that there was the same proportion of serious offenders aged 18–25 as in the group aged 10–17 (Home Office Statistical Bulletin 2006), and frequent offenders were actually slightly more represented among the older group. Only the smaller sub-groups of serious and frequent offenders were a little more prevalent among juveniles. Research in other countries reveals similar patterns (van der Laan 2010).

Recidivism rates also suggest that young adulthood requires as much attention as youth. For example, Figure 6.2 contains the reoffending rates over a two-year follow-up period of a 2002 cohort of offenders in England and Wales who had been released from prison or commenced a community sentence. In accordance with the age–crime curve, the rate of reoffending declines after age 18–19; however, the curve remains very flat during the early 20s.

Although any similarities between adolescent and young adult offenders may vary over time and cultures, the above-mentioned findings and research suggest that the differentiation between 'youth' and 'adult' offenders at age 18 is arbitrary. Problems of a strict age cut-off also become obvious when one compares offenders aged 18–20 with the rest of the adult group (age 21 or older). For example, in a recent national longitudinal cohort study that investigated the problems and needs of 1,457 newly-sentenced adult prisoners in England and Wales (Stewart 2008), it was shown that a much larger proportion of offenders aged 18–20 (referred to as 'young offenders') received a sentence of one to four years than was the case from age 21 onwards (52 per cent vs. 29 per cent). On top of this, it was that a higher rate of young offenders had also been sentenced for violent offences (22 per cent vs. 17 per cent) or robbery (11 per cent vs. 1 per cent). With regard to demographic characteristics, a majority of the young offenders lived with their parents or step-parents (59 per cent vs. 20 per cent) and, as is to be expected, only a small group was married or lived with a partner (15 per cent vs. 38 per cent). Most of the young offenders had been regular truants (70 per cent vs. 55 per cent) and approximately half of them had been excluded from school (52 per cent vs. 37 per cent). Although slightly fewer young offenders had ever been employed (82 per cent vs. 89 per cent), more were employed in the year before custody (63 per cent vs. 51 per cent). More young offenders also showed good physical health (83 per cent vs. 66 per cent), although they were also more prone to heavy drinking (42 per cent vs. 35 per cent). The rates for psychosis (8 per cent vs. 10 per cent) were a little lower in the young group, while the pattern for drug use was mixed (e.g. young offenders used more cannabis, ecstasy and cocaine).

These and other data suggest that young adult prisoners differ in various aspects from older inmates. Their serious offending and frequent other problems speak against an extended adolescence-limited pathway, in the sense that the concept is used by Moffitt (1993). Nevertheless, their criminal careers are not yet as consolidated as in persistent older offenders. Therefore, young adulthood seems to be a very important period in which treatment and support programmes can be used to contribute to processes of desistance. For example, the protective effects of marriage (Sampson and Laub 2003) seem to be stronger at this age (Theobald and Farrington 2009) and a high base rate of reoffending may lead to larger programme effects (Lipsey and Cullen 2007; Lösel 2007). Many young adult offenders are also in the early phases of founding their own families and, without successful intervention, their lifestyle and imprisonment will increase the risk of developmental problems for their children (Murray and Farrington 2008). For all these reasons, sound programmes for this age group are not only necessary, but also particularly promising.

Offender treatment and rehabilitation

Despite there being so many good reasons for special efforts to be made in the rehabilitation of young adult offenders, there is not much systematic knowledge about what works for this group. Indeed, the rapid increase in controlled evaluations and systematic reviews on the effects of correctional treatment over the last two decades has mainly addressed either juveniles or adult offenders in general. Another area that has been addressed is specific types of crime or criminals, such as drug dependent, sexual or violent offenders or – to a much lesser degree – female offenders (Dowden and Andrews 1999). The fact that young adult offenders did not receive specific attention may be partially due to the above-mentioned international differences in age thresholds and legal practice in this area. However, even on the national level it looks as if this offender group is 'lost in transition'. For example, in England and Wales they do not feature heavily in the British Crime Reduction Programme (Carter 2003; Maguire 2004), nor in the current government's Green Paper 'Breaking the Cycle' (Ministry of Justice 2010). Still, it is encouraging that the latter document aims for a 'revolution' of the criminal justice system and, although it places a strong emphasis on cost-effective interventions, it strongly supports the key topic of offender rehabilitation.

Effective rehabilitation requires adequate decisions in sentencing and an evidence-based, coordinated approach in the prison and probation services. The goal of achieving an effective 'end to end' management of offenders has been indicated by the creation of the National Offender Management Service (NOMS) in 2004. Similar to some other countries, NOMS programmes follow seven (plus two for females) pathways to reduce reoffending and meet the needs of offenders, victims, diverse other groups and the general public:

1 accommodation
2 education, training and employment
3 mental and physical health
4 drugs and alcohol
5 finance and debts
6 children and families
7 attitudes, thinking and behaviour

A core element of this policy is the accreditation and quality implementation of a range of offending behaviour programmes (Maguire *et al.* 2010). Typically, they contain more-or-less structured approaches to changing offenders' attitudes, their thinking patterns and their behaviour (and, partially, also aim to improve the offender's mental health). The present chapter mainly addresses these types of intervention. More than 40 custodial and community programmes have been accredited in England and Wales and more than 25,000 offenders participate in one or another of these programmes per-annum. However, there is not much that can be concluded from this development with regard to our target group, as the evidence-driven policy to reduce reoffending has not led to specific programmes being implemented for young adult offenders. Likewise, the Youth Justice Board (YJB) has not adopted a policy of accredited programmes (with the exception of Juvenile Enhanced Thinking Skills; JETS) for juvenile offenders. Instead, its concept of rehabilitation is based on relationship formation, intensive case work, education, elements of therapeutic communities and less structured approaches. Although there are various reasons for a more integrated approach to be used with youth, evidence-based reviews suggest that the YJB should apply more accredited programmes (Wikström and Treiber 2007). The termination of the independent status of the YJB in 2011 offers the opportunity for a more integrated approach to now be introduced; however, it remains to be seen whether this reorganization will lead to an improvement at the day-to-day service level.

At age 18–20, offenders in England and Wales are accommodated in more prison-like YOIs or regular prisons, and this is definitely the case at age 21. Although young adult offenders may then participate in treatment programmes, the few relatively well-controlled evaluations of accredited programmes that have been carried out did not specifically address our target group (Harper and Chitty 2005). The situation in other countries is similar. Therefore, the present chapter can only review the general findings of the 'what works' literature and draw some specific conclusions for young adult offenders where possible.

General effects of correctional interventions

Since the 1990s, a substantial number of systematic reviews and meta-analyses on the effects of correctional treatment and offender rehabilitation have been carried

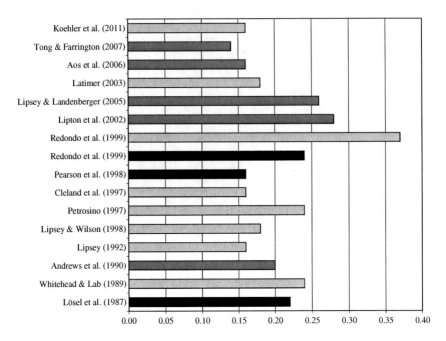

Figure 6.3 Mean effect sizes (*d*) of selected meta-analyses on a broad range of programmes to reduce reoffending.

Note: black = adult offenders; dark grey = adult & juvenile offenders; light grey = juvenile/young offenders.

out. Altogether, this body of research probably incorporates more than 700 primary studies. Although the number of studies included, the programme types adopted, the target groups studied, the methodological quality of the research, the settings for the research and the outcome measurements used vary substantially across these reviews, the most consistent outcome is a mean positive effect (Lipsey and Cullen 2007; Lösel 1995a; McGuire 2002a). Figure 6.3 shows the average effect sizes of some of the many meta-analyses in the field. The data confirms early estimates about the typical effects of correctional interventions (Lösel 1993) as the mean effect sizes vary between *d*-coefficients of approximately 0.10 and 0.30, with an estimated mean of *d* = 0.20 plus/minus 0.05. Although this is only a small effect in Cohen's (1988) classification, it is by no means trivial. For example, if the recidivism rate in the control group was 50 per cent, the respective rate in the treated group would be 40 per cent; this is a reduction of 10 percentage points.

Unfortunately, a systematic comparison between the results for different age groups is not possible. Although there are specific meta-analyses of programmes for juvenile offenders, the respective programmes differ from the ones used in reviews of studies on mixed or purely adult groups. A comparison of age groups is also complicated by other moderators such as institutional context or research methods (see below). Such confounded variables can easily lead to inconsistent conclusions for different age groups. Some reviews found no significant relation between offenders' age and programme effects, while others showed a small negative correlation. Generally, the treatment effects for juvenile/young offenders seem to be a little greater than those for adults only (Lipsey and Cullen 2007; Lösel 1995a).

The variation in outcomes of different research syntheses seems to be larger in specific areas of treatment, such as in programmes for sexual offenders. For such offenders, a comparison of 11 meta-analyses revealed mean effect sizes between $d = 0.10$ and $d = 0.54$, with four of them above $d = 0.30$ (Lösel and Schmucker 2008). This larger variation may be due to a lower number of studies, their smaller sample sizes and the large differences in the research design of different projects. The mean effect sizes of the two most comprehensive reviews were $d = 0.12$ (Hanson *et al.* 2002) and $d = 0.29$ (Lösel and Schmucker 2005), which is within the above-mentioned typical range of effects for correctional treatment. The difference between these two reviews seems to be due to the inclusion of hormonal treatment in the Lösel-Schmucker study. However, although this study showed stronger effects, it also had methodologically weaker research designs. A recent updated review of good quality studies in this area shows a mean of $d = 0.20$: i.e. 27 per cent less sexual recidivism for psychosocial interventions (Schmucker and Lösel 2009).

Sceptics of offender treatment may state that mean effect sizes in such ranges are rather small in comparison to psychotherapy in general, where meta-analyses reveal mean effects of up to $d = 0.85$ (e.g. Lipsey and Wilson 1993; Smith *et al.* 1980). However, this comparison is inappropriate for a number of reasons. First, the framing conditions in both areas are very different; for example, whereas patients with conditions such as anxiety or depression often have a primary motivation to change and are treated in a supportive clinical or community context, offender treatment is more-or-less forced upon the individual and frequently embedded in a non-therapeutic milieu. Second, most offenders are not well educated, self-reflective or verbally skilled, and they may have multiple psychiatric problems, such as personality disorders and substance misuse, which are particularly difficult to treat (even outside the criminal justice system). Third, the main outcome measure of offender treatment is official recidivism after several years, whereas general psychotherapy research often uses more subjective indicators of success after shorter periods of follow-up that normally lead to larger effects (Glass and Kliegl 1983). Fourth, many evaluations of psychotherapy are carried out as analogue or demonstration studies in university contexts, where effects are typically larger than in studies with real patients in routine practices (Donenberg 1999). Fifth, when psychotherapy is compared with placebo treatment (Prioleau *et al.* 1983) or with other active treatments (Luborsky *et al.* 2002) effect sizes are substantially lower (with effects of around $d = 0.20$). Sixth, measures of reducing reoffending do not only contain treatment and rehabilitation, but also punitive and deterrent elements whose effects may be quite different. For these and other reasons, therefore, it is not appropriate to make simple comparisons between offender treatment and other areas of mental health treatment.

Potential moderators of outcome

Total mean effects, however, only give a very rough picture of the success of correctional interventions, as all systematic reviews show a large variation of outcomes. Typically, the effects in primary studies range from large positive effects to small negative effects, with a majority in the small to moderate positive area of the distribution. Such variation does not occur only in analyses that amalgamate heterogeneous types of interventions, but also in reviews of programmes that have roughly similar contents. This can be seen, for example, in meta-analyses of relatively homogeneous cognitive-behavioural programmes for sexual offenders (Schmucker and Lösel 2009) or even in reviews of a single programme for general offenders (Reasoning and Rehabilitation; Tong and Farrington 2006). Such variations clearly demonstrate that the outcome of correctional intervention is linked not only to the content of programmes, but also to many other factors as well. Particularly important are methodological study characteristics; often, they can explain a large proportion of the variances in effect size (Lipsey and Wilson 1998; Lipsey *et al.* 2007; Lösel and Schmucker 2005). In addition to the methods of evaluation, many other issues play a role, including: characteristics of the programme, the offenders, the staff, the setting, the research context and so forth. The impact of these factors is shown in systematic reviews or primary evaluations and case studies. Although more research is needed, the following factors seem to be important moderators of effect size:

1 Content of the programme: Differences between various types of programmes will be intensively discussed in the next sections of this chapter. Here it is only worth noting that the type of programme is, of course, important, but not always the major source of outcome variation. In addition, there may not be enough reported details to evaluate what programme components are most relevant for effectiveness (Koetzle, Shaffer and Pratt 2009; Lösel 1995a).

2 Integrity of programme implementation: Integrity is a summary label for the reliability of programme implementation (Lösel and Wittmann 1989). It is related to quality features such as staff competence, staff motivation, staff supervision and programme monitoring (Hollin 1995; see also below). Research shows that effect sizes are larger when programmes are implemented in a high quality manner (Andrews and Dowden 2005; Gendreau *et al.* 1999; Goggin and Gendreau 2006; Lipsey *et al.* 2007).

3 Programme intensity: Programme intensity contains various issues such as overall duration, number of sessions and/or their frequency per-week. As far as these factors are concerned, there seems to be a tendency for larger effects to result from more intensive programmes (Lipsey *et al.* 2007). However, treatment intensity should not be evaluated in absolute terms, but should instead be analysed with regard to its fit to the offenders' risk level (Andrews and Bonta 2010).

4 Content of the control condition: It is rarely noted that the content of the control condition (e.g. imprisonment or probation) can be as important for effectiveness as the actual treatment itself (Lösel and Egg 1997). Indeed, when the control group receives no rehabilitative measures at all, the effects of a programme may be particularly strong. Similarly, some treatment in the control group may lower effect sizes (Holloway *et al.* 2008). Although treatment programmes improved over time, more positive control conditions and the transfer of 'what works' knowledge into routine practice seem to contribute to lower effects in some more recent studies (Tong and Farrington 2006). Smaller effects in more recent studies may also be due to more rigorous research designs (Jolliffe and Farrington 2009).

5 Quality of the research design: Design quality (internal validity) is the key issue when it comes to drawing causal inferences. The quality of evaluation studies is often rated on summary scales, such as the Maryland Scale of Methodological Rigour (Sherman *et al.* 1997), and meta-analyses of various criminal justice and surveillance measures suggest that larger effects emerge in weaker studies (Weisburd *et al.* 2011; Welsh *et al.* 2011). However, reviews in the specific field of offender rehabilitation show less consistent results in terms of relations with effect size (Lipsey and Cullen 2007; Lösel 1995a). A similar trend is observed with regard to randomized control trials (RCTs) in relation to quasi-experimental designs (Lipsey and Wilson 1998; Lösel and Schmucker 2005). These inconsistent findings are perhaps due to the other moderator variables (Lipsey 2003) or to confounded methodological issues in one single dimension of design quality (Lösel 2007). For example, sometimes differences in outcome indicators or length of follow-up are more important than randomization alone. Therefore, general design quality ratings should be complemented by more differentiated ratings of the internal, statistical, construct, external and descriptive validity of different surveys (Farrington 2006; Lösel and Köferl 1989).

6 Length of follow-up: Effect sizes often decrease when longer follow-up periods are in place (Lösel 1995a; Lösel and Schmucker 2005). This may be due to the reduced impact of treatment programmes over time, along with the compensatory influence of natural protective factors on desistance in the control groups. Although 'sleeper effects' are sometimes reported in developmental prevention, rehabilitation studies very rarely analyse the possibility of a delayed programme impact.

7 Type of outcome measures: Although indicators of official recidivism (e.g. arrest or reconviction) contain various problems, they are politically the most important. Some reviews suggest larger treatment effects in more serious offences (Morales *et al.* 2010) or in non-official indicators of success (Lösel and Schmucker 2005). Frequency of reoffending may also be more sensitive than prevalence, and psychometric measures of personality or social skills seem to reveal better outcomes (Lipsey 1992b; McDougall *et al.* 2009). This is partially due to the fact that they are directly addressed in the programmes (e.g. impulsivity, deviant attitudes). However, one must also take into account

the fact that self-reporting measures are more vulnerable to social desirability than other response sets. Both issues may be responsible for low correlations between intermediate self-reporting measures and longer-term behavioural outcomes in recidivism (Barnett *et al.* 2010; Lipsey 1992b).

8 Sample size: Systematic reviews have shown stronger programme effects in smaller samples than in larger ones (Lipsey *et al.* 2007; Lipsey and Wilson 1998; Lösel and Schmucker 2005). There are two main reasons for this finding. First, because effects in small samples must be larger to reach levels of statistical significance, it may be indicative of a pressure by authors, reviewers or journal editors for researchers to produce significant findings. However, larger effects in small samples have also been observed in unpublished studies. A second explanation is that the larger effects are due to better programme integrity in small-scale studies (Lösel and Beelmann 2003).

9 Demonstration projects vs. routine practice: Related to the previous issue, it has been shown that demonstration projects reveal larger effects than evaluations of routine practice (Lipsey and Landenberger 2006; Lipsey and Wilson 1998; Lösel and Schmucker 2005). Such model projects are typically carried out by universities and contain a careful selection of participants and closely monitor programme implementation. This is more easily done in studies of smaller size.

10 Involvement of programme developers in evaluation: Another related variable is the involvement of programme developers in the evaluation. Studies with programme developers often show larger effects than those that are carried out by independent evaluators. This seems to be a general trend in criminological programme evaluations (Eisner 2009; Petrosino and Soydan 2005). In this instance, one must not assume intentional faking, but in any evaluation research there are processes of data grouping and data analysis, within which many decisions might be more or less consciously made in favour of one's own programme. It should also be appreciated that researchers who evaluate their own programme may be particularly interested in high-quality implementation (Lösel and Beelmann 2003; Sherman and Strang 2009).

11 Social relations and institutional climate: In psychotherapy research it is well documented that social relations and emotional bonds between clients and therapists are as important as specific therapeutic techniques (Orlinsky *et al.* 1994). Although these relational features have been emphasized with regard to programme-based offender rehabilitation (Lösel 1995a; Ward and Maruna 2007), they are still less investigated than in general psychotherapy research. There is also not much attention given to the linkage between treatment programmes and the wider institutional climate or prison regimes. Research in this area suggests that mutual respect, humanity, support, relationship-orientation and trust play an important role in the prevention of conflicts, suicides and other problems (Liebling and Arnold 2002, 2005). Similarly, a thorough assessment and management of situational risk factors is highly relevant for reducing violence in custodial settings (Cooke *et al.* 2008; Cooke and Johnstone 2010; Cregg and Payne 2010). Although such factors

are particularly targeted in therapeutic communities, they may be similarly relevant for specific offending behaviour programmes.

12 Staff competence and training: The institutional context also depends on staff characteristics. Some research, as well as practical experience, suggests that correctional treatment effects are larger when staff shows good relationship- and problem-solving skills and when there is adequate reinforcement and dis- approval of offenders' behaviour and other indicators of social competence (Dowden and Andrews 2004; Goggin and Gendreau, 2006). Accordingly, it is important that programme deliverers, managers and other staff are well selected, trained and supervised (Antonowizc and Ross 1994; Gendreau *et al.* 1999).

13 Custodial vs. community settings: On average, evaluations of programmes in the community reveal larger effect sizes than studies on prison interven- tions (Andrews and Bonta 2010; Lipsey and Cullen 2007; Schmucker and Lösel 2009). It should, however, be noted that both groups of studies con- tain comparisons with the respective control groups and not between custodial and community measures. Custodial and community programmes normally address offender groups that differ with regard to risk level and potential harm, while community programmes have the advantage that programme contents can be more directly and immediately transferred to the real world.

14 Risk level of offenders: Systematic reviews show larger effects in high risk offender groups than in low risk ones (Andrews and Bonta 2010; Andrews and Dowden 2006; Lipsey 2009; Lipsey *et al.* 2007; Lipsey and Wilso 1998; Lösel and Schmucker 2005). At first glance, this may appear counter-intuitive because one would expect that offenders with a lower risk for reoffending are easier to change. From a methodological perspective, however, the result is fully plausible. First, groups at high risk have a higher base rate of reoffending and therefore contain a larger range for potentially positive programme effects. Second, many low risk offenders have access to natural protective resources and therefore do not need a treatment programme. Although larger effects for high risk offenders are replicated, it is questionable whether such findings can be generalized to include extremely high risk groups such as psychopaths. As a result, Lösel (1996) has proposed an inverted U-shaped relationship between risk level and programme effectiveness.

15 Offender motivation: Traditional views on psychotherapy assume that clients must have a genuine wish to change. In current approaches, however, treat- ment motivation is seen as a much more dynamic process (Porporino 2010; Prochaska and Levesque 2002; Wormith *et al.* 2007). It incorporates, amongst other things, aspects of willingness, readiness and ability, all of which should be continuously monitored and strengthened. Accordingly, some research sug- gests no clear outcome differences between fully voluntary and more-or-less mandatory participation (Schmucker and Lösel 2009).

16 Proportion of treatment dropouts: Typically, treatment dropouts and non- starters show larger rates of recidivism than regular programme completers (Lösel 1995a; Lipsey and Cullen 2007) and in many studies they do even worse than the control group. This may be due to the more problematic characteristics

of dropouts as well as their stigmatization due to failure. In any case, there are smaller programme effects in intent-to-treat analyses in which the dropouts and non-starters are conservatively allocated to the treatment group than in studies that only define completers as those treated (Jolliffe and Farrington 2009; Lipsey and Wilson 1998).

17 Age of offenders: With regard to young adult offenders, the moderator effects of age could be particularly interesting. However, as mentioned previously, there is little empirical data on this issue. This is partially due to a lack of differentiated analyses within the group of adult offenders and partly due to natural processes of desistance when offenders get older. There is also a lack of systematic comparisons of treatment effects for adults vs. juveniles. Typically, programmes for juvenile offenders seem to show larger effects than programmes for adult offenders only (Lipsey and Cullen 2007; Redondo *et al.* 2002). This could be due to the less consolidated and, thus, more modifiable criminal dispositions of younger people and/or reflective of a higher base rate of reoffending that goes along with larger effects (Lösel 2007).

Many of the above mentioned potential outcome moderators are not specific for correctional rehabilitation, but can also be found in the fields of criminal justice, social work, clinical psychology and psychiatry. In all areas, it is difficult to disentangle the specific impact of one factor from another. Many moderators are confounded and there are not enough studies on a specific combination of characteristics (Lipsey 2003). As a consequence, we must be aware that the 'what works' question cannot simply be reduced to the type of programme. Therefore, the following comparison of the effects of various programme types contains an unavoidable reduction of complexity.

Punishment, deterrence and intensive supervision

Among the general public, tough sanctioning and intensive control are often seen as the most appropriate reactions to offending. Typical examples of measures of this type are longer prison sentences or incarceration instead of community sanctions. However, differences in offender characteristics and legal restrictions make it difficult to carry out well-controlled studies on this topic. Therefore, the evidence for this area is rather limited. Systematic reviews show that custodial sanctions (rather than community ones) and longer prison sentences (rather than shorter ones) lead to slightly higher reoffending rates or non-significant differences (Killias *et al.* 2006; Pearson *et al.* 1997; Smith *et al.* 2002). Single studies with matching procedures (Nieuwbeerta *et al.* 2009; Wermink *et al.* 2010) and experimental comparisons of security level placement (Gaes and Camp 2009) also suggest that prison sentences seem to have more of a criminogenic effect than a deterrent or rehabilitative one. However, further experimental research on differentiated outcomes – notably the prevalence and frequency of reoffending – is needed.

Correctional boot camps are specific forms of custodial regimes which temporarily became popular for juveniles and adults. These institutions have tough regimes and adopt the structures of basic military training camps (i.e. strict execution of command and obedience, highly challenging physical exercise and immediate punishment of misbehaviour). Boot camps are intended to achieve a number of different aims: to function as a deterrent against further criminal behaviour; to provide structure and order for the inmates, who often have a chaotic life history and lifestyle; to increase positive experiences of competence by mastering physical demands; and to promote conformity within the group. The programme details vary widely between institutions and sometimes a tough regime is combined with psychosocial treatments and education elements. Despite the popularity of boot camps (particularly in the US), systematic reviews revealed no effect on rehabilitation (Aos *et al.* 2001; MacKenzie *et al.* 2001). The reported mean effect size is around zero, with a large variation from positive to negative outcomes in single studies. Although there is not a simple explanation for this variation, it looks as if only the 'second generation' boot camps with educational and treatment components may have had a rehabilitative effect (MacKenzie 2006). As the first generation boot camps reduced neither reoffending nor imprisonment rates, a number of US States recently abandoned them (Cullen *et al.* 2005).

Other deterrent measures are shock incarceration, or so-called 'Scared Straight', programmes. Here, juvenile offenders make visits to, or have short stays in, prisons with particularly tough regimes that contain prolific offenders with intimidating behaviour. In contrast to the expectation of a negative reinforcement or deterrent effect being produced, meta-analyses actually demonstrate higher instead of lower reoffending for those who have been put through these programmes (Lipsey and Wilson 1998; Petrosino *et al.* 2003); suggesting, perhaps, that the young men become impressed and attracted by the violent inmates and the macho subculture.

Less daunting are findings on intensive supervision and intermediate sanctions, or 'smart punishment', programmes in the community. Various reviews revealed zero to very small positive effects of such measures in comparison to routine parole, probation, fines or diversion (Aos *et al.* 2001, 2006; Lipsey and Wilson 1998; Pearson *et al.* 1997; Smith *et al.* 2002). Other reviews even found a criminogenic effect for these types of measures (Andrews *et al.* 1990a; Gendreau *et al.* 2000). Indeed, intensive community supervision, based around a reduced case load for probation officers, only seems to be effective when it is accompanied by some kind of treatment (Aos *et al.* 2006). Intensive supervision and intermediate sanctions also run the risk that potentially positive effects are negated because of the closer monitoring and violation of licensing orders used. The same problem applies to the more recent tactic of electronic monitoring and, although there are some promising findings, better controlled studies are needed in this area (Renzema and Mayo-Wilson 2005). The mean effect size in the meta-analysis by Aos *et al.* (2006) was zero.

In conclusion, the research does not prove that programmes of pure punishment, deterrence and supervision reduce reoffending. Indeed, some have even been shown to produce negative outcomes. These findings are similar for both juvenile and adult offenders and may, therefore, be generalized across different age groups. As a consequence, there is no evidence base for the currently popular calls for tougher punishments for young adult offenders.

Cognitive-behavioural programmes

As in general psychotherapy research, the majority of methodologically sound evaluations of offending behaviour programmes address cognitive-behavioural treatment (CBT). These programmes are based on theories of social learning, information processing, action and moral reasoning. They contain modules on self-reflection, anger management, self-control, social skills training, interpersonal problem solving, considering action alternatives, value-orientation, perspective taking (empathy) and pro-social roles (Hollin and Palmer 2009). The CBT programmes differ in the number or structure of such components and in the emphasis placed on cognitive or behavioural techniques. Typical examples of CBT programmes include: Reasoning and Rehabilitation, Aggression Replacement Training, Enhanced Thinking Skills, Interpersonal Problem Solving and the new, integrated Thinking Skills Programme of the NOMS.

Nearly all meta-analyses have found that, on average, CBT programmes reduce both general and violent reoffending (Aos *et al.* 2006; Garrett 1985; Koehler *et al.* 2011; Landenberger and Lipsey 2005; Lipsey and Cullen 2007; Lipsey and Wilson 1998; Pearson *et al.* 2002; Redondo *et al.* 2002; Tong and Farrington 2006). The research also suggests that no one single programme is clearly superior to another. Therefore, one should not advertise a specific programme as the gold standard or magic bullet (Lösel 2007).

Nevertheless, detailed studies do suggest that some CBT components are more relevant than others and, although there is not much research on this issue, elements of anger control and interpersonal problem solving (Landenberger and Lipsey 2005) and cognitive skills training (Jolliffe and Farrington 2009) seem to contribute most to positive outcomes. According to some studies, classical behaviour modification elements even correlated negatively with effect size. However, it is not yet clear whether the latter finding can be generalized. In a recent meta-analysis of programmes for juvenile offenders, Lipsey (2009) found a clear effect (22 per cent reduction in reoffending) for behavioural techniques (e.g. reinforcement management or contingency management). Moreover, in a review of programmes for serious and violent juvenile offenders the mean effect for behavioural programmes was particularly large at 44 per cent (Lipsey and Wilson 1998). Most recently, a meta-analysis of programmes for young offenders conducted by the present author and colleagues (including juveniles and young adults) confirmed that CBT has also been successful in a number of European countries (Koehler *et al.* 2011).

CBT also proved to be successful with more specific groups of offenders; having, for example, positive effects for female offenders (Dowden and Andrews 1999). Various reviews have demonstrated mean positive outcomes in the treatment of drug- or alcohol-addicted offenders (Lipsey and Wilson 1998; Pearson and Lipton 1999; Mitchell *et al.* 2007). Positive average effects were also found for drug courts, which often combine judicial action and intensive supervision with cognitive-behavioural elements of education and treatment (Wilson *et al.* 2006; Lowenkamp *et al.* 2005). Various meta-analyses further demonstrated that CBT is effective for sexual offenders (Hall 1995; Hanson *et al.* 2002; Lösel and Schmucker 2005). However, it is not yet fully apparent what programme elements are most relevant. For example, there is some inconsistency with regard to the independent impact of behaviour modification techniques and relapse prevention components that are not linked to CBT (Lösel and Schmucker 2005).

In spite of such issues, however, there is much evidence that CBT programmes work for a broad range of offenders. This relatively solid evidence base also makes CBT programmes particularly appropriate for working with young adult offenders. Moreover, most CBT programmes are standardized and are, therefore, applicable to different offender groups. However, as many young adult offenders seem to have similar needs and problems as adolescent offenders, uniformity may not always be appropriate. It is probable that the most success will occur when the strength of well-structured group programmes is combined with some sort of individualization (e.g. specific modules and one-to-one sessions). Deliverers of CBT programmes should also analyse whether the age range and psychological heterogeneity of young adult offenders may be an advantage or perhaps a risk, especially when they are a minority in groups of serious adult offenders.

Therapeutic communities, milieu therapy and social-therapeutic prisons

In contrast to circumscribed CBT programmes, therapeutic communities (TCs) and milieu therapies aim to create a comprehensive rehabilitative milieu that can be implemented in custody as well as in community residential care institutions (Cullen 1997). There are various concepts of TCs (Kennard 1994; Roberts 1997), but, typically, people live together, have informal non-hierarchical relationships, share information, are committed to the goal of learning, strive for an open resolution of problems and conflicts, are sensitive to the psychodynamic of individual and group processes and follow a basic set of rules concerning roles, time and place (Kennard 1994). Originally, TCs placed much emphasis on democratic processes and inmate self-governing, but current concepts vary widely with regard to such principles and many TCs are now more hierarchic and structured. They now often contain a therapeutic social climate and regime, provide intensive contact between staff and inmates, have relatively large numbers of therapeutic staff, are sensitive to group dynamics, adopt various modes of therapy, define appropriate responsibilities, operate control and reward systems and provide graduated openings to the world outside. In this way, the therapeutic process has become less idiosyncratic; meaning that the basic principles could even be formally accredited in England and Wales. Social-therapeutic prisons in Germany are similar to hierarchical TCs, but share basic organizational structures with regular custody services (Lösel and Egg 1997). Although TCs and social-therapeutic prisons do not focus on manual-based offending behaviour programmes, these can be integrated as one element of treatment if need be.

Because of the more complex nature of treatment in these institutions, they are less easy to evaluate than structured CBT programmes. However, this is not a sufficient explanation for the low number of methodologically rigorous studies carried out in this area; particularly for offenders with serious personality disorders (Lees *et al.* 1999). Taking this limitation into account, meta-analyses have shown overall positive effects for rehabilitation (Lösel 1995b; Lees *et al.* 1999; Lipton *et al.* 2002), although the mean effects are smaller than those of sound CBT programmes (Aos *et al.* 2001). TCs and social-therapeutic prisons seem to work not only for groups of general and violent offenders, but also for drug-addicted offenders (Holloway *et al.* 2008, Mitchell *et al.* 2007; Pearson and Lipton 1999). For sexual offenders they can also provide a helpful therapeutic environment, although offence-specific treatment programmes need to be included in these cases (Lösel 2000; Lösel and Schmucker 2005).

In conclusion, the evidence for TCs, milieu therapy and social-therapeutic prisons suggests that they could be useful for the treatment of young adult offenders. Although the necessary staff numbers and staff qualifications make them relatively costly, this investment is particularly worthwhile for serious young adult offenders. Indeed, because young adult offenders often come from very difficult family backgrounds, the therapeutic climate in institutional or community TCs may have a buffering effect that reduces the risk of long criminal careers. However, TCs are relatively broad approaches to reduce reoffending and, therefore, they should be combined with structured offending behaviour programmes for offenders with particular needs (e.g. specific CBTs for violent, sexual or alcohol-addicted offenders).

Multisystemic therapy

The idea that the social milieu is particularly important for intervention programmes also forms the basis for Multisystemic Therapy (MST) and other similar programmes. These are intensive, short-term, family- and community-based interventions which were originally designed for juvenile offenders and drug abusers. Over time they also became popular for groups with other behavioural problems and were used as a measure of developmental prevention. The MST from Henggeler and his group (Henggeler *et al.* 2009; Borduin *et al.* 1995) aims to reduce reoffending, drug misuse, out-of-home placements, school failure and other youth and family problems. The programme works with the young people, with the family members and with other relevant social systems (such as peer groups, schools, extended families, neighbourhoods, community service providers, health care workers and juvenile justice organizations. Similar to milieu therapy, it requires qualified therapeutic staff (psychologists, social workers etc.). However, the basic vehicle for lasting behaviour change is the youth's own social system; particularly their family. The approach is structured and based on a manual, but it is not as standardized as a typical CBT programme. Instead of concrete modules or lessons it uses nine broader therapeutic principles:

1 match the youngster's problems with his/her systemic context
2 focus on their strengths, not only on their deficits
3 increase responsibility
4 be present-focused and action-oriented
5 target behavioural sequences in the system
6 developmental appropriateness
7 continuous effort
8 evaluation and accountability
9 generalization (i.e. learning general principles from specific incidents)

The details of the measures depend on the respective problems and protective factors that are identified in each case. A number of relatively well-controlled evaluations have demonstrated the positive effects of MST on delinquency, violence, substance abuse, school achievement and other behaviour problems (Curtis *et al.* 2004; Henggeler *et al.* 2009). Cost-benefit ratios of 1:5 US $ also seem to be particularly positive. On top of this, independent meta-analyses on juvenile offender treatment also confirmed significant reductions in recidivism for MST and similar multimodal family-based therapeutic approaches (Aos *et al.* 2001; Farrington and Welsh 2003; Latimer 2001; Lipsey and Wilson 1998). Indeed, in some reviews the effects of MST were exceptionally strong (Curtis *et al.* 2004; Schmucker and Lösel 2009). However, a number of critical issues also need to be raised; like, for example, the fact that a number of studies on MST have not been very well controlled and have been carried out by the programme developers themselves, whereas independent evaluations have revealed less positive effects (Littell 2006; Littell *et al.* 2005;). These are important issues that are not only relevant for MST, but for other programmes as well (see above).

Overall, though, MST and similar multimodal family- and community-based programmes seem to work well. Nevertheless, the model addresses juveniles and cannot simply be transferred to young adult offenders as the latter have looser, or already broken, family ties and, partially, different needs and lifestyles. However, if the principle of developmental appropriateness is taken into account, the systems- and strength-oriented approach can still be of relevance for young adult offenders. Targeting family relations, peer-contacts and other parts of the individual's social system would be particularly relevant for those young offenders whose psychosocial development is not much different from that of adolescents. The broader approach of MST-type programmes is also important for relapse prevention and successful processes of desistance (Lösel and Bender 2003; Maruna 2001; Porporino 2010; Sampson and Laub 2003; see also Shapland *et al.* in chapter 8 of this volume).

Low-structured, psychodynamic and counselling approaches

Although cognitive-behavioural programmes are now prevailing in offender rehabilitation, it is important not to overlook psychodynamic, humanistic and theoretically unspecific modes of counselling, treatment and case work. Typically, these programmes are less structured and are not based on manuals. They aim instead to realize basic therapeutic principles, such as emotional acceptance, empathy, openness and mutual bonding and support between clients and therapists or within treatment groups. Psychodynamic approaches, in particular, address core conflicts and defence mechanisms in the individual's development. Indeed, right from the start Sigmund Freud and his colleagues emphasized that antisocial individuals not only have deficits in bonding and emotional transference but also in cognitive, verbal and other ego competences. Therefore, the classical 'talking cure' is seen as being less appropriate than more structured and educational approaches (Aichhorn 1925).

Perhaps for these reasons, the well-known rivalries between different therapeutic schools seem to be less prevalent in the treatment of offenders than in other areas of psychotherapy. However, the empirical evidence for low-structured and psychodynamic approaches to offender rehabilitation is weaker than that for cognitive-behavioural approaches. Various reviews suggest that the effects of such interventions are very slight in comparison to CBT (Andrews *et al.* 1990a; Garrett 1985; Gottschalk *et al.* 1987; Lipsey 1992a; Lipsey and Wilson 1998; Pearson *et al.* 1997; Redondo *et al.* 1999). This has led to a widespread belief that they are not relevant in our field. However, one must bear in mind that we are dealing with particularly heterogeneous types of interventions which are difficult to compare because of their more individualized and less replicable content. The above-mentioned therapeutic principles – basic acceptance, cooperation and empathy – are important for all kinds of psychotherapy (Orlinsky *et al.* 1994) and can, therefore, provide value in structured cognitive-behavioural and other offending behaviour programmes. They can also play a role in therapeutic communities and systemic approaches, and may be applicable for multiple disordered young adult offenders (Mueller 1953). Indeed, as Lipsey (2009) has shown, a therapeutic philosophy plays a key role in interventions with juvenile offenders and, although evidence-oriented experts would not recommend Freudian psychotherapy or Roger's nondirective therapy as key approaches to reducing reoffending, the 'what works' movement should not ignore helpful contributions from outside the CBT mainstream. One should also remember that some 'psychodynamic' concepts, such as Adler's individual psychology, have much in common with goal-directed modern CBT. However, all theoretical arguments still have to undergo rigorous empirical tests before they can be applied in practice.

More research is also needed on mentoring programmes for young offenders and at-risk youth which contain core elements of counselling and relationship-formation. Such measures have shown small positive effects on aggression and delinquency (DuBois *et al.* 2002; Tolan *et al.* 2008), but there is not yet sound evidence that they reduce reoffending in the longer term (Jolliffe and Farrington 2008). Instead, mentoring seems to be primarily of worth as part of more comprehensive interventions; this is in accordance with the above arguments on relationship formation and treatment. Therefore, mentoring may be a promising additional approach in programmes for those young adult offenders who do not have a protective reference person in their natural social network.

The R-N-R and other principles of appropriate programmes

The above-mentioned results from evaluations of offender treatment led to the development of core principles for successful programmes. These went beyond a specific type of programme, although cognitive-behavioural approaches played a key role. Most influential became the Risk-Need-Responsivity (R-N-R) principles formulated by Andrews *et al.* (1990b). This approach suggested that clinically meaningful 'appropriate programmes' must: match the offender's risk for reoffending (R); address his/her specific criminogenic needs (N); and contain methods that fit to his/her learning style (R). According to Andrews *et al.* (1990a), programmes that fulfilled these three principles showed up to 60 per cent reduction (compared to untreated control groups) in reoffending. Later analyses revealed more realistic effects of approximately one-third less recidivism (Andrews and Bonta 2010). It was also shown that effect sizes systematically increased with the number of principles realized in the respective programmes. Whereas appropriate programmes – ones that incorporated all three principles – on average showed a medium effect size, programmes without any of the three characteristics had a slightly negative effect. A similar relationship between the R-N-R principles and effect size was reported for sexual offender treatment (Hanson *et al.* 2009). Most recently, a European meta-analysis on young offender treatment also confirmed that programmes that fulfilled all three R-N-R principles were most successful. They showed a 30 per cent reduction in reoffending whereas interventions with a medium or low fit to R-N-R principles revealed positive but non-significant mean effects (Koehler *et al.* 2011).

Despite the empirical evidence for the great value of the R-N-R concept for the development of sound rehabilitation programmes, one should not neglect various problems of this approach. First, the risk principle is only a rough guide to an appropriate dosage and is mainly applied on the group and not the individual level; whether a specific client needs additional treatment or support measures is not often addressed in standardized programmes. Second, the issue of responsivity partially confounds programme and person characteristics because it is often not really assessed on the individual level, but more-or-less generally assumed for specific types of programmes (e.g. CBT). However, in some cases, verbally and intellectually competent offenders may benefit from classical therapeutic approaches and not only from a fixed group programme. A third issue relates to the potential discrepancies between the programme concept and its actual implementation. This problem is not only relevant for the R-N-R approach, but is typical in correctional treatment more generally.

Other authors have questioned the R-N-R concept more fundamentally (Ward and Brown 2004; Ward and Maruna 2007). Amongst other things, it is argued that the R-N-R model: does not tell offenders the positive rewards in desisting from crime; tends to neglect the role of identity and the self-directed intentional actions of offenders; ignores the need for specific experiences; does not appreciate the role of treatment alliances in the therapeutic process; is fundamentally a psychometric model; and is often implemented in a one-size-fits-all manner (Ward and Brown 2004). However, some of these arguments sound more like stereotypes than actual comments about the current practice of R-N-R-oriented offender rehabilitation. For example, most sound programmes contain modules on the potential life-benefits of desistance from crime. The role of identity and intended actions is also addressed in CBT programmes. Likewise, whether the theoretical bases of social-cognitive learning theories (Bandura 1993; McMurran and Hollin 2005) are less appropriate for offender treatment than general concepts of human motivation seems to be a matter of taste and should be compared empirically (see next section). Furthermore, whilst sound risk assessment is unavoidable in any criminal justice system, psychometric measurements are actually much less important for CBT than is often assumed.

However, the other critical arguments of Ward and his colleagues are more important. In particular, there is indeed less reflection on differential indication, therapeutic processes and individualization in correctional treatment than in other areas of psychotherapy. Nevertheless, one should also take into account that the R-N-R principles only form a part of the basis of current offending behaviour programmes. This is obvious with regard to therapeutic communities, milieu therapy or Multisystemic Therapy. One should also recognize that the R-N-R concept had, by the 1990s, already been widened to include other factors that emerged from research and practical experience on effective offending behaviour programmes (e.g. Andrews 1995; Lösel 1995a; most recently: Andrews *et al.* 2011). These characteristics were transformed into detailed criteria that could be applied in the accreditation of programmes and a number of countries (including Canada, England and Wales, the Netherlands, Scotland and Sweden as well as some US States) subsequently introduced accreditation processes for correctional programmes. In England and Wales, for example, the Correctional Services Accreditation Panel stipulated that accredited programmes must:

1 be based on a clear model of change
2 have a thorough selection of eligible offenders
3 target a range of dynamic risk factors
4 use effective learning and teaching methods
5 enhance concrete behavioural skills
6 be appropriate with regard to sequence, intensity and duration
7 promote offender engagement and motivation
8 care for continuity of programmes and services
9 maintain programme integrity
10 take measures for an on-going evaluation

As mentioned previously, England and Wales adapted or developed many offending behaviour programmes that are now delivered to thousands of offenders per-annum. In accordance with the accreditation criteria, programme delivery is accompanied by supervision and auditing (in custody) and other measures of quality management. Although the fast and large-scale roll-out of programmes led to various problems – such as frequent staff changes, violations of inclusion criteria, high dropout rates and a lack of auditing in the community; (Maguire *et al.* 2010) – the accredited programmes approach in England and Wales is probably the world's most comprehensive rehabilitation policy that is based on the R-N-R and related 'what works' principles. Unfortunately, however, less effort was made to evaluate this policy in a methodologically sound way. Several studies used quasi-experimental designs with non-equivalent treatment and control groups, but for many programmes there is no UK outcome evaluation at all. Some findings on well-implemented cognitive-behavioural programmes for medium to high risk offenders, on aggression replacement training in probation, on sex offender treatment and on drug treatment programmes were encouraging (see Harper and Chitty 2005), but other evaluations revealed mixed results and led to controversies about various methodological issues (Hollin *et al.* 2004; Hollin 2008).

More experimental outcome evaluations are urgently needed as reviews consistently suggest that the efficacy in demonstration studies is larger than the effectiveness in day-to-day routine practice (Lipsey and Wilson 1998; Lösel and Schmucker 2005). Therefore, the recent attempts by the NOMS to reduce duplications in programme portfolios and to aim for better evaluations of core programmes – like the new Thinking Skills Programme and Sex Offender Treatment Programmes – are meaningful steps forward. On the other hand, concentrating on evidence-based core programmes may inevitably increase a 'one size fits all' tendency. Overall, one must concede that there is no definite solution to this problem. From a purely therapeutic perspective one could, of course, argue for highly individualized interventions, but, with regard to evaluation and policy, more general approaches are required. Against this background, it is important that less methodologically controlled, more practice-oriented data seems to support the accredited programmes policy.

One indirect indicator of programme effectiveness is a recent decrease in adult reoffending rates in England and Wales. Figure 6.4 shows the percentage of offenders committing at least one offence within one year of discharge from prison or after commencement of probation supervision. As can be seen, from 2000 to 2006 there was a reduction of 11 per cent and the number of offences per-100 offenders actually decreased to 23 per cent.

Of course, such developments cannot simply be attributed to the increased roll-out of accredited programmes, and may be linked to other factors such as the falling crime rate, general improvements in the criminal justice system, a better composition of the offender population, better police discretion in making decisions and more favourable social conditions (including, at that date, the labour market). Although there is no clear data on such potential influences, the programme-related hypothesis is at least indirectly supported. For example, from 2000 to 2004 there was only a substantial decrease in reoffending rates for those offenders who received prison sentences of at least one year (HMPS 2007). In 2004 the difference between the actual and predicted (taking changes

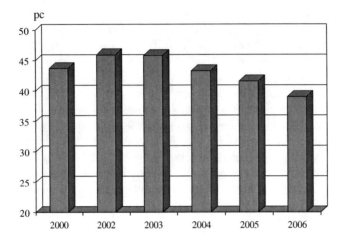

Figure 6.4 Percentage of offenders in England and Wales who committed at least one offence within one year of discharge from prison or the start of probation supervision.

Note: No valid data available for 2001.
Source: Ministry of Justice Evidence Digest (2009).

in population risk levels into account) offending rates was substantial for offenders serving between one and two years (−6.2 per cent), larger for those serving between two and four years (−10.1 per cent) and particularly strong for sentences of four or more years (−13.6 per cent). In contrast, there was nearly no improvement (−0.2 per cent) for offenders who received a sentence of less than one year. This group rarely receives accredited treatment programmes and has the highest rates of reoffending. Although the lower reoffending rates in the groups with longer sentences could partially be attributed to increased age, it is not plausible to assume that longer sentences became more of a deterrent within a period of a few years.

There is also some encouraging data on reductions of reoffending for offenders who participated in treatment programmes in the community (Hollis 2007). Compared to expected reoffending rates, the overall decrease was more than 10 per cent, with significantly positive results from programmes for sexual offenders, for drink-impaired drivers, for anger management, for general offending and for substance misuse treatment. However, these results are weakened by incomplete data, particularly as regards dropout rates.

More recently, there have been very promising findings in comparisons of treated groups with offenders from untreated cohort samples who were matched according to risk level and sentence length. Those offenders who participated in the Enhanced Thinking Skills programme showed significantly less reconvictions than predicted (according to risk) and also less convictions than the matched groups from the cohort (Travers *et al.* 2011). Similarly positive results were observed in a smaller study with propensity score matching (Sadlier 2010). Comparisons between treated sexual offenders and a national cohort of untreated sexual offenders also revealed desirable outcomes (Wakeling *et al.* 2011). Although such studies are only post-hoc, quasi-experimental evaluations and may, therefore, be less empirically valid than randomised experiments, they do address large samples on treatment programmes in day-to-day practice (and not only demonstration projects). Together with the above-mentioned meta-evaluations, they provide substantial evidence for R-N-R and related approaches as a core concept of offender rehabilitation. However, this does, of course, not mean that such accredited programmes are the one and only route to reducing reoffending.

The Good Lives Model and the desistance 'paradigm'

Although accredited and other offending behaviour programmes contain much more than the R-N-R approach, there is increasing discussion about whether this model is too narrow. Whilst not questioning the basic advantages of quality management by programme accreditation, systematic monitoring and auditing, members of accreditation panels have stated that there is a need for a wider perspective (e.g. Maguire and Raynor 2006; Maguire *et al.* 2010). In particular, they have emphasized the necessity of providing broader system concepts of rehabilitation that overcome the 'silo approach' of isolated programmes. Nevertheless, it should be noted that this widened view is not opposed to the principles of effective rehabilitation outlined above, as its focus is on integrated patterns of programmes and their linkage to multilevel influences in the process of desistance. Moreover, no serious researcher and practitioner of the recent 'what works' movement has ever doubted that R-N-R-based programmes are the only measures capable of reducing reoffending or telling the whole story of how people change their behaviour. The above-mentioned moderate effect sizes of positive evaluations clearly speak against any such omnipotent fantasies.

In addition to critical arguments against the recent 'what works' movement, various authors have also argued for a more fundamental 'paradigm change'. For example, Ward and his colleagues have proposed the 'Good Lives Model' (GLM) as an alternative to the R-N-R approach to offender rehabilitation (Ward and Brown 2004; Ward and Maruna 2007). Similar to Multisystemic Therapy, the GLM incorporates basic life goals and protective resources as it is assumed that offenders – much like non-offenders – want to achieve legitimate goals. In order to tackle their antisocial lifestyles they need skills, knowledge and resources to achieve nine basic 'goods':

1 Life-management (including healthy living and functioning)
2 knowledge
3 excellence in work and play
4 excellence in agency (autonomy, self-directedness)

5 inner peace (freedom from emotional turmoil, stress)
6 friendship and community (intimate partner, family relations)
7 spirituality (finding meaning and purpose in life)
8 happiness
9 creativity

The GLM is recommended as a relatively general approach for different types of offenders, including sexual offenders, as it uses a more resource-oriented concept of reducing reoffending that relates to various perspectives in clinical psychology and developmental psychopathology; particularly, to the concepts of humanistic psychology (Maslow 1954; Rogers 1961), salutogenesis (instead of pathogenesis) (Antonovsky 1987) and positive psychology (Seligman *et al.* 2005). The GLM also rightly emphasizes motivational issues of change. However, the list of nine explicit and general goods (motives) is a little arbitrary and is not much related to the empirical research on motivation and its often implicit components (Schultheiss and Brunstein 2010). Although the GLM has important clinical implications for rehabilitation (Ward *et al.* 2007), there are not yet strong evidence-based measures that demonstrate how offenders can successfully acquire the knowledge and skills for reaching the GLM's nine basic human goals. Admittedly, the more narrative and individualized GLM approach cannot simply be reduced to a portfolio of programmes. Nevertheless, research on differential indications has questioned whether humanistic approaches of psychotherapy are the most appropriate choice in cases where patients demonstrate high impulsivity and aggression (Beutler and Harwood 2000). Therefore, it is important that elements of traditional rehabilitation programmes are related to the GLM framework (Ward *et al.* 2007). For this reason, explicitly GLM-driven treatment programmes need to be systematically evaluated because, so long as sound empirical evaluation is not undertaken, it is difficult to judge the specific value of the GLM as an approach to reducing reoffending (Andrews *et al.* 2011; Ogloff and Davis 2004).

The GLM is also tied in with the research on desistance from offending. This has shown that even serious and persistent offenders reach turning points in their life and give up criminal careers (Bottoms and Shapland 2011; Farrall and Calverley 2006; Laub and Sampson 2003; Maruna 2001; McNeill 2006; Sampson and Laub 1993; Ward and Maruna 2007; see also chapter 8 of this volume). Marriage to the 'right' person, support from non-deviant relatives or friends, stable employment, positive experiences in education or at work, adequate accommodation, the triggering of motivational experiences, experiences of sense and meaning in non-criminal activities and other social and personal resources in the natural environment may all contribute to desistance from crime (Lösel and Bender 2003). Such findings are particularly relevant for young adult offenders because the high reoffending rates at this age are often due to maturation gaps (Graham and Bowling 1995; McNeill 2006; Maruna 2001), which may be reduced by significant intimate partnerships, stable employment and other resources.

Desistance research has also demonstrated that there is less continuity and more change in criminal development than sometimes assumed. It has also showed that not only official rehabilitation programmes, but also natural protective factors make an important contribution in stopping reoffending. As a consequence, some authors have proposed a 'desistance paradigm' as an alternative to the risk-need-oriented 'what works' movement (McNeill 2006; Ward and Maruna 2007; Brayford *et al.* 2010; Farrall *et al.* 2011). Such a paradigm shift is not primarily informed by empirical facts, because typical effect sizes in desistance research are not stronger than in intervention studies, but is instead based on other reasons and concerns, that seem to include the following: a concern that the prevailing 'what works' approach reduces diversity and creativity in rehabilitation; a worry that it applies too demanding accreditation and audit processes; a belief that it goes along with centralization and top-down administration; a concern that it gives too much priority to quantitative evaluations instead of qualitative methods; a notion that it focuses more on individual characteristics than on institutional issues; and a worry that it adheres to a risk- and deficit-oriented image of humankind. Some of these arguments are more plausible than others. For example, accreditation is open for all types of programmes as long as they provide sound information with regard to effectiveness. Likewise, the recent history of criminal justice in the UK does not show a linear trend of centralization, but rather a series of pendulum swings with currently more emphasis on de-centralization. Furthermore, it should be noted that even CBT programmes do not only address offender deficits (which are indeed often serious), but also aim to strengthen protective resources. However, more important than one or the other argument is the question of whether a shift towards a desistance paradigm is really necessary.

Many social scientists seem to like major controversies about the 'right' paradigms, which attract more attention than the more piecemeal progress being made in theoretical and empirical knowledge. According to Kuhn (1962), a paradigm shift (a moment of revolutionary science) occurs when an old and a new paradigm are incommensurable (i.e. when there are fundamentally different epistemologies and processes in the socialization of scholars). Applied to our topic, this could mean that, if a paradigm shift were to occur, the accumulated knowledge of the previous 'what works' research may get diluted. Therefore, one should be cautious with regard to shifts in rehabilitation approaches. In my view, neither the 'what works' research (including the R-N-R approach), nor the recommended concept of desistance are paradigms in the sense of Kuhn's philosophy of science. They both contain a more-or-less eclectic integration of theories, hypotheses, assessments and intervention measures that can be applied to reducing reoffending. Instead of allowing a paradigm shift to take place, then, it would be more appropriate to use the GLM and the desistance approach to widen perspectives on offender rehabilitation and expand the evidence base (see also Porporino 2011).

A stronger focus on desistance research must also take into account the fact that the respective findings stem from correlation designs and not from experimental or quasi-experimental studies as in the intervention literature. Therefore, one cannot draw causal inferences and must instead ask how the findings can be transferred into measures that promote desistance. As in the field of drug addiction, motivation and first steps to desist from crime are often counteracted by individual and social barriers (Bottoms and Shapland 2011, and chapter 8 of this volume). Overcoming such obstacles requires interventions that strengthen or complement protective factors. This is exactly the aim of rehabilitation programmes which the NOMS has classified into the above mentioned seven pathways (see page 79).

Both the GLM and the desistance concepts are closely related to the field of research on protective factors and resilience in human development (Lösel and Bender 2003; Luthar *et al.* 2000; Werner and Smith 1992). It is surprising, therefore, that this area only plays a marginal role in criminological research. Indeed, it actually emerged from different research strands over two decades ago that the following factors may have a relatively broad and consistent protective function in cases of adversity (Lösel and Bliesener 1990; Werner 1989):

1 stable emotional relationship with at least one reference person
2 acceptance and supervision in social contexts
3 adequate social support
4 social models that encourage constructive coping
5 appropriate social responsibilities
6 cognitive competencies such as realistic future planning
7 an easy temperament and ego resiliency
8 experiences of self-efficacy and an adequate self-concept
9 active coping with stressors and strains
10 experience of sense and meaning in life

Such concepts can be addressed in programmes designed to promote desistance and a good life. They also relate to the risk-need-oriented approaches because many of the protective factors are not that different from (causal) risk factors. Analyses of non-linear relationships are needed, however, to disentangle such different effects (Loeber *et al.* 2008; Lösel and Farrington 2011). Promotive and protective factors also seem to be less general across different developmental periods, contexts and outcomes than the above-mentioned list or the GLM suggests (Lösel and Bender 2003; Lösel and Farrington 2011) and factors that may be a risk for reoffending at one time can have a desirable function at another.

In summary, then, one should not view GLM, desistance, R-N-R and other 'what works' concepts as incommensurable and all-encompassing alternatives. Rather, we need thoroughly planned interventions and empirical evaluations that address the specific and combined influences of these programmes on reducing reoffending.

Discussion and conclusions

This chapter has identified young adult offenders as an important target group for correctional treatment. Like serious juvenile offenders, they show a particularly high risk of recidivism and differ in various biographical and psychological aspects from older adult offenders. Because their criminal careers are often not yet consolidated and because their family networks may still be able to contribute to desistance, effective interventions at this stage could be particularly beneficial in the long term. However, specific intervention research on this group has rarely been conducted. Therefore, this chapter answered the 'what works' question by extrapolating information and evidence from the more general evidence base on correctional interventions.

A broad range of approaches to offender rehabilitation have been addressed. The first and most general conclusion of this analysis is rather simple: namely, that measures of correctional treatment do work (i.e. they significantly reduce the rate of reoffending amongst those who participate in the respective programmes compared to those who do not). Of course, this is not a very original or thrilling conclusion to make, as a number of other reviews over the last two decades have concluded that the 'nothing works' doctrine is wrong and ineffective. However, with regard to the target group of young adult offenders, this positive conclusion is not trivial, because public discussions in many countries still argue for tougher sanctions to be imposed on young people. The present analyses clearly show that just 'getting tough' on crime is not a promising policy. Indeed, punitive and deterrent measures, alongside more intensive supervision, were the only types of measures that did not reduce reoffending. In fact, for deterrent measures such as these, there is frequently a zero and sometimes even a negative effect in comparison to other types of intervention. Although the results of these controlled evaluations and systematic reviews are not specifically derived from studies on groups of young adult offenders, there is no reason why they may not be generalized to our target group.

In public discussions, arguments against punitive and deterrent measures are often attributed to a 'soft' vs. a 'tough' position in polarized concepts of crime policy. Placing the present conclusion into this framework, however, would be a misinterpretation. Correctional treatment programmes – particularly in custody – are certainly not 'mild' or 'lenient' reactions; instead, they reflect the punitive sentiments of society. As such, retribution and the other punitive aims of criminal justice are always inherent when rehabilitative measures are applied. Moreover, as stated in the introduction, a future-oriented crime policy does not give up the other aims of criminal justice, but asks what can reduce reoffending.

With regard to this question, it has been shown that interventions based on sound concepts of criminology and psychology show, on average, positive effects. This proved to be particularly the case for cognitive-behavioural programmes, structured therapeutic communities, social-therapeutic prisons, milieu therapy programmes, Multisystemic Therapy approaches and other multimodal programmes that address well-replicated causal risk factors and offender needs. Low-structured case work, counselling and psychodynamic interventions showed weaker effects, but could still be useful with regard to relationship issues.

Beyond specific types of programmes, the more complex R-N-R approach and its extensions (Andrews *et al.* 2011) proved to be a core route to effective rehabilitation. This was particularly the case when the approach also took other moderators of effectiveness into account (e.g., quality of programme delivery, staff factors, interpersonal relationships, offender characteristics, context features, research methodology and so forth). Such a broader view is highly important for programme accreditation and quality assurance and, although the appropriateness of a programme's content remains a key issue, the 'what works' question should not be reduced to it. The 'multiple factors perspective' that is presented in this chapter overcomes the limits of 'silo' approaches in offender rehabilitation by analysing specific programmes within frameworks that look at other influences that are relevant to an offender's behavioural change and desistance from crime. It also helps to appreciate, as has been frequently pointed out elsewhere, that even sound evidence-based programmes do not show positive outcomes in all situations or contexts.

Although an increased sensitivity for the complex patterns and processes of intervention is becoming more and more relevant, one should not overlook its potential flaws. For instance, such complex approaches to reducing reoffending are more difficult to evaluate in a well-controlled manner than single programmes that are implemented in isolation from other measures. However, this should not be used as an excuse for not carrying out experimental or sound quasi-experimental evaluations as far as is possible under the given circumstances. These issues were evident in recent discussions on offender rehabilitation programmes such as the GLM. Although there are sound reasons for complementing risk- and deficit-oriented approaches to rehabilitation with concepts from positive psychology, the GLM and research on protective factors and desistance, the respective interventions still need to be as rigorously evaluated as the more traditional R-N-R and other 'what works' programmes. This is not yet the case. The same must be stated with regard to a number of other programmes (e.g faith-based interventions that were not discussed here, see Aos *et al.* 2006; Baier and Wright 2001).

Systematic reviews have shown, for example, that academic education and vocational training programmes make a significant contribution to reducing reoffending (MacKenzie 2006; Wilson *et al.* 2000). However, in contrast to popular opinion, there is not yet consistent evidence for the rehabilitative effects of prison work and non-custodial employment programmes (MacKenzie 2006; Visher *et al.* 2006; Wilson *et al.* 2000) and more controlled evaluations and differentiated analyses of essential programme features are needed in this area. As Romig (1978) noted in an early review of programmes for young offenders, employment and work programmes may only be successful if the respective qualifications are useful in the labour market and accompanied by the personal skills needed to keep a post.

There is also clear evidence for using Restorative Justice (RJ), particularly for face-to-face conferences with offenders and victims organized by mediation experts of the police or criminal justice system (Sherman and Strang 2007). Recently, Shapland *et al.* (2008) carried out randomized and matched-pairs experiments on three RJ schemes that applied direct and/or indirect mediation in Britain. The results showed a desirable tendency in the likelihood of reconviction and a significant reduction in the frequency of reoffending. Overall, there was a financial payoff of the RJ schemes and no differential impact in various offender groups. However, evaluations in Australia have revealed that the RJ may not work under specific circumstances and for specific clients (such as aborigines) (Sherman and Strang 2007). Such findings support the view expressed in this chapter that the 'what works' question should not be limited simply to the type of programme, but should take a broader pattern of relevant change factors into account. Against this background it is noteworthy that various elements of RJ – perspective taking, cognitive restructuring, motivational change and so forth – are also key elements of the more intensive CBT programmes that address relatively persistent offenders with a higher risk of recidivism.

Although this article has shown various pathways for the effective treatment of young adult offenders, it does not recommend specific organizational structures. Whether a country should keep this age group in prisons for juveniles, treat them in separate young adult offender institutions or give them specific attendance in adult custody depends on the respective age thresholds and legal regulations. However, as a core principle, the criminal justice system should allow for adequate differentiation and continuity of care, either within or across institutions. It is also not necessary to develop a range of new programmes to meet the needs of young adult offenders; rather, current evidence-based approaches should be adapted to fulfil this task (i.e. by the inclusion of more targeted modules). One should also aim to create a social-therapeutic context that provides a supportive learning milieu for these offenders.

Of course, adequate correctional programmes and institutional contexts require financial resources. This is currently problematic because Britain and many other countries are still having to cope with the consequences of the financial crisis. However, one should bear in mind that successful correctional interventions can not only reduce the harm done to potential victims, but also save money for that society in the long run. As demonstrated in this chapter, evidence-based interventions show roughly 10 per cent less reoffending than in the untreated control groups and other appropriate treatment factors may further increase success rates up to 20 per cent. Treatment in many areas of medicine is often no more effective, but it is more accepted because of the lack of alternatives. One should apply a similar perspective to offender rehabilitation. Detailed cost-benefit analyses on measures of crime prevention have shown that effect sizes in the above-mentioned range may well pay-off for the society (Welsh *et al.* 2001). This is also reflected in simple figures: whereas a sound cognitive-behavioural offending behaviour programme may cost approximately £3,000 per offender, a serious and long-term criminal career can lead to costs of more than £1 million (Cohen and Piquero 2009; Muñoz *et al.* 2004). Against this background there is no plausible alternative to effective intervention in childhood and youth and – if this is not possible or has failed – as early as possible in young adulthood.

References

Aichhorn, A. (1925). *Verwahrloste jugend: Die psychoanalyse in der fürsorgerziehung [Wayward youth: Psychoanalysis in correctional education]*. Vienna, Austria: Internationaler Psychoanalytischer Verlag.

Andrews, D. A. (1995). 'The psychology of criminal conduct and effective treatment,' in J. McGuire (ed.), *What works: Reducing reoffending: guidelines from research and practice*. New York: Wiley.

Andrews, D. A. and Bonta, J. (2010). *The psychology of criminal conduct, 5th ed.* Cincinatti. OH: Anderson.

Andrews, D. A., Bonta, J. and Hoge, R. D. (1990b). 'Classification for effective rehabilitation'. *Criminal Justice and Behavior*, 17, 19–52.

Andrews, D. A., Bonta, J. and Wormith, S. (2011). 'The Risk-Need-Responsivity (RNR) model: Does adding the Good Lives Model contribute to effective crime prevention?'. *Criminal Justice and Behavior*, 38: 735–755.

Andrews, D. A., Zinger, I., Hoge, R. D., Bonta, J., Gendreau, P. and Cullen, F. T. (1990a). 'Does correctional treatment work? A clinically relevant and psychologically informed meta-analysis'. *Criminology*, 28, 369–404.

Andrews, D. A. and Dowden, C. (2006). 'Risk principle of case classification in correctional treatment: a meta-analytic investigation'. *International Journal of Offender Therapy and Comparative Criminology*, 50: 88–100.

Antonovsky, A. (1987). *Unraveling the mystery of health: How people manage stress and stay well.* San Francisco: Jossey-Bass.

Antonowicz, D. H. and Ross, R. R. (1994). 'Essential components of successful rehabilitation programs for offenders'. *International Journal of Offender Therapy and Comparative Criminology*, 38: 97–104.

Aos, S., Phipps, P., Barnoski, R. and Lieb, R. (2001). *The comparative costs and benefits of programs to reduce crime.* Olympia, WA: Washington State Institute of Public Policy.

Aos, S., Miller, M. and Drake, E. (2006). *Evidence-based adult corrections programs: What works and what does not.* Olympia, WA: Washington State Institute of Public Policy.

Baier, C. J. and Wright, B. R. E. (2001). 'If you love me, keep my commandments: a meta-analysis of the effect of religion on crime'. *The Journal of Research in Crime and Delinquency*, 38: 3–20.

Bandura, A. (1973). *Aggression: A social learning analysis.* New York: Prentice Hall.

Barnett, G. D., Wakeling, H. C., Mandeville-Norden-R. and Rakestrow, J. (2010). *What does change in psychometric test scores tell us about risk of reconviction in sexual offenders?* Unpublished manuscript. Rehabilitation Services Group, NOMS, London.

Beutler, L. E. and Harwood, T. M. (2000). *Prescriptive psychotherapy: A practical guide to systematic treatment selection.* New York: Oxford University Press.

Borduin, C. M., Mann, B. J., Cone, L. T., Henggeler, S. W., Fucci, B. R., Blaske, D. M. and Williams, R. A. (1995). 'Multisystemic treatment of serious juvenile offenders: Long-term prevention of criminality and violence'. *Journal of Consulting and Clinical Psychology*, 63: 560–578.

Bottoms, A. and Shapland, J. (2011). 'Steps towards desistance among young male adult offenders,' in S. Farrall, M. Hough, S. Maruna and R. Sparks (eds.), *Escape routes: Contemporary perspectives on life after punishment.* Milton Park, UK: Routledge.

Brayford, J., Cowe, F. and Deering, J. (eds.) (2010). *What else works? Creative work with offenders.* Cullompton, UK: Willan.

Carter, P. (2003). *Managing offenders, reducing crime: A new approach.* London: Strategy Unit.

Cohen, J. (1988). *Statistical power analysis for the behavioral sciences.* New York: Academic Press.

Cohen, M. A. and Piquero, A. R. (2009). 'New evidence on the monetary value of saving a high risk youth'. *Journal of Quantitative Criminology*, 25: 25–49.

Cooke, D. J. and Johnstone, L. (2010). 'Somewhere over the rainbow: Improving violence risk management in institutional settings'. *International Journal of Forensic Mental Health*, 9: 150–158.

Cooke, D. J., Wozniak, E. and Johnstone, L. (2008). 'Casting light on prison violence in Scotland: Evaluating the impact of situational risk factors'. *Criminal Justice and Behavior*, 35: 1065–1078.

Cregg, M. and Payne, E. (2010). 'PRISM with incarcerated young people: Optical illusion or reflection of reality?' *International Journal of Forensic Mental Health*, 9: 173–179.

Cullen, E., Jones, L. and Woodward, R. (eds.) (1997). *Therapeutic communities for offenders*. Chichester, UK: Wiley.

Cullen, F. T. (2005). 'The twelve people who saved rehabilitation: How the science of criminology made a difference'. *Criminology*, 43: 1–42.

Cullen, F. T., Blevins, K. R., Trager, J. S. and Gendreau, P. (2005). 'The rise and fall of boot camps: a case study in common-sense corrections'. *Journal of Offender Rehabilitation*, 40 (3/4): 53–70.

Curtis, N. M., Ronan, K. R. and Borduin, C. M. (2004). 'Multisystematic treatment: a meta-analysis of outcome studies'. *Journal of Family Psychology*, 18: 411–419.

Donenberg, G. R., Lyons, J. S. and Howard, K. I. (1999). 'Clinical trials vs. mental health services research: Contributions and connections'. *Journal of Clinical Psychology*, 55: 1135–1146.

Dowden, C. and Andrews, D. A. (1999). 'What works for female offenders: A meta-analytic review'. *Crime and Delinquency*, 45: 438–452.

— (2004). 'The importance of staff practices in delivering effective correctional treatment: A meta-analysis of core correctional practices'. *International Journal of Offender Therapy and Comparative Criminology*, 48: 203–214.

DuBois, D. L., Holloway, B. E., Valentine, J. C. and Cooper, H. M. (2002). 'Effectiveness of mentoring programs for youth: A meta-analytic review'. *American Journal of Community Psychology*, 30: 157–197.

Eisner, M. (2009). 'No effects in independent prevention trials: Can we reject the cynical view?'. *Journal of Experimental Criminology*, 5: 163–183.

Farabee, D. (2007). *Rethinking rehabilitation: Why can't we reform our criminals?* Washington, DC: American Enterprise Institute.

Farrall, S. and Calverley, A. (2006). *Understanding desistance from crime: Theoretical directions in resettlement and rehabilitation*. Maidenhead, UK: Open University Press.

Farrall, S., Hough, M., Maruna, S. and Sparks, R. (eds.) (2011). *Escape routes: Contemporary perspectives on life after punishment*. Milton Park, UK: Routledge.

Farrington, D. P. (2006). 'Methodological quality and the evaluation of anticrime programmes'. *Journal of Experimental Criminology*, 2: 329–337.

Farrington, D. P. and Welsh, B. C. (2003). 'Family-based prevention of offending: A meta-analysis'. *Australian and New Zealand Journal of Criminology*, 36: 127–151.

Gaes, G. G. and Camp, S. D. (2009). 'Unintended consequences: experimental evidence for the criminogenic effect of prison security level placement on post-release recidivism'. *Journal of Experimental Criminology*, 5: 139–162.

Garrett, C. J. (1985). 'Effects of residential treatment on adjudicated delinquents: a meta-analysis'. *Journal of Research on Crime and Delinquency*, 22: 287–308.

Gendreau, P., Goggin, C., Cullen, F. T. and Andrews, D. A. (2000). 'Does "getting tough" with offenders work? The effects of community sanctions and incarceration'. *Forum on Corrections Research*, 12: 10–13.

Gendreau, P., Goggin, C. and Smith, P. (1999). 'The forgotten issue in effective correctional treatment: Program implementation'. *International Journal of Offender Therapy and Comparative Criminology*, 43: 180–187.

Glass, G. V. and Kliegl, R. M. (1983). 'An apology for research integration in the Study of psychotherapy'. *Journal of Consulting and Clinical Psychology*, 51: 28–41.

Goggin, C. and Gendreau, P. (2006). 'The implementation and maintenance of quality services in offender rehabilitation programmes', in C. Hollin and E. Palmer (eds.), *Offending behaviour programmes*. Chichester, UK: Wiley.

Gottschalk, R., Davidson, W. S. II., Mayer, J. and Gensheimer, G. K. (1987). 'Behavioral approaches with juvenile offenders: a meta-analysis of long-term treatment efficacy', in E. K. Morris and C. J. Braukmann (eds.), *Behavioral approaches to crime and delinquency: A handbook of application, research, and concepts*. New York: Plenum.

Graham, J. and Bowling, B. (1995). *Young people and crime*. London: Home Office.

Hall, G. C. N. (1995). 'Sexual offender recidivism revisited: A meta-analysis of recent treatment studies'. *Journal of Consulting and Clinical Psychology*, 63: 802–809.

Hanson, K., Burgon, G., Helmus, L. and Hodgson, S. (2009). 'The principles of effective correctional treatment also apply to sexual offenders: A meta-analysis'. *Criminal Justice and Behavior*, 36: 865–891.

Hanson, R. K., Gordon, A., Harris, A. J. R., Marques, J. K., Murphy, W., *et al.* (2002). 'First report of the collaborative outcome data project on the effectiveness of psychological treatment for sex offenders'. *Sexual Abuse: A Journal of Research and Treatment*, 14: 169–194.

Harper, G. and Chitty, C. (eds.) (2005). *The impact of corrections on re-offending: a review of 'what works'. Home Office Research Study 291.* London: Home Office.

Henggeler, S. W., Schoenwald, S. K., Borduin, C. M., Rowland, M. D. and Cunningham, P. B. (2009). *Multisystemic treatment of antisocial behavior in children and adolescents, 2nd ed.* New York: Guilford Press.

Hollin, C. R. (2008). 'Evaluating offending behaviour programmes: Does only randomization glister?'. *Criminology and Criminal Justice*, 8: 89–106.

Hollin, C. and Palmer E. J. (2009). 'Cognitive skills programmes for offenders', *Psychology Crime and Law*, 15: 147–164.

Hollin, C., Palmer, E., McGuire, J., Hounsome, J., Hatcher, R., Bilby, C. and Clark, C. (2004). *Pathfinder Programmes in the Probation Service: a retrospective analysis. Home Office Online Report 66/04.* London: Home Office.

Hollis, V. (2007). *Reconviction analysis of interim accredited programmes software (IAPS) data.* London: NOMS.

Holloway, K., Bennett, T. H. and Farrington, D. P., (2008). *Effectiveness of treatment in reducing drug-related crime.* Stockholm: Swedish National Council for Crime Prevention.

Hood, R. (1974). 'Young adult offenders. Comments on the Report of the Advisory Council on the Penal Reform'. *British Journal of Criminology*, 14: 388–395.

Jolliffe, D. and Farrington, D. P. (2008). *The influence of mentoring on reoffending.* Stockholm: Swedish National Council for Crime Prevention.

— (2009). *Effectiveness of interventions with adult male violent offenders.* Stockholm: Swedish National Council for Crime Prevention.

Kennard, D. (1994). 'The future revisited: New frontiers for therapeutic communities'. *Therapeutic Communities*, 15: 107–113.

Killias, M., Villettaz, P. and Zoder, I. (2006). *The effects of custodial vs. non-custodial sentences on reoffending: A systematic review of the state of knowledge.* [online report] The Campbell Collaboration: www.campbellcollaboration.org/reviews_crime_justice/index.php.

Koehler, J., Akoensi, T., Humphries, D. and Lösel, F. (2011). *A systematic review and meta-analysis of the effectiveness of treatment programmes to reduce juvenile reoffending in Europe. Research report of the STARR Project.* Cambridge: Institute of Criminology.

Koetzle Shaffer, D. and Pratt, T. C. (2009). 'Meta-analysis, moderators, and treatment effectiveness: The importance of digging deeper for evidence of program integrity'. *Journal of Offender Rehabilitation*, 48: 101–119.

Kuhn, T. S. (1962). *The structure of scientific revolutions.* Chicago, IL: University of Chicago Press.

Landenberger, N. A. and Lipsey, M. W. (2005). 'The positive effects of cognitive-behavioral programs for offenders: A meta-analysis of factors associated with effective treatment'. *Journal of Experimental Criminology*, 1: 451–476.

Latimer, J. (2001). 'A meta-analytic examiniation of youth delinquency, family treatment, and recidivism'. *Canadian Journal of Criminology*, 43: 237–253.

Laub, J. H. and Sampson, R. J. (2007). *Shared beginnings, divergent lives: Delinquent boys to age 70.* Cambridge, MA: Harvard University Press.

Lees, J., Manning, N. and Rawling, B. (1999). *Therapeutic community effectiveness: A systematic international review of therapeutic community treatment for people with personality disorders and mentally disordered offenders*. University of York, UK: Centre for Research and Dissemination.

Liebling, A. and Arnold, H. (2002). *Measuring the quality of prison life. Research Findings 174*. London: Home Office.

— (2005). *Prisons and their moral performance: A study of values, quality, and prison life*. Oxford: Oxford University Press.

Lipsey, M. W. (1992a). 'Juvenile delinquency treatment: A meta-analytic inquiry into variability of effects', in T. D. Cook, H. Cooper, D. S. Cordray, H. Hartmann, L. V. Hedges, R. L. Light, T. A. Louis and F. Mosteller (eds.), *Meta-analysis for explanation*. New York: Russell Sage Foundation, 83–127.

— (1992b). 'The effect of treatment on juvenile delinquents: Results from meta-analysis', in F. Lösel, D. Bender and T. Bliesener (eds.), *Psychology and law: International perspectives*. Berlin: de Gruyter, 131–143.

— (2003). 'Those confounded moderators in meta-analysis: Good, bad, and ugly'. *Annals of the American Academy of Political and Social Science*, 587: 69–81.

— (2009). 'The primary factors that characterize effective interventions with juvenile offenders'. *Victims and Offenders*, 4: 124–147.

— (2009). 'The primary factors that characterize effective interventions with juvenile offenders: A meta-analytic overview'. *Victims and Offenders*, 4: 124–147.

Lipsey, M. W. and Cullen, F. T. (2007). 'The effectiveness of correctional rehabilitation: A review of systematic reviews'. *Annual Review of Law and Social Science*, 3: 297–320.

Lipsey, M. W. and Landenberger, N. A. (2006). 'Cognitive-behavioral interventions', in B. C. Welsh and D. P. Farrington (eds.), *Preventing crime: What works for children, offenders, victims, and places*. Dordrecht, NL: Springer, 57–71.

Lipsey, M. W., Landenberger, N. A. and Wilson, S. (2007). 'Effects of cognitive-behavioral programs for criminal offenders'. [online report] Systematic review for the Campbell Collaboration: >www.campbellcollaboration.org/reviews_crime_justice/index.php<.

Lipsey, M. W. and Wilson, D. B. (1993). 'The efficacy of psychological, educational, and behavioral treatment: Confirmation from meta-analysis'. *American Psychologist*, 48: 1181–1209.

Lipsey, M. W. and Wilson, D. B. (1998). 'Effective intervention for serious juvenile offenders', in R. Loeber and D. P. Farrington (eds.), *Serious and violent juvenile offenders*. Thousand Oaks, CA: Sage, 313–345.

Lipton, D. S., Pearson, F. S., Cleland, C. M. and Yee, D. (2002). 'The effects of therapeutic communities and milieu therapy on recidivism', in J. McGuire (ed.), *Offender rehabilitation and treatment*. Chichester: Wiley, 39–77.

Littell, J. H. (2006). 'The case for Multisystemic Therapy: Evidence or orthodoxy?'. *Children and Youth Services Review*, 28: 458–472.

Littell J. H., Campbell M., Green S. and Toews B. (2005). 'Multisystemic Therapy for social, emotional, and behavioral problems in youth aged 10–17'. *Cochrane Database of Systematic Reviews 2005*, Issue 4.

Loeber, R., Farrington, D. P., Stouthamer-Loeber, M. and White, H. R. (2008). *Violence and serious theft: Development and prediction from childhood to adulthood*. New York: Routledge.

Lösel, F. (1993). 'The effectiveness of treatment in institutional and community settings'. *Criminal Behaviour and Mental Health*, 3: 416–437.

— (1995a). 'The efficacy of correctional treatment: A review and synthesis of meta-evaluations', in J. McGuire (ed.), *What works: Reducing reoffending*. Chichester, UK: Wiley, 79–111.

— (1995b). 'Increasing consensus in the evaluation of offender rehabilitation? Lessons from research syntheses'. *Psychology, Crime and Law*, 2: 19–39.

— (1996). 'Changing patterns in the use of prisons: An evidence-based perspective'. *European Journal on Criminal Policy and Research*, 4: 108–127.

— (1998). 'Treatment and management of psychopaths', in D. J. Cooke, A. E. Forth and R. B. Hare (eds.), *Psychopathy: Theory, research and implications for society.* Dordrecht: Kluwer Academic Publishers, 303–354.

— (2000). 'The efficacy of sexual offender treatment: A review of German and international evaluations', in P. J. van Koppen and N. H. M. Roos (eds.), *Rationality, information and progress in psychology and law.* Maastricht, NL: Metajuridica Publications, 145–170.

— (2007). 'It's never too early and never too late: Towards an integrated science of developmental intervention in criminology'. *Criminologist*, 35 (2): 1–8.

Lösel, F. and Beelmann, A. (2003). 'Effects of child skills training in preventing antisocial behavior: A systematic review of randomized experiments'. *The Annals of the American Academy of Political and Social Science*, 587: 84–109.

Lösel, F. and Bender, D. (2003). 'Protective factors and resilience', in D. P. Farrington and J. Coid (eds.), *Prevention of adult antisocial behaviour.* Cambridge, UK: Cambridge University Press.

Lösel, F. and Bliesener, T. (1990). 'Resilience in adolescence: A study on the generalizability of protective factors,' in K. Hurrelmann and F. Lösel (eds.), *Health hazards in adolescence.* Berlin: De Gruyter, 299–320.

— (1997). 'Zur Altersgrenze strafrechtlicher Verantwortlichkeit von Jugendlichen aus psychologischer Sicht' ['The age threshold of criminal responsibility from a psychological perspective']. *DVJJ-Journal* [*Journal of Juvenile Criminal Law and Youth Welfare*], 8: 388–395.

Lösel, F. and Egg, R. (1997). 'Social-therapeutic institutions in Germany: Description and evaluation,' in E. Cullen, L. Jones and R. Woodward (eds.), *Therapeutic communities in prisons.* Chichester, UK: Wiley.

Lösel, F. and Farrington, D. F. (2010). 'Promotive and protective factors in the development of youth violence'. Paper for the project *Protective and promotive factors for youth violence of the U.S. Centres of Disease Control and Prevention.* Atlanta, GA: CDC.

Lösel, F. and Köferl, P. (1989). 'Evaluation research on correctional treatment in West Germany: A meta-analysis,' in H. Wegener, F. Lösel and J. Haisch (eds.), *Criminal behavior and the justice system.* New York: Springer, 334–355.

Lösel, F. and Schmucker, M. (2005). 'The effectiveness of treatment for sexual offenders: A comprehensive meta-analysis'. *Journal of Experimental Criminology*, 1: 117–146.

Lösel, F. and Schmucker, M. (2008). 'Meta-analyzing the effects of sex offender treatment: A systematic integration of research syntheses'. Paper presented at the *Stockholm Criminology Symposium*, 16–18 June 2008, Stockholm, Sweden.

Lösel, F. and Wittmann, W. (1989). 'The relationship of treatment integrity and intensity to outcome criteria'. *New Directions for Program Evaluation*, 42: 97–107.

Lowenkamp, C. T., Holsinger, A. M. and Latessa, E. J. (2005). 'Are drug courts effective: a meta-analytic review'. *Journal of Community Corrections*, 28: 5–10.

Luborsky, L., Rosenthal, R., Diguer, L., Andrusyna, T. P., Berman, J. S., Levitt, J. T., Seligman, D. A. and Krause, E. D. (2002). 'The dodo bird verdict is alive and well – mostly'. *Clinical Psychology: Science and Practice*, 9: 2–12.

Luthar, S. S., Cicchetti, D. and Becker, B. (2000). 'The construct of resilience: A critical evaluation and guidelines for future work'. *Child Development*, 71: 543–562.

MacKenzie, D. L. (2006). *What works in corrections? Reducing the criminal activities of offenders and delinquents.* Cambridge, UK: Cambridge University Press.

MacKenzie, D. L., Wilson, D. B. and Kider, S. B. (2001). 'Effects of correctional boot camps on offending'. *The Annals of the American Academy of Political and Social Science*, 578: 126–143.

Maguire, M. (2004). 'The Crime Reduction Programme: Reflections on the vision and the reality'. *Criminology and Criminal Justice*, 4: 213–238.

Maguire, M., Grubin, D., Lösel, F. and Raynor, P. (2010). 'What works' and the Correctional Services Accreditation Panel: Taking stock from an inside perspective'. *Criminology and Criminal Justice*, 10: 37–58.

Maguire, M. and Raynor, P. (2006). 'How the resettlement of prisoners promotes desistance from crime: Or does it?'. *Criminology and Criminal Justice*, 6: 19–38.

Maruna, S. (2001). *Making good: How ex-convicts reform and rebuild their lives.* Washington, DC: American Psychological Association Books.

Maslow, A. (1954). *Motivation and personality.* New York: Harper.

McDougall, C., Perry, A. E., Clarbour, J., Bowles, R. and Worthy, G. (2009). *Evaluation of HM Prison Service Enhanced Thinking Skills Programme. MoJ Research Series 3/09.* London: Ministry of Justice.

McGuire, J. (ed.) (1995). *What works: Reducing reoffending – guidelines for research and practice.* Chichester: Wiley.

McGuire, J. (ed.) (2002a). *Offender rehabilitation and treatment: Effective programmes and policies to reduce re-offending.* Chichester, UK: Wiley.

McGuire, J. (2002b). 'Integrating findings from research reviews', in J. McGuire (ed.), *Offender rehabilitation and treatment.* Chichester, UK: Wiley, 4–38.

McMurran, M. and McGuire, J. (eds.) (2005). *Social problem solving and offending: Evidence, evaluation and evolution.* Chichester, UK: Wiley.

McNeill, F. (2006). 'A desistance paradigm for offender management'. *Criminology and Criminal Justice*, 6: 39–62.

Mitchell, O., Wilson, D. B. and MacKenzie, D. L. (2007). 'Does incarceration-based drug treatment reduce reoffending? A meta-analytic synthesis of research'. *Journal of Experimental Criminology*, 3: 353–375.

Moffitt, T. (1993). 'Adolescence-limited and life-course-persistent antisocial behavior: A developmental taxonomy'. *Psychological Review*, 100: 674–701.

Morales, L. A., Garrido, V. and Sanchez-Meca, J. (2010). *Treatment effectiveness in secure corrections of serious (violoent or chronic) juvenile offenders.* Stockholm: Swedish National Council for Crime Prevention.

Mueller, G. O. W. (1953). 'Resocialization of the young adult offender in Switzerland'. *The Journal of Criminal Law, Criminology, and Police Science*, 43: 578–591.

Muñoz, R., Hutchings, J., Edwards, R. T., Hounsome, B. and O'Ceilleachair, A. (2004). 'Economic evaluation of treatments for children with severe behavioural problems'. *Journal of Mental Health Policy Economics*, 7: 177–189.

Murray, J. and Farrington, D. P. (2008). 'The effects of parental imprisonment on children'. *Crime and Justice A Review of Research*, 37: 133–206.

Nieuwbeerta, P. D., Nagin, D. and Blokland, A. (2009). 'The relationship between first imprisonment and criminal career development: A matched samples comparison'. *Journal of Quantitative Criminology*, 25, 227–257.

Ogloff, J. R. P. and Davis, M. R. (2004). 'Advances in offender assessment and rehabilitation: Contributions of the risk-needs-responsivity approach'. *Psychology, Crime and Law*, 10: 229–242.

Orlinsky, D. E., Grawe, K. and Parks, B. K. (1994). 'Process and outcome in psychotherapy', in A. E. Bergin and S. L. Garfield (eds.), *Handbook of psychotherapy and behavior change, 4th ed.* New York: Wiley, 270–376.

Palmer, T. (1992). *The re-emergence of correctional intervention.* Newbury Park, CA: Sage.

Pearson, F. S. and Lipton, D. S. (1999). 'A meta-analytic review of the effectiveness of correction-based treatments for drug abuse'. *Prison Journal*, 79: 384–410.

Pearson F. S., Lipton, D. S. and Cleland, C. M. (1997). 'Rehabilitative programs in adult corrections: CDATE meta-analysis'. Paper presented at the Annual Meeting of the American Society of Criminology, San Diego, California 19–22 November.

Pearson, F. S., Lipton, D. S., Cleland, C. M. and Yee, D. S. (2002). 'The effects of behavioral/cognitive-behavioral programs on recidivism'. *Crime and Delinquency*, 48: 476–496.

Petrosino, A. and Soydan, H. (2005). 'The impact of program developers as evaluators on criminal recidivism: results from meta-analyses of experimental and quasi-experimental research'. *Journal of Experimental Criminology*, 1: 435–50.

Petrosino, A., Turpin-Petrosino, C. and Buehler, J. (2003). 'Scared straight and other juvenile awareness programs for preventing juvenile delinquency: a systematic review of randomized experimental evidence'. *Annals of the American Academy of Social and Political Science*, 589: 41–62.

Porporino, F. (2010). 'Bringing sense and sensitivity to corrections: from programmes to 'fix' offenders to services to support desistance', in J. Brayford, F. Cowe and J. Dering (eds.), *What else works? Creative work with offenders*. Cullompton, UK: Willan, 61–85.

Prioleau, L., Murdock, M. and Brody, N. (1983). 'An analysis of psychotherapy vs. placebo studies'. *Behavioral and Brain Sciences*, 6: 275–285.

Prochaska, J. O. and Levesque, D. A. (2002). 'Enhancing motivation of offenders at each stage of change and phase of therapy' in M. McMurran (ed.), *Motivating offenders to change*. Chichester, UK: Wiley, 57–73.

Redondo, S., Sánchez-Meca, J. and Garrido, V. (1999). 'The influence of treatment programmes on the recidivism of juvenile and adult offenders: A European meta-analytic review'. *Psychology, Crime and Law*, 5: 251–278.

— (2002). 'Crime treatment in Europe: A review of outcome studies', in J. McGuire (ed.), *Offender rehabilitation and treatment: Effective programmes and policies to reduce reoffending*. Chichester, UK: Wiley, 113–141.

Renzema, M. and Mayo-Wilson, E. (2005). 'Can electronic monitoring reduce crime for moderate to high-risk offenders?'. *Journal of Experimental Criminology*, 1: 215–237.

Roberts, J. (1997). 'History of the therapeutic Community', in E. Cullen, L. Jones and R. Woodward (eds.), *Therapeutic communities for offenders*. Chichester, UK: Wiley, 3–22.

Rogers, C. R. (1961). *On becoming a person: A therapist's view of psychotherapy*. London: Constable.

Romig, A. D. (1978). *Justice for our children: An examination of juvenile delinquent rehabilitation programs*. Lexington, MA: Lexington Books.

Rutter, M. (1985). 'Resilience in the face of adversity. Protective factors and resistance to psychiatric disorder'. *British Journal of Psychiatry*, 147: 598–611.

Sadlier, G. (2010). *Evaluation of the impact of the HM Prison Service Enhanced Thinking Skills programme on reoffending outcomes of the Surveying Prisoner Crime Reduction (SPCR) sample. Ministry of Justice Research Series 19/10*. London: Minsisty of Justice.

Sampson, R. J. and Laub, J. H. (1993). *Crime in the making: Pathways and turning points through life*. Cambridge, MA: Harvard University Press.

Schmucker, M. and Lösel, F. (2009). 'A systematic review of high-quality evaluations of sexual offender treatment'. Paper presented at the *Annual Conference of the European Society of Criminology*, 9–12 September 2009, Ljubljana, Slovenia.

Schultheiss, O. and Brunstein, J. C. (2010). *Implicit motives*. New York: Oxford University Press.

Seligman, E. P., Steen, T. A., Park, N. and Peterson, C. (2005). 'Positive psychology progress: Empirical validation of interventions'. *American Psychologist*, 60: 410–421.

Shapland, J., Atkinson, A., Atkinson, H., Dignan, J., Edwards, L., Hibbert, J., Howes, M., Johnstone, J., Robinson, G. and Sorsby, A. (2008). *Does restorative justice affect reconviction? The fourth report from the evaluation of three schemes. Ministry of Justice Research Series no. 10/08*. London: National Offender Management Service.

Sherman, L. W. and Strang, H. (2007). *Restorative justice: The evidence*. London: The Smith Institute.

— (2009). 'Testing for analysts' bias in crime prevention experiments: Can we accept Eisner's one-tailed test?'. *Journal of Experimental Criminology*, 5: 185–200.

Sherman, L. W., Gottfredson, D. C., MacKenzie, D. L., Eck, J. E., Reuter, P. and Bushway, S. D. (1997). *Preventing crime: What works, what doesn't, what's promising*. Washington, DC: U.S. Department of Justice, National Institute of Justice.

Smith, M. L., Glass, G. V. and Miller, W. R. (1980). *The benefits of psychotherapy*. Baltimore: John Hopkins Press.

Smith, P., Goggin, C. and Gendreau, P. (2002). *The effects of prison sentences and intermediate sanctions on recidivism: General effects and individual differences. Research Report JS42–103/2002*. Ottawa: Public Works and Government Services Canada.

Stewart, D. (2008). *The problems and needs of newly sentenced prisoners: results from a national survey. Ministry of Justice Research Series 16/08*. London: Ministry of Justice.

Theobald, D. and Farrington, D. P. (2009). 'Effects of getting married on offending: Results from a prospective longitudinal survey of males'. *European Journal of Criminology*, 6, 496–516.

Tolan, P., Henry, D., Schoeny, M. and Bass, A. (2008). 'Mentoring inteventions to affect juvenile delinquency and associated problems'. [online document] Campbell Collaboration www.campbellcollaboration.org/reviews_crime_justice/index.php.

Tong, L. S. J. and Farrington, D. P. (2006). 'How effective is the Reasoning and Rehabilitation programme in reducing offending? A meta-analysis of evaluations in four countries'. *Psychology, Crime and Law*, 12: 3–24.

Toynbee, P. (2003). *Hard work: Life in low-pay Britain*. London: Bloomsbury.

Travers, R., Wakeling, H. C., Mann, R. E. and Hollin, C. R. (2010). 'Reconviction following a cognitive skills intervention: An alternative quasi-experimental methodology'. *Legal and Criminological Psychology*, 17 (published online).

Van der Laan, P. (2010). 'Probation supervision and young adults'. Paper presented at the *Stockholm Criminology Symposium*, 14–16 June, 2010, Stockholm, Sweden.

Visher, C. A., Winterfield, L. and Coggeshall, M. B. (2006). 'Systematic review of non-custodial employment programs: Impact on recidivism rates of ex-offenders'. [online document] Campbell Collaboration www.campbellcollaboration.org/reviews_crime_justice/index.php.

Wakeling, H. C., Mann, R. E. and Travers, R. (2011). *Reconviction following sex offender treatment: An alternative quasi-experimental methodology*. Unpublished research report. London: NOMS.

Ward, T. and Brown, M. (2004). 'The good lives model and conceptual issues in offender rehabilitation'. *Psychology, Crime and Law*, 10: 243–257.

Ward, T. and Maruna, S. (2007). *Rehabilitation: Beyond the risk-paradigm*. London: Routledge.

Ward, T., Mann, R. E. and Gannon, T. A. (2007). 'The good lives model of offender rehabilitation: Clinical implications'. *Aggression and Violent Behavior*, 12: 87–107.

Webster, C., Simpson, D., MacDonald, R., Abbas, A., Cielsik, M. and Shildrick, T. (2004). *Poor transiations: Young adults and social exclusion*. Bristol, UK: Policy Press.

Weisburd, D., Lum, C. M. and Petrosino, A. (2001). 'Does research design affect study outcomes in criminal justice?' *The Annals of the American Academy of Political and Social Science*, 578, 50–70.

Welsh, B. C., Farrington, D. P. and Sherman, L. W. (eds.) (2001). *Costs and benefits of preventing crime*. Oxford, UK: Westview Press.

Welsh, B. C., Peel, M. E., Farrington, D. P., Elffers, H. and Braga, A. A. (2011). 'Research design influence on study outcomes in crime and justice: a partial replication wit public area surveillance'. *Journal of Experimental Criminology*, 7.

Wermink, H., Blokland, A., Nieuwberta, P., Nagin, D. and Tollenaar, N. (2010). 'Comparing the effects of community service and short-term imprisonment on recidivism: A matched samples approach'. *Journal of Experimental Criminology*, 6, 325–349.

Werner, E. E. (1989). 'Vulnerability and resiliency: A longitudinal perspective', in M. Brambring, F. Lösel and Helmut Skowronek (eds.), *Children at risk: Assessment, longitudinal research, and intervention.* Berlin: de Gruyter, 157–172.

Werner, E. E. and Smith, R. S. (1992). *Overcoming the odds.* Ithaca, NY: Cornell University Press.

Wikström., P.-O. and Treiber, K. (2007). *Assessing the evidence of young offender-oriented therapies: Cognitive-behavioural and multisystemic therapies. Report to the Youth Justice Board.* London: Youth Justice Board.

Wilson, D. B., Gallagher, C. A. and MacKenzie, D. L. (2000). 'A meta-analysis of correction-based education, vocation, and work programs for adult offenders'. *Journal of Research on Crime and Delinquency,* 37: 347–368.

Wilson, D. B., Mitchell, O, and MacKenzie, D. L. (2006). 'A systematic review of drug court effects on recidivism'. *Journal of Experimental Criminology,* 2: 459–487.

Wormith, J. S., Althouse, R., Simpson, M., Reitzel, L. R., Fagan, T. L. and Morgan, R. D. (2007). 'The rehabilitation and reintegration of offenders: The current landscape and some future directions for correctional psychology'. *Criminal Justice and Behavior,* 34: 879–892.

7 Young women in transition

From offending to desistance

Monica Barry

The fact that offending behaviour is primarily the preserve of youth has challenged criminologists for the best part of a century to date and will no doubt continue to do so. Burt's (1925) pioneering psychological study initiated a wave of positivist research that focussed on young people as, in the words of Sheila Brown (2005: 29), 'the hapless population upon which much of the emphasis of "scientific criminology" and "administrative criminology" was to come to rest'. Children and young people have been set apart from adults by dint of their age and status rather than their capacities and competences (Archard 1993; Franklin 2002). There are special measures in place to protect them from harm (whether this be self-inflicted or imposed by others), they are herded into institutionalised educational establishments from the age of five purportedly to improve their life chances, and they can be denied access to opportunities afforded 'adults' in mainstream society until they are well into their twenties. They are the main focus of criminal enquiry and their behaviour is often seen as abnormal, rebellious or pathological rather than a manifestation of the power imbalances inherent in society. This chapter argues, however, that young people strive towards conventionality and integration (MacDonald 1997; Williamson 1997), albeit often held back by the attitudes and practices of adults which can be both discriminating and disempowering (Barry 2005).

Youth transitions

Young people adopt diverse pathways in the transition to adulthood but are often restricted by structural constraints, notably in relation to their legal status as young adults as well as their opportunities for further education and employment. The importance of social inequalities and social institutions in determining or undermining youth transitions is becoming increasingly apparent. Many young people are excluded from higher education (through a lack of qualifications or financial support), from employment opportunities and from housing. Nevertheless, the fact is that the majority of young people who are marginalised or otherwise disadvantaged, within the labour market as elsewhere, do not actively rebel against their predicament and indeed aspire towards mainstream goals (MacDonald 1997; Williamson 1997; Wyn and White 1997).

Traditionally, transitions research has portrayed a linear, psychosocial movement towards conventional goals, summarised by Coles (1995) as the school-to-work transition; the domestic transition from family of origin to family of destination; and the housing transition from living at home to living independently. Prior to this increasing sociological interest in youth transitions, however, anthropologists had been examining the experiences of adolescents in small-scale societies and the 'rites of passage' through which they progress in preparation for adulthood. Whilst the term 'youth' was not seen as a middle phase between childhood and adulthood in such anthropological studies, Van Gennep (1960, quoted in Turner 1967) nevertheless identified three elements in the transition from childhood to adulthood in terms of 'rites of passage', namely:

Separation – the detachment of the individual from an earlier fixed point in the social structure;
Margin – a 'liminal' period when there are few commonalities with the past or coming state;
Aggregation – the individual once more has rights and obligations vis-à-vis others that are clearly defined.

Turner (1969) describes individuals within the 'margin' or 'liminal' phase as: 'persons or principles that (1) fall in the interstices of social structure, (2) are on its margins, or (3) occupy its lowest rungs' (Turner 1969: 125). The elements of transition described by Turner, van Gennep and Coles, amongst others, are predominantly structurally defined and determined, as well as linear, but Stephen and Squires (2003), for example, argue that young people's transitions in late modernity are neither linear nor predictable but are fragmented, prolonged and cyclical. Equally, young people are increasingly seen as being proactive in defining, negotiating and making sense of their own transitions, within the confines of structural constraints. Many recent accounts of young people's experience of youth transitions (see, amongst others, Holland *et al.* 2007; Barry 2001, 2006) suggest that their narratives and transitional experiences are guided as much by personal agency and responsibility as they are by structural factors, not least because of the 'risk society' notion (Beck 1992) that young people now have to resolve their own problems, overcome structural constraints and 'individualise' their own life projects (Cote 2002). Whilst the concept of individualisation describes both structure and agency, the individual is nevertheless at the centre (albeit structurally defined), and factors such as class, gender and social networks are peripheral. Furlong and Cartmel (1997: 114), however, warn against an over-emphasis on individualisation at the expense of social and structural change, suggesting that it would be an 'epistemological fallacy' to focus on individual responsibility and self-determination without taking into account the powerful impact of existing social structures. Likewise, Shildrick and MacDonald (2006) argue that post-subcultural studies epitomise the move within a postmodern theoretical environment towards less interest in social inequalities and an over-emphasis on individualistic solutions. Nevertheless, as long as young people experience 'ageism' – socially, legally and economically – within society, they will continue to have a low status as 'liminal beings' (Turner 1967), however much they determine their own transitional pathways.

If, as Beck (1992) suggests, agency is given as much emphasis as structure in youth transitions, then it would seem reasonable to assume that the timing of such transitions would vary greatly between individuals, depending on their capacity to progress their life projects. However, there tends to be continuity in the overall timing of transitions, not least as reflected by the age–crime curve in criminology where offending could be seen to increase and decrease over time in line with fluctuations in power and social status for young people. This general continuity between age and the transition to adulthood suggests that structural factors are more constraining than individual factors are enabling, but that offending in youth gives a semblance of self-determination in an otherwise constraining environment, a topic returned to later in this chapter.

Offending and capital in transition

It is argued here that the three phases of transition (childhood, youth and adulthood) run parallel to the three phases of offending, namely onset, maintenance[1] and desistance. As criminological theory currently stands, there seems to be a lack of congruence and continuity between those factors influencing onset and those influencing desistance. On the one hand, it is other people that are predominantly seen as influencing children and young people to start offending (e.g. subcultural theories, social control theory, differential association), and yet, on the other hand, individual agency tends to be seen as the most influential element in young people's desistance from offending (e.g. narrative theory, rational choice theory). This anomaly – that interdependence is associated with onset but not with desistance – requires further attention, not least when young people seem to desist from crime in order to achieve mainstream goals.

One possible concept which may enable a greater understanding of offending and desistance as a process is the concept of 'capital' as espoused by Pierre Bourdieu (1977, 1986). Bourdieu identifies four types of capital to explain how individuals gain power through social action. These are:

- *Social capital* – valued relations and networks with significant others.
- *Economic capital* – the financial means to at least the necessities of everyday living.
- *Cultural capital* – legitimate competence, skills or status arising from knowledge of one's cultural identity and lifestyles.
- *Symbolic capital* – an overarching resource that brings prestige and honour gained from the collective, legitimate and recognised culmination of the other three forms of capital.

These four types of capital are, it is argued here, difficult to accumulate in the transition to adulthood. Young people have few permanent friendships at that age;

they are limited in opportunities to earn money or respect; and they are either con-fined to full-time education or largely segregated from the adult labour market. However, they can gain some capital within the peer group, through the kudos and reputation gained from being a successful offender or having money and consum-ables as a result. But such capital is difficult to sustain through offending over time, not least because of the negative connotations of being labelled an 'offender' or being constantly embroiled in the criminal justice system; hence, young people's desire to find alternative sources of capital as they get older.

Most theorists in criminology support the proposition that social integration, whether this be by individual, structural or political means, is an important factor influencing the behaviour and attitudes of young people in transition today. Most theorists also agree that young people are keen, eventually, to adjust to conven-tional society, to strive to achieve their aspirations and to be recognised by society as a whole for their efforts.

However, subcultural and other criminological theories on their own, whilst allowing a description and analysis of why young people may choose deviant means to conventional ends, do not take full cognisance of young people's expec-tations and aspirations as well as their lack of opportunities, rights, capital and status during the transition to adulthood. Whilst research on youth transitions has been used relatively sparsely in the field of criminology,[2] it is argued that such lit-erature can provide a better understanding of youth offending as perceived and experienced by young people. Not only are the phases of transition important markers to young people, but they should also be important markers to criminol-ogists keen to understand the usually temporary and youthful nature of offending. Studying youth transitions in parallel with youth offending enables an exploration of the dynamics of age, power, interdependence and integration in the transition to full citizenship in adulthood. Equally, adding the capital component enables a greater understanding of the 'liminality' of youth transitions and the age–crime curve. The successful transition from the world of youth to that of adulthood, encouraged by an accumulation of legitimate and sustainable capital, is one of the crucial factors in reducing offending behaviour by young people. The follow-ing findings from a Scottish study of youth offending by both young men and young women (Barry 2006) illustrate this argument, although the focus here is specifically on young women.

The Scottish Desistance Study

In 2000–2001, the author explored the reasons for, and advantages and disadvan-tages of, starting, continuing and stopping offending amongst 40 persistent young offenders in Scotland, 20 male and 20 female, aged 18–33. All of the men and seven of the women were approached via the auspices of a voluntary organisa-tion running intensive probation projects in Scotland, and the remaining thirteen women were ex-probation clients referred to the researcher via various social work departments. All had been on probation in the past and the mean average number of previous offences for the men was 24 and for the women 12. The majority of the sample had been high-tariff, persistent offenders for a substantial part of their lives, on average 10 years in childhood and youth. Fourteen of the women started offending before the age of 16.

Most interviews were conducted in respondents' own homes, and the interview lasted on average one and a half hours. It involved in-depth discussion of offending histories, biographies, reasons given for onset, maintenance and desistance, the advantages and disadvantages of starting, continuing and stopping offending, and future expectations and aspirations.

The onset phase

The main influence on both the young men and the young women in the onset phase of offending was the fact that their peers were offending and they wanted to be seen as part of that friendship group. Having friends was a crucial source of social capital as they moved away from the influence of the family and into the secondary school environment, and having a reputation as an offender also gave them symbolic capital. The women were more likely to start offending specifically for the attention of usually a male partner who was offending, because this gave them social and symbolic capital, as one 23-year-old woman suggested:

> [My first boyfriend] was a drug dealer and I admired him. . . I fancied him and I thought he was cool because everybody respected him, and all the people my age respected me because I was mucking about with this person.

Gilligan (1982) suggests that young women are more likely to be influenced by their need for attention from and interaction with other young people in the transition to adulthood, but the influence of male drug-using partners in particular was a key risk factor for the young women in this study. They were much more likely to be influenced to take drugs by partners who were themselves using drugs – not least if those partners wanted the women to offend in order to feed a drug habit. This often resulted in the women becoming not only dependent on drugs but also dependent on those relationships with drug-using partners for love and attention, however violent they became, as one 21-year-old woman explained:

> I got forced into it. Basically my boyfriend turned round and said do you love me? I said aye, I love you. He said, if you love me, try this. I said I don't want to. And he said he'd batter me if I didn't.

Although sociability and relationships were the main impetus for these young women starting offending, they were also much more likely than the men to see the monetary advantages of offending (for consumables, clothes and drugs), whereas the men were more likely to see the personal advantages of relieving boredom and keeping in with their friends. For the women in particular, the economic and symbolic capital gained from offending was more apparent in the starting phase, as one 29-year-old woman explained about why she started offending at the age of 17:

> [Shoplifting] gave me confidence. I felt going with somebody else's cheque book and getting all dressed up and going in [to a shop], I could spend what I wanted, they treated me well because they thought I had enough money. They had a different outlook... It was like a power trip.

The women were also more likely to cite the latent adverse effects of traumatic childhoods, such as sexual abuse or family illness or bereavement, as major factors in their starting offending, which may in turn have exacerbated their drug use:

> When I was younger I got interfered with. That's got a lot to do with it, with anger and that... I was only four.
>
> (20-year-old female)

> It was a horrible childhood... my mum and dad split up when I was 14 – happiest day of my life when my mum and dad split up because she was just a punch bag to him.
>
> (33-year-old female)

The women were more than twice as likely as the men to see the advantages of starting offending. Indeed, their calculation of the monetary gain in starting offending makes the fact that they eventually stop offending all the more incongruent, given that they seemingly stopped more easily than the men. Likewise, given that the men could see few advantages in starting offending, it is perhaps surprising that they carried on with such activity for so long. When asked what they perceived as the disadvantages of starting to offend, the women were more likely than the men to cite disadvantages, namely becoming embroiled in the criminal justice system (e.g. getting caught, having court appearances and being detained) and losing the trust of their family and local community. As will be seen in the following section, however, the balance of advantages to disadvantages changes dramatically between the sexes as these young people move into the maintenance phase of offending.

The maintenance phase

Once offending became a routine, there was a marked change in attitude to offending between the men and women. Offending may have brought capital initially, but the majority realised over time that the capital gained from offending was short-lived and eventually created more difficulties for them than going straight. This was much more apparent for the women than the men. The men seemed to think less about what they were actually doing by offending (and became increasingly opportunistic about it) whereas the women seemed to think more about their behaviour and its adverse consequences, but nevertheless continued to offend out of necessity or pragmatism.

At the time of interview, over half the respondents had been involved in offending for between six and nine years, although the majority had since stopped offending. Whilst the type of offence committed varied minimally between onset and maintenance, the frequency and sophistication of that behaviour increased over time, as did the reasons and justifications for that behaviour. For example, whilst most offending initially was for sociability reasons or for money for consumables, it increasingly became a solitary activity and a means of funding only a drug habit, especially for the women. The longer they offended, necessity overtook sociability and routine replaced excitement. Offending often became a business, with customers replacing friends as the raison d'etre. Money for drugs became increasingly important to many of these young women in the maintenance phase, with many adapting their offending to maximise the economic gains anticipated:

> As my face got known for shoplifting, I stopped that and went into house breaking... I went on to fraud, credit card fraud... I was making about £300 to £400 a day and it was just going on purely drugs... I was a prostitute and using credit cards to go buy clothes to work in.
>
> (27-year-old female)

It could be argued that this 'force of habit' has wider connotations, in that the status quo may be more secure and preferable to a change in lifestyle or peer group. The need to uphold a reputation could also be seen as wanting to maintain the status quo amongst existing friends as a 'face-saving' mechanism, rather than giving up what is known for something that is uncertain: 'I think it was because nobody knew me... I felt as if I had to make a name for myself' (24-year-old male). Bromley (1993: 11) highlights this need to maintain a reputation gained in the past because to do otherwise would draw adverse attention to their seemingly changed persona: 'The autonomy of reputation, as a process distinct from the personality it is supposed to reflect, is the cause of much ambivalence'.

Whilst consumption of clothes, leisure, cigarettes and alcohol were important to these young people in youth, many of the women required money to maintain a developing drug addiction. They spoke of relationships with partners who were also offending for drugs, and this created a dichotomy for many of the women who wanted to support their partner's lifestyle, but did not necessarily want to match their partner's drug habit. Often when a relationship had started out as a source of love and attention, it rapidly became a liability, often resulting in domestic violence and addiction as well as stigmatisation within these women's wider social networks.

Amongst others, Covington (1985) and Barry (2006) suggest that drug-related offending by women is often partner-induced, initially to please the partner but often latterly because of coercion through abuse or the women becoming addicted to drugs themselves. For the majority of the young women (18 out of the 20), drug or alcohol use was seen as the main reason for, or an influence in, their offending in the past. Early offending, both in terms of experimenting with drugs or committing other offences such as theft, tended to be for friendship for these respondents. When substance use became a problem for them, it increased their propensity to offend over time. There was then a noticeable shift in the reasons for offending if the individual became addicted to a substance and needed money to fund their usage:

> I was getting addicted to speed. When I was 16 years old, I was on an ounce a day, which is £80 so I had to steal to get my habit.
>
> (23-year-old female)

> I didn't realise it was killing me. I didn't think there was anything wrong with me but it got to a point every day you wake up, you do the same thing, you get up, you've the clothes on you had on from the night before, you get up, you find where you're going to get money from, you'd walk for miles and miles, you'd climb a mountain for a tenner at the top of it and you'd walk back down it again and buy yourself a bag [of heroin]. You wouldn't eat. The only thing you would eat was chocolate. If you never had money for chocolate... you'd steal a bar of chocolate to keep your sugar level up.
>
> (21-year-old female)

The men and women diverged in their 'choice' of whether to offend or not in the maintenance phase. The men were more likely to be dependent on *status* gained from offending whereas the women were more likely to be dependent on *drugs* as a result of starting to offend, and therefore chose to commit specific offences in the maintenance phase to fund their habit. Substance misuse and crime have tended to show a close association that cannot be put down to chance alone. Whilst crime rates have apparently dropped over the last 20 years or so in most developed countries (Leonardsen 2003, 2010; van Dijk 2010), there have been 'alarming trends' in increased substance misuse since the Second World War (Pudney 2002).

Just as many of the young women in this sample suggested that a methadone programme to stabilise their drug use would have precluded any need to offend, likewise many suggested that offending would not have been so necessary if they had found employment. However, legitimate employment was elusive to the majority of them, who seldom had the skills, qualifications or social networks necessary to find paid work. However, in the transition between school and eventual employment, offending was one way of ensuring some form of income, however precarious such activity was. Equally, whilst offending may have initially been seen a source of kudos and status for these young people, as their offending became more persistent, their reputations were undermined greatly by their involvement in the criminal justice system, thus further undermining their chances of finding employment. The disadvantages of offending eventually outweighed the advantages at a time when wider social networks and responsibilities (to themselves and their families) became increasingly valuable to them. They seemed no longer to value the advantages of offending accrued in the childhood and early youth phases but wanted to progress to adulthood and more conventional opportunities and responsibilities.

Thus, what had started out as generally sociable and enjoyable criminal activity in the onset phase had become isolating, habitual and increasingly risky behaviour for many in the maintenance phase. The reasons given for *continuing* offending were rarely synonymous with the reasons for *starting* offending, and it seems that the initial kudos, sociability or excitement gained from offending soon wore off as drug use increased, practical need took over or 'criminal justice system fatigue' set in. These respondents' offending seemed to become very much a pragmatic means of sustaining a certain lifestyle or habit in the seeming absence of an alternative lifestyle, and few were currently satisfied with their situation. Thus, many of the respondents talked of distancing themselves from offending peers in the latter stages of the maintenance phase, suggesting the beginning of the process of desistance.

The desistance phase

Eighteen of the 20 young women suggested they had stopped offending at the time of interview and the majority of them also suggested they had done so within a year prior to interview. This was broadly supported by the official data collated two years after interview which suggested that 15 of the 20 women had, according to official criminal records, maintained an offence-free lifestyle since their decision to stop. Reasons for stopping offending revolved around the risks of being incarcerated and of losing people close to them. The women often had children for whom they felt increasingly responsible and whose welfare was linked to the mother being both in the community and free of a drug addiction. Not only losing a child through the mother's potential death from drugs but also losing the child to the care of social services were both concerns voiced by some of these young women.

There were few perceived 'pull' factors involved in their decision to stop offending, with a drug addiction, the criminal justice system, loss of trust within the family and a deteriorating reputation being the main 'push' factors. The main pull factor was the dream of leading a normal life, with a loving relationship, a house and a job. This striving for normality and independence was much more noticeable amongst the women than the men, and the means of achieving it seemingly more readily available and attractive to the women – such as through being able to give their love and attention to another person – whether that be a partner or their own children.

Because of the drug problems that many of the women in this sample had, desistance was only seen as possible if and when their drug use reduced, stabilised or stopped altogether. If they did not need drugs, the majority said they would not need to offend, and this has been borne out in other studies of offending (for example, Jamieson *et al.* 1999). Therefore, their main preoccupation in the desistance phase was to give up drugs. A high proportion of the women (8 out of 20) were prescribed methadone in the later stages of an addiction. They suggested that this was a saving grace in their fight to stop drug taking and offending – although they recognised that methadone was also an addictive drug in its own right.

The 'hassle factor' which accompanied offending (e.g. getting caught, getting tired and disillusioned or having a criminal record or reputation) was also a major factor in their reasons for stopping:

> I had just grown up, realised the serious trouble I had been in... and well, at 20, I had my own house at this point... At the start, I had all nice stuff in it and then like with the heroin, I had sold it all for £20 at a time. Everything, and then I just thought to myself 'what am I doing here? I've got nothing. I'm in my twenties'. Do you know what I mean?... and I was 'right, that's enough, time to grow up here'... the police knew... it was this house I was dealing in, right, and they were sitting right outside... the door was going constantly... that was enough. That was enough after that.
>
> (23-year-old female)

The advantages of no longer offending were mainly to do with no longer being the focus of police attention and no longer fearing imprisonment: 'Not having to worry about anything, about the police coming to the door. Nobody can come to me now and say "you've done this" because I've not done nothing' (27-year-old female).

Those close to these young people seemed to become increasingly important as they moved into early adulthood. Social and symbolic capital seemed also more influential for the young women in the sample, for example, over half the women suggested they stopped offending because of now having responsibilities for children, because of the positive impact of a relationship or because of the support from family more generally:

> Reasons for stopping? Well the kids, know what I mean. To try and make a family... I just didn't want to hurt them anymore. I knew I had hurt them enough. [My daughter] had seen so much... She hadn't seen the needle or nothing, know what I mean, but kids aren't stupid.
>
> (27-year-old female)

The women suggested that they were more determined to stop offending if such offending meant jeopardising a loving relationship with a non-offending partner. Generally, it could be said that desistance for the women in this study resulted more from *actual* commitments (to children, partners or parents), whereas for the men desistance was more in *preparation* for potential commitments (aspirations for employment or raising a family). Having real rather than imaginary responsibilities was no doubt a potential factor which precipitated earlier desistance amongst the women.

The women were also nearly three times as likely as the men to mention having freedom, control, pride and a 'normal' life again and were twice as likely to mention having improved relationships with family, children and partners and improved reputations within the community:

> I don't feel like scum anymore... [I] feel worth something now. I can make something of myself now. Get on with my life. I want to have babies and I want to get married. I just want all the normal things in life and I feel now that I'm grown up a wee bit and my head's more clearer. I've got a lot of loss of memory with drugs and I've still got a lot of very bad depressions but I've sort of got my family back a wee bit. I don't want to ever lose that, it's so sad.
>
> (23-year-old female)

The increasing pragmatism and disenchantment in the desistance phase was closely related to the 'hassle factor' mentioned above, but was also associated with a developing realisation that offending was not compatible with their increased need and desire to achieve conventional goals. The vast majority of this sample had similar conventional aspirations to those of young people more generally, namely a job, a house of their own and a family of their own (Barnardo's 1996; Barry 2001; Webster *et al.* 2006). Thirteen women mentioned wanting a job, and ten women wanted a house of their own. Five women mentioned having a settled family life, but only after they had gained stable employment.

Employment is often cited in the desistance literature as being a major precursor or trigger to desisting, and yet 16 of the 18 young women who said they had stopped offending did not have employment but still considered that they were desisters. Of the two young women who were employed at the time of the interview, neither equated their desistance with actually finding employment, although one commented that the job gave her the opportunity to prove herself as reliable and trustworthy.

Discussion

These findings suggest that young women may start offending as a means, however misguided or short-sighted, of social integration, whether this be through friendships or relationships. Offending offered possible status and identity in moving from the confines of the family in childhood to the wider social network of the school milieu. However, in the maintenance phase, sociability and status were overtaken by necessity, resignation and addiction. Although they may not have had a lot to lose materially in the youth phase, the 'hassle factor' of the criminal justice system became increasingly inhibiting and relationships with family, partners and children became stronger and more empathic. Thus, the two key factors associated with desistance for these young women tended to be practical or social: that is, criminal justice system 'fatigue' or because of relationships with, or the support of, family, friends and significant others.

These young people eventually realised that their offending was losing them the trust of significant others, was losing them their freedom and was resulting in more costs than benefits as they moved into adulthood. Offending offered them 'informal' legitimation by their peers and some continuity and recognition in the absence of more conventional and formal legitimation by the wider society, but as they moved into adulthood offending became less likely to give them longer-term capital. Such capital was more likely to be gained from legitimate sources, and for the women this was more often through opportunities to take on responsibilities for children or partners, rather than through employment per se. The women were more concerned about their reputations within the wider community, their need to be good mothers and the possibility of further involvement in the criminal justice system if they continued to offend or take drugs. This new sense of responsibility and care in adulthood was a much more viable source of legitimate capital to the women than the men and they thus tended to move away from offending peers and emphasised renewed contact with, and support from, family members or non-offending partners. State benefits also became an alternative source of income for those aged over 18 and those prescribed methadone found the economic savings considerable.

However, it is acknowledged that many who *had* not stopped offending also had access to such opportunities for accumulating capital (in Bourdieau's sense: see above) – a loving relationship, children to look after, maybe a job – but were unable or unwilling, for varying reasons, to desist from crime. This anomaly has been a constant and major source of concern for criminologists and suggests that capital accumulation on its own cannot account for desistance. It is therefore suggested here that capital *expenditure* is a missing link in the chain of events surrounding both youth transitions and youth offending. Taking on responsibilities for themselves or others – giving their own capital to others or being needed by others – gave them the impetus to stop offending. What was particularly striking about these young people's narratives, especially the women's, was their emphasis, once they had stopped offending, on taking on responsibilities for others and wanting to give back to others for the damage or hurt they had caused them in the past, however indirectly. The two main ways in which expenditure of capital can be achieved for young people are through taking on responsibility and 'generativity':

- *Taking on responsibility* means having the desire, opportunity, incentive and capacity to be trusted with a task of benefit to others. Examples would be having employment, or having responsibility for one's own children or family.
- *Generativity* means the passing on of care, attention or support to others based on one's own experiences, through, for example wanting to become a drugs counsellor or probation worker; wanting to ensure that their own children have a better life than they had; and wanting to make restitution to the local community for past offending (see Maruna 2001).

In this study, it seemed that those who had desisted from crime were more likely to have opportunities for responsibility-taking and generativity than those who were still persistent offenders. Thus, it may be that a combination of expenditure and accumulation of capital is necessary not only in the transition to adulthood but also in the transition to desistance. This combination of accumulation and expenditure of durable and legitimate capital is what I would call 'social recognition'. The concept of social recognition suggests that young people recognise the needs of others (generativity) and are concurrently recognised by others in addressing those needs (responsibility-taking).

The young women seemed to have greater opportunities not only to accumulate capital as they got older but also to spend it – by taking on responsibilities or through looking after a partner or children, for example. The young men, on the other hand, had fewer opportunities to both accumulate and spend legitimate capital in youth. They were more likely to hold onto the capital they gained from offending as a means of feeling socially integrated and having a stake in that micro-society of their peers.

Constraints to capital expenditure

However, opportunities for accumulating and spending capital are not always available to young people, not least in the transition to adulthood. There are several structural constraints which are beyond the control of more disadvantaged young people, which reduce their ability to accumulate and spend legitimate capital in the youth phase, and thereby also reduce their likelihood of giving up crime. For example:

Liminal status – young people have few rights or opportunities as full citizens. They are marginalised in the labour market, have limited access to state benefits and limited opportunities to be trusted with responsibility for themselves or others.

Reputation – their reputation as an offender made them less likely to be trusted with responsibility, and such discriminatory attitudes were far from easy to shift. Coping with 'bad friends' or police harassment when one lives in the same neighbourhood requires a great deal of patience and determination.

Housing status – living at home was a financial necessity for some, which meant reduced autonomy and remaining in close proximity to the adverse influences of their peers or the police, as mentioned above. And yet to find a job often meant moving area but not having money for accommodation.

Unemployment – many suggested if they could find work and a steady income, offending would no longer be necessary, but few of them had experienced sustained periods of employment. This was partly because of their criminal record, partly the uncertainties of the youth labour market.

Criminal justice system – involvement in the criminal justice system was no doubt an eventual deterrent to offending but its repercussions were immense: a criminal record, police harassment and pending court cases made the accumulation and expenditure of capital more difficult. These young people needed a 'clean slate' to sustain a non-offending lifestyle but had little encouragement from the system in order to do that.

In conclusion, young people need opportunities to take on responsibilities for themselves and others, and to gain respect and trust in youth as well as in adulthood. Social inclusion is not enough: it requires reciprocity and social recognition, but social recognition can only come from durable and legitimate opportunities to spend as well as to accumulate capital. The key to desistance, therefore, may be in offering young people responsibility and respect: legitimate opportunities to spend capital, thereby allowing them to be recognised as valued members of society rather than merely liminal beings in transition.

The implications of this research for policy in the criminal justice system are two-fold. First, given that the period of transition from childhood to adulthood runs a seemingly parallel course to that of onset, maintenance and desistance, it would seem logical to extend a welfare-based rather than punishment-based criminal justice system until the age of at least 21, if not 25. Such a system would also need to review the keeping and divulging of criminal records: for example, certain criminal records should only be divulged for judicial purposes and not for employment purposes. Second, pending the rejuvenation of the labour market, it may well be worth encouraging young people to take on volunteering work which could foster reciprocity and trust between young people and their communities, as well as offering opportunities for taking on responsibilities and for generativity.

Notes

1 I choose to use the word 'maintenance' rather than 'persistence' since the latter often suggests not only dogged obstinacy or purposefulness, but also increased frequency of offending. Maintenance, on the other hand, suggests the possibility of merely keeping going with offending, with or without purpose, and can imply a reduction as well as an increase in offending behaviour.
2 Although see Bottoms *et al.* (2004), Harada (1995), McAra and McVie (2010), MacDonald and Marsh (2005) and Smith (2006).

References

Archard, D. (1993) *Children: rights and childhood*. London: Routledge.
Barnardo's (1996) *Young People's Social Attitudes: having their say – the views of 12–19 year olds*. Ilford: Barnardo's.
Barry, M. (2001) *A Sense of Purpose: care leavers' views and experiences of growing up*. London: Save the Children/Joseph Rowntree Foundation.
— (2005) 'Introduction', in M. Barry (ed.) *Youth Policy and Social Inclusion: critical debates with young people*. London: Routledge.
— (2006) *Youth Offending in Transition: the search for social recognition*. Abingdon: Routledge.
Beck, U. (1992) *Risk Society: towards a new modernity*. London: Sage.
Bottoms, A., Shapland, J., Costello, A., Holmes, D. and Mair, G. (2004) 'Towards desistance: theoretical underpinnings for an empirical study'. *Howard Journal of Criminal Justice*, 43: 368–89.
Bourdieu, P. (1977) *Outline of a Theory of Practice*. Cambridge: Cambridge University Press.
— (1986) 'The forms of capital', in J. G. Richardson (ed.) *Handbook of Theory and Research for the Sociology of Education*. Westport, CT: Greenwood Press.
Bromley, D. (1993) *Reputation, Image and Impression Management*. Chichester: Wiley.
Brown, S. (2005) *Understanding Youth and Crime: listening to youth?* Buckingham: Open University Press.

Burt, C. (1925) *The Young Delinquent*. London: University of London Press.
Coles, B. (1995) *Youth and Social Policy: youth citizenship and young careers*. London: UCL Press.
Cote, J. (2002) 'The role of identity capital in the transition to adulthood: the individualization thesis examined'. *Journal of Youth Studies*, 5: 117–34.
Covington, J. (1985) 'Gender differences in criminality among heroin users'. *Journal of Research in Crime and Delinquency*, 22: 329–54.
Dijk, J. van (2010) 'The European crime falls: security driven?'. *Criminology in Europe*, 9: 12–13.
Franklin, B. (ed.) (2002) *The New Handbook of Children's Rights: comparative policy and practice*. London: Routledge.
Furlong, A. and Cartmel, F. (1997) *Young People and Social Change: individualization and risk in late modernity*. Milton Keynes: Open University Press.
Gilligan, C. (1982) *In a Different Voice: psychological theory and women's development*. Cambridge, MA: Harvard University Press.
Harada, Y. (1995) 'Adjustment to school, life course transitions, and changes in delinquent behaviour in Japan', in Z. S. Blau and J. Hagan (eds), *Current Perspectives on Aging and the Life Cycle: delinquency and disrepute in the life course*. Greenwich, CT: JAI.
Holland, J., Reynolds, T. and Weller, S. (2007) 'Transitions, networks and communities: the significance of social capital in the lives of children and young people'. *Journal of Youth Studies*, 10: 97–116.
Jamieson, J., McIvor, G. and Murray, C. (1999) *Understanding Offending Among Young People*. Edinburgh: The Stationery Office.
Leonardsen, D. (2003) 'The Moral Dimension in Crime – the Japanese experience'. Paper presented at the British Society of Criminology Conference, June (unpublished).
— (2010) *Crime in Japan: paradise lost?* London: Palgrave Macmillan.
MacDonald, R. (1997) 'Youth, social exclusion and the millennium', in R. MacDonald (ed.) *Youth, The 'Underclass' and Social Exclusion*. London: Routledge.
MacDonald R. and Marsh, J. (2005) *Disconnected Youth? Growing up in Britain's Poor Neighbourhoods*. Basingstoke: Palgrave Macmillan.
McAra, L. and McVie, S. (2010) 'Youth crime and justice: key messages from the Edinburgh Study of Youth Transitions and Crime'. *Criminology and Criminal Justice*, 10: 179–209.
Maruna, S. (2001) *Making Good: how ex-convicts reform and rebuild their lives*. Washington DC: American Psychological Association.
Pudney, S. (2002) *The Road to Ruin?: sequences of initiation into drug use and offending by young people in Britain*. Home Office Research Study 253, London: Home Office.
Shildrick, T. and MacDonald, R. (2006) 'In defence of subculture: young people, leisure and social divisions'. *Journal of Youth Studies*, 9: 125–40.
Smith, D. J. (2006) *Social Inclusion and Early Desistance from Crime*. Edinburgh Study of Youth Transitions and Crime, No. 12, Edinburgh: Centre for Law and Society.
Stephen, D. and Squires, P. (2003) ' "Adults don't realise how sheltered they are": a contribution to the debate on youth transitions from some voices on the margins'. *Journal of Youth Studies*, 6: 145–64.
Taylor, A. (1993) *Women Drug Users: an ethnography of a female injecting community*, Oxford: Clarendon Press.
Turner, V. (1967) *The Forest of Symbols: aspects of Ndombu ritual*. Ithaca, NY: Cornell University Press.
— (1969) *The Ritual Process: structure and anti-structure*. Chicago: Aldine.
Webster, C., MacDonald, R. and Simpson, M. (2006) 'Predicting criminality? Risk factors, neighbourhood influence and desistance'. *Youth Justice*, 6: 7–22.
Williamson, H. (1997) 'Status Zero youth and the "underclass": some considerations', in R. MacDonald (ed.) *Youth, the 'Underclass' and Social Exclusion*. London: Routledge.
Wyn, J. and White, R. (1997) *Rethinking Youth*. London: Sage.

8   Perceptions of the criminal justice system among young adult would-be desisters[1]

Joanna Shapland, Anthony Bottoms and Grant Muir

It would seem that one of the few constants in the criminological world is the age–crime curve, which, in essence, appears to be similar between countries and over time. Starting from childhood, it shows how the proportion of people who are convicted of a criminal offence initially rises steeply and then peaks in late adolescence, declining thereafter through the early 20s and onwards into middle age.[2] Figure 8.1 is an age–crime curve from England and Wales; it shows the proportion of both men and women from each age group convicted of, or officially cautioned for, an offence (excluding motoring offences) in the year 2000. This type of age–crime curve – the kind typically presented in criminological text books – provides a snapshot at a given point in time; or, to put it more technically, it provides a cross-sectional overview. There is, however, no necessary reason why individuals should, over their lifetime, follow the same kind of curve (i.e. becoming more delinquent during adolescence and then lessening their offending in their 20s, 30s and 40s).[3]

To establish whether such a pattern exists, one needs a longitudinal study that follows a considerable number of initial offenders over their whole adolescent and adult lives. Unfortunately, there have been relatively few such studies carried out. One exception is the American study started over half a century ago by the Gluecks (1950) and – after a significant hiatus – subsequently continued by Laub and Sampson (2003) (see also Sampson and Laub 1993). The initial sample used in the Gluecks' research consisted of boys, already identified as offenders, who were resident in correctional schools for juveniles.[4] Their lifetime age–crime curve (up to the age of 70) is shown in Figure 8.2, which, as can be seen, has an almost identical shape to that of Figure 8.1 (even though Figure 8.2 is longitudinal and Figure 8.1 is cross-sectional). Such a curve suggests that early adulthood may be a watershed period; a time at which people start to desist and, thus, a time at which the criminal justice system could be influential in helping or hindering these moves towards desistance.

These considerations prompted us to undertake a longitudinal study of persistent young adult offenders. We started investigating them when they were aged about 20 and then followed their lives, as well as looking at the ways in which they understood their own lives, over the next three to four years. During their

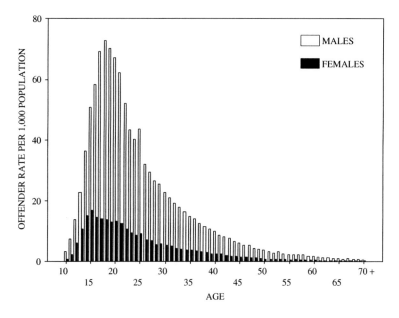

Figure 8.1 A cross-sectional age–crime curve for England and Wales, 2000 (recorded offender rates by age and gender per 1,000 of the relevant population).

Source: *'Perceptions of the Criminal Justice System...'*

early 20s, they are not only considering their relation to crime, but also working out how to earn a living, how to cope with adult relationships and so on; it is a time of significant social transition. The Barrow Cadbury Trust has pointed to exactly the same period as being of interest to criminal policy in its report *Lost in Transition* (Barrow Cadbury Commission 2005). The early 20s is an age when people have left behind the relatively ordered world of school, but have often not yet settled into adult patterns of living.

For persistent offenders, this is also a time when they are, for the first time, in sustained contact with the adult criminal justice system: that system aims to prevent reoffending (and, thus, encourage desistance). But is this how the justice system is perceived by offenders from this age group? Are its current practices really directed towards maximising the processes of desistance or do they, inadvertently, hinder such processes? In this chapter, we shall try and tackle these issues by considering the social contexts of the lives of persistent offenders in their early 20s, the contacts that our research sample had with the criminal justice system and the effects those contacts appeared to be having.

Desistance in adulthood

The greatest degree of criminological attention has traditionally been focused on childhood and adolescence; the ages at which some people move into delinquency

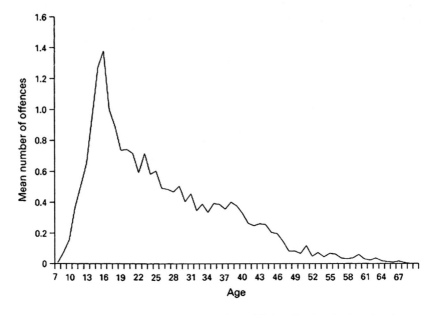

Figure 8.2 A longitudinal age–crime curve for recidivist offenders in America showing actual mean number of offences for total crime (total criminal events =
9,548) from age 7 to age 70. Reprinted by permission of the publisher from
Shared Beginnings, Divergent Lives: Delinquent Boys to Age 70 by John
H. Laub and Robert J. Sampson, P. 86, Cambridge, Mass: Harvard University Press, Copyright © 2003 by the President and Fellows of Harvard
College.

and criminality.[5] By contrast, tracking the criminality of adults has been relatively
rare. One important reason for this is that, after adolescence, it becomes more difficult to study criminality using a general population sample. In the Cambridge
Study of Delinquent Development – one of the most well-known longitudinal
criminal career studies, which followed 411 boys from one area in London from
age 8–9 – it was found that the number of offences and offenders peaked at age
17 (Farrington *et al.* 2006). But when we consider the next part of the curve, from
age 18 onwards, we rapidly find that a general population study produces relatively
few offenders at each age. Persistent offenders (those who have been convicted of
several offences at different times) are, of course, rarer still. Yet, despite the difficulties presented by such small numbers, the Cambridge Study has indicated that
there are some interesting age-related differences in offending and social life from
the 20s onwards; as David Farrington describes in more detail in chapter 4 of this
volume. For example, in terms of life success (employment, family, housing, etc.),
those who had only ever been convicted before the age of 20 had by the age of 48
became indistinguishable from those who were never convicted (Farrington *et al.*

2006). Hence, it seems that obtaining a conviction in adolescence can be overcome. However, those who received a criminal conviction *both* before *and* after the age of 21 fared far worse in terms of life success and continuing criminality after adolescence seemed to be a definite indicator of potential future difficulties.

The Sheffield Desistance Study

Our own research has concentrated upon persistent young adult male offenders, beginning a little after the peak of the age–crime curve.[6] It is not easy to obtain any form of random sample for persistent offenders because there is no widely accepted definition of who is a persistent offender and who is not, nor any easily available means of accessing such a group. We were fortunate in this case that the South Yorkshire Police were able to search the Police National Computer database to produce an overall population of offenders with particular characteristics and that the then National Probation Service (South Yorkshire) was prepared to contact those on this list of offenders with whom they were in contact to see whether they would consent to take part in the research. We specified that the population initially selected needed to have been born in certain years (to locate them in relation to the age–crime curve) and that they should have at least two separate convictions (which were not just for motoring offences). This latter requirement was made in order for the idea of desistance from criminality to have meaning (and, by fixing this minimum requirement, we knew that most of the sample would probably also have received at least one caution). The search for such offenders produced a total of 679 males born between the years 1982–1984, convicted of a standard list offence on at least two occasions, who were living in Sheffield at the time of their last conviction and who were recently known to the criminal justice system through having been in prison or being on a community sentence.[7] From this population, 113 male offenders agreed to be interviewed and they took part in up to four long interviews at intervals of 9–12 months over the next 3–4 years.[8] In this chapter, we use the results from the first two interviews.[9] The sample is of course not a random sample, nor a proportionate sample, nor can it be seen as representative of the population from which it was drawn; in fact, we know that it was, on average, more recidivistic than that population. We can however reasonably say that, if we find particular patterns of criminality, lifestyles or attitudes in our sample, then they are likely to be present in other samples of highly offending males. So, for example, if we find that people in this sample are helped to desist by some particular circumstances, then this should be the case for others also.

Our sample showed high levels of previous offending. The Home Office used to define a persistent young offender as someone who had been 'sentenced by any criminal court in the UK on three or more occasions for one or more recordable offences and within three years of the last sentencing occasion is subsequently arrested or has an information laid against him for a further recordable offence' (Home Office 1997). The offenders in our sample had been convicted by a court for a standard list (recordable) offence on an average of 8.05 occasions (s.d. 4.51).

As such, our sample had on average double the threshold number of convictions required to be termed 'persistent' in accordance with the Home Office definition. Moreover, their own self-reported offending over the 12 months prior to the first interview[10] was so high that we divided them into three categories: an 'extremely active' group made up of those who admitted 100 or more offences in the preceding 12 months ($n = 46$); a 'moderately active group' made up of those who admitted between 50 and 99 offences ($n = 29$); and a 'low active' group made up of those who admitted less than 50 offences ($n = 37$).

Although there is considerable evidence from criminal career studies that an early age of onset tends to lead to longer criminal careers (Farrington 1989; Farrington *et al.* 1998), the young adults in our sample in fact varied quite widely in the age of their first official act of criminality (caution or conviction): from age 9 (one offender from Scotland) to age 18. Overall, about a third had had their first official contact with the law at ages 13 or 14, a third below this age and a third at age 15 or above.

The stereotype of persistent offenders in the UK is that they are also addicted to drugs and that much offending is drug-related. However, this particular group of persistent offenders were not all dependent on drugs. Virtually everyone in the sample said that they might take soft drugs such as cannabis or ecstasy on a social basis. However, at the first interview only around a third (35 per cent) admitted to taking hard drugs more than purely socially and only 8 per cent to taking soft drugs in a similar fashion ($n = 112$). In a separate question, 41 per cent said they had been dependent on drugs in the last year. Overall, a slight majority self-reported that they had no drug problem (whether measured through perceived drug dependency or taking drugs more than purely socially).[11] When we correlated problem drug use against types of self-reported criminality, there was a link with 'other theft' (primarily shop theft) and burglary. These are offences known to be committed to feed a drug habit, but they did not form the majority of criminality revealed in our study.

This sample may not be typical of persistent offenders in England and Wales in general, but we need to bear in mind that encouraging desistance from persistent offending is not simply a matter of treating drug dependence (although that is clearly very important where there is dependence). Instead, for many in our study, desistance seems to rely upon helping them to create other aspects of a different lifestyle.

Wishing to desist

What would constitute desistance for this sample of high offenders? Although the most absolute measure of desistance would, clearly, be if someone were to stop offending and never to commit another offence in their lifetime, this is quite simply unrealistic for those who have persistently offended at the level that many of the young adult men in our sample had. Nor is it, technically, possible to judge whether this measure of desistance has been achieved until the whole sample dies. It is possible that some offenders do indeed have sudden and dramatic conversions and stop offending entirely. For most, however, our evidence shows that desistance will be a gradual process: a gradual decrease in the frequency of offending or an increasing number of crime-free periods (West 1963). Desistance should, therefore, be seen as a process; one which may be rather like the process of treatment from an addiction – not easy and not immediate (Bottoms *et al.* 2004).

We can reasonably ask, however, whether the offenders in our sample were intending or trying to desist or whether they, by contrast, enjoyed or saw as inevitable a life in which offending played a considerable part? An important finding from our study, in this respect, is that most said that they did want to stop offending and to change their lives. At the first interview, a majority said they had made a definite decision to try to stop (56 per cent). Some others wanted to stop but, realistically, said that they did not know if they could (37 per cent). Only a few said they were unlikely to stop (7 per cent). This is a sample of would-be desisters.

There is a tendency in some circles to believe that once someone has reached the stage of being a really persistent offender, then they are likely to continue to offend and to live their lives in and out of jail. We think it is very important to stress that, as far as our sample were concerned, this was not their choice. This makes it even more important to consider what may happen in young offenders lives and which social and criminal justice interventions are likely to encourage (or discourage) them to keep on trying to desist. The small amount of available research evidence in this area suggests that the factors influencing the paths out of offending may not be identical to the ones that lead to offending in adolescence. Hence, the choices people make which influence the paths out may, in some respects, be different, not just the reverse, of those on the paths in (Stouthamer-Loeber *et al.* 2004; Sampson and Laub 1993).[12] If this is so, then effective strategies to promote desistance among young adult offenders may not be the same as the strategies that should be used to prevent people turning to crime in the first place. However, in order to consider the impact that criminal justice agencies and sentences have upon these would-be desisters, we need first to outline their social and economic situation.

Changing social contexts

In our sample, diversity and change seemed to be characteristic of lifestyles in the early 20s. If we look at the social contexts in which these men were living, a majority said, perhaps surprisingly for such a highly offending sample, that they were living with their parents. Others were living with girlfriends or partners or were in hostels or staying on friends' floors (Table 8.1). Many were in a steady relationship or said that they had been in the past 12 months. Indeed, 31 per cent had fathered children, although some were not in contact with their children. Generally, their partners (girl friends) disapproved of the men's offending; as did almost all of the offenders' parents. Overall, therefore, three-quarters of our sample, when not in prison, were living with people who were important to them, such as parents or girl friends (many actually still turned to parents for advice), *and* who made it clear to them that they were opposed to their offending.

Table 8.1 The social and economic contexts of lifestyles of the young adult men in the Sheffield Desistance Study at the time of first interview

Social and Economic Context	%
Current living circumstances (*n* = 112)	
Living with parents	56
Living with girlfriend/partner	21
Other (with friends, alone, in a hostel, etc.)	23
Relationships (*n* = 112)	
Currently in a steady relationship with girlfriend/partner	42
Had a previous steady relationship in last year	35
Father of one or more children	31
Mates (*n* = 108)	
Mates very important	63
Mates less important	37
Whether mates had been in trouble with the police (*n* = 108)	
Mates 100% in trouble with the police	32
Mates 75–99% in trouble with the police	37
Mates less than 75% in trouble with the police	32
Employment (*n* = 112)	
No job of any kind in the last year	58
'Regular' job at some time in the last year	24
'Regular' job for the full year	10
Cash in hand/casual jobs only	18
Qualifications and schooling (*n* = 108)	
Left school without qualifications	86
Obtained qualifications since school	51
Excluded from school at some point	93
Excluded permanently or for more than a month	46
Driving (*n* = 112, but for licences *n* = 110)	
Driving licence held	5
Disqualified from driving	27
Had committed driving offence in the last 12 months	72
Victim of vehicle theft/theft from vehicle	24

The Tübingen desistance study, which adopted a qualitative methodology, has produced similar findings (Kerner 2006). It seems that even though people may become quite estranged from their parents in late adolescence, they still often retain some parental ties, which can become reactivated in the 20s and can help to pull people away from crime. As we can see, therefore, the 20s is a period of change, during which different people may move at different speeds and, at one point in time, have different lifestyles. But, encouragingly, when we asked the Sheffield sample what they wanted for the future, their goals and values were mostly very conventional: to find a partner, have children, live in a decent flat or house, find some work and have a bit of respect in the community.

Where they differed from the general population (and where there were potential tensions between their different relationships), however, was in respect of their 'mates' (friends). For most, 'mates' were very important to them and were often highly trusted, but were also very likely to have been in trouble with the police. A third of our sample said *all* their mates had been in trouble with the police, while another third said three-quarters of their mates had been in trouble (Table 8.1). These were often criminogenic bonds and indeed many had offended with their mates. Some respondents also ruefully confessed that they knew that if they went out with their mates on a Friday or Saturday night, then they might well end up committing offences. There were, therefore, significant tensions in these men's lives between, on the one hand, their parents and girlfriends and their aspirations which stressed a mostly conformist and mainstream lifestyle, and, on the other hand, their mates, who often exerted a pull towards offending behaviour (see also Warr 2002).

Economic contexts: starting again?

In contrast to their social contexts, which were very diverse (from rough sleepers to being close to parents) the economic context for our sample was fairly uniform, and mostly dire (Table 8.1). At the first interview, 58 per cent had had no job of any kind in the past year (before going into prison, if they were in prison). Only a quarter had had a regular job (meaning that they received a pay-packet) at some time in the last year and only a tenth had had a regular job for the full year. Another fifth had cash-in-hand or casual jobs only. The informal economy played some part in their lives, but not a major part.

When we asked respondents to tell us about their income and expenditure, it became clear that there was often a gap between income (work, benefits) and spend; and this gap was frequently filled by crime. Given this picture, it is not surprising that, when we asked them what difficulties there might be in going straight, the major obstacles (for 87 per cent of the survey) were a lack of money, a lack of work or coming across opportunities to make easy money. Personal problems also featured heavily in the list of obstacles, but the material dimension was very strong.

Some may respond to this by asking 'why couldn't they stir themselves and just go out and get a job'? However, trying to find a job for many in this sample would be difficult as they were a very low-achieving group (so far as qualifications for employment are concerned). Not only did virtually none have any higher or further education qualifications, but as many as 86 per cent had left school without any qualifications at all. This is possibly linked to the fact that almost all (93 per cent) had been excluded from school at some point and that 46 per cent had been excluded permanently or for a month or more. However, half of the sample had later acquired (sometimes in prison or during a community sentence) some qualifications, mostly of a vocational skills nature.

For young men without many (or any) paper educational qualifications, one real employment possibility is a job that requires driving. However, though it was clear that many of this sample did sometimes enjoy driving vehicles, it was also clear that most were not driving legally. Between them, they could only muster one full driving licence and five provisional licences. Over a quarter were disqualified from driving because of previous vehicle-related offences (some of which were committed more than a year earlier, and by no means all of which were for moving-vehicle offences such as careless driving). Despite these bans, however, many of the men were driving on the roads and during their normal social lives. In fact, in the victimisation section of our first interview, nearly a quarter said that they had in the last year had a vehicle under their control stolen or had had something stolen from it. This also means that they were driving without insurance (because with no driving licence they were necessarily uninsured). Cars were socially important to them but they were not driving legally.

So the position is that, if they wanted to do things legally (i.e. desist from crime), the majority had a poor employment history and few skills; hence, economically, they needed a new start. Some were trying to do just that; over half had obtained qualifications since leaving school, several in prison. In this respect, one rather radical suggestion would be for the criminal justice system to try to provide some help towards this fresh start. For instance, should driving bans be automatically reviewed at some point (say at age 21) with disqualifications stemming from much earlier car-related offences quashed if there is evidence of moves being made towards desistance? Should those running community sentences be in the business of teaching people to drive legally and obtain licences? A fresh, full licence might be a real incentive for some to desist. Some readers might react strongly against these suggestions, but we need to think what we want the purpose of rehabilitative programmes within criminal justice to be. Are they intended – as their official aims state – to promote desistance and prevent reoffending? Or are our goals really that while we state that correctional measures should aim to prevent reoffending, in reality we are unwilling to see offenders become full members of civil society at the end of their sentences? Do we think that it is somehow unfair that offenders, if they desist, should be able to drive, to acquire a job or to become mainstream members of society? In short, do we wish punishments to be served or in a sense to remain in force?

The role of the criminal justice system

On the evidence we have presented so far, the criminal justice system – a very present element for our sample – is working in a context of young adult offenders wishing to desist, but having few material possibilities to acquire a different lifestyle. What, then, should be the role of the criminal justice system for such persistent offenders, most of whom (82 per cent) were in prison at the time of our first interview and how did the offenders themselves perceive the system?

In the criminological literature, the criminal justice system has not been noted for its prowess in promoting desistance, even though this is one of its key aims.[13] Sentencers do not have readily available choices between a host of proven sentences which they know will reduce reoffending to a considerable extent (Shepherd and Whiting 2006). If we were being controversial, we might say that the criminal justice system in England and Wales has, for many offenders anyway, settled for more modest goals; namely, to function as a general deterrent, to reduce revictimization by the incapacitation of offenders through longer prison sentences, to monitor and try to reduce risk and to enforce breach. We would like to suggest from our early results, however, that maybe concentrating upon the age band of those in their early 20s might provide a means to do something rather more positive as well; namely, to encourage desistance when people are starting to show signs of wanting to desist and, more particularly, to not discourage desistance.

Deterrence and experience of prison

For the more persistent offenders, this process may start in prison. Many people in our sample said that prison had made them think hard about their life (65 per cent said 'yes, definitely it had'; 18 per cent said, 'yes, a little'; whilst 18 per cent said 'not really' or 'no'). So, for this age-group, then, prison may well help to provide a turning point in opening them up to an opportunity for change.

This is buttressed by our findings on deterrence. The criminological literature is clear that, objectively, people are deterred more by a greater probability of being caught than by the likelihood of a longer sentence (von Hirsch *et al.* 1999; Pratt *et al.* 2006). However, these two elements are linked as it is not possible to be sentenced unless one is caught. In our sample, there was a high correlation between saying they would be deterred by more severe sentences or by a higher likelihood of being caught (Pearson $r = 0.46$, $p < 0.001$). Additionally, our results showed that, in the subjective assessments of our sample, a more severe sentence – which in the case of these persistent offenders would be highly likely to be a prison sentence – was seen by many as far more of a deterrent than a greater likelihood of being caught. Moreover, those who said that they were trying to desist were significantly more likely to find the prospect of a longer sentence more of a deterrent.[14]

We think that there may be a positive feedback loop here; a spell in prison may provide time to think about (and to regret) one's lifestyle, especially as prison experiences for young adult offenders are frequently stressful (see chapter 5 of this volume). Future prison sentences are, then, very much seen as something to be avoided if possible and those who are deciding to desist become more deterred by the likelihood of prison. A small German study by researchers at Tübingen University similarly showed that young adult prisoners regarded future imprisonment as much more of a deterrent than other criminal sanctions; though they also regarded imprisonment as being one of the least meaningful sanctions in social terms (Kerner 2006: 45–47).

So prison can, albeit in a slightly negative way, be seen as having positive effects.[15] However, the Sheffield study also provides supporting evidence for some of the known negative effects of incarceration. Prison made it harder for the young men in our sample to retain the positive relationships they had with those on the outside (parents, girl friends, relatives, children). Indeed, at the second interview, 45 per cent of our sample said that the hardest thing about being in prison was not seeing people, particularly your family. Prison also provided a new supply of potentially offending mates who, by definition, had been in trouble with the police. Most (71 per cent) of our sample said that they had made new mates in prison; of whom 48 per cent were still keeping up with them and a quarter, who were still in prison, said they intended to see their new friends when they were out. As such, while prison can provide cognitive space to rethink one's life and some opportunities for change, it can also weaken helpful relationship bonds and create fresh potentially criminogenic bonds.

Experience of community criminal justice agencies

In relation to desistance, the other problem with prison, as both we and the Tübingen study have found, is that though prison may create an opportunity for change, it often does not show people *how* to change. Desisting is working out a non-offending life outside prison. As Sampson and Laub (1993) have shown (see also Laub and Sampson 2003), a significant part of beginning to forge a desisting path are the desister's social bonds and relationships outside prison.

Members of our sample were clear about this. When asked 'What might help you to go straight?', the men gave a whole range of different and sometimes individual answers. The major elements were getting a job (25 per cent); moving out of the area (13 per cent, recognising that they needed to get away from their criminal mates and away from places where they might offend); a partner (6 per cent) or family (5 per cent); and staying off drugs (only 4 per cent). The men very rarely mentioned any element of the criminal justice system, even though we know (because it was a criterion for being in the sample) that all of them had recently had contact with the probation service. Only 2 per cent mentioned probation or prison staff as potentially helping them to go straight. Likewise, only 2 per cent mentioned educational or prison programmes aimed at changing behaviour. Either these offenders did not see the criminal justice system as providing a primary source of help or their experience of it was that it was not helpful in enabling them to desist.

What, then, was their experience of the probation service and of contact with probation staff? At the first interview, 20 of the 112 offenders interviewed were at that time on a community sentence (the others were in prison or in a Young Offenders' Institution).[16] At the second interview, 20 of the 98 respondents were on licence from prison and 12 on community sentences (either the same one or a new one). When asked what they had to do in relation to their order, respondents usually said something like 'attend probation' (those on community service/unpaid work orders or conditions said 'work' as well). Different respondents had been given varying frequencies as to how often they had to attend probation, but no respondent mentioned any other kind of probation-related activity; such as having to attend treatment programmes or do something in relation to employment.[17] The frequencies with which they had to 'attend probation' were very similar between those on licence and those on community sentences and it seemed as though, from the perspective of offenders, the experience of being on licence was almost identical to that of being on a community sentence.

At our second interview, we asked respondents about their experience of 'attending probation'. These were the visits made by offenders to probation offices, rather than visits made by the probation officer to the offender's home because, in common with recent probation practice nationally (Canton and Hancock 2007: 138), home visits were rare. Those currently on licence or on a community sentence ($n = 45$) were asked how long they spent with their probation officer on each visit. The great majority said either 5–15 minutes (42 per cent) or 15–30 minutes (42 per cent), with a few having longer visits of 30–45 minutes (7 per cent) or 45 minutes (9 per cent). Clearly, the length of visits will vary during the time on supervision. For instance, the initial meeting, particularly ones in which the OASys risk and needs assessment tool has to be filled in (Robinson 2003; Mair *et al.* 2006), is likely to take longer. However, on average, four out of five offenders said they would normally spend less than 30 minutes with the probation officer.

If the average time for visits is around a quarter of an hour to half an hour, then there will inevitably be limits as to what can be done in that time to encourage desistance. Some of the lower time periods for meetings may be due to respondents seeing duty officers rather than their own probation officer. This tended to happen where the person being supervised had a requirement to meet with a probation officer on a particular day and then either the probation officer was not available or the offender came late, or perhaps the next day, and was allowed to see duty staff. As this last example illustrates, respondents themselves were sometimes at fault here; and we know from our own personal experiences of trying to interview them that getting them to keep appointments could be really hard, even though they were not, in general, leading rootless or chaotic lives (they just were not always where they said they would be.) Nevertheless, seeing a duty officer will inevitably not provide the consistent relationship and support that may be needed to facilitate desistance; particularly if offenders are just out of prison.

What did our respondents say when asked what they talked about in these meetings with probation staff? Mostly they described it as 'general stuff' (36 per cent) or 'how I am managing' (24 per cent), though a few mentioned more specific elements, such as offending, drink or drug rehabilitation, or getting a job or finding accommodation. In this regard, it is interesting that those experiencing shorter meetings (perceived as being less than 15 minutes on average) rated meetings as significantly less useful than those who had longer meetings.[18] These offenders tended to say that probation officers just made general enquiries as to how they were doing. A similar point is made in a quote from one young man in the *Lost in Transition* report (Barrow Cadbury Commission 2005: 16):

> Most of the time they just ask you to come in, ask a couple of questions "What have you been doing? Have you been in trouble?" I say "no". "Alright, go home". Not that I mind about that because I don't like sitting in probation for hours on end... But really they should be saying "What do you want to do?" "What can we help you with?"

We therefore obtained the strong impression that some probation staff were not fully probing desistance-related issues, such as employment, accommodation, being led into trouble by mates or relationships.

To check whether practical issues were being addressed, we asked the sample whether they had asked probation staff to sort out a problem for them in the period between the first and second interviews. Only a third (33 per cent) had done so, while two thirds had not. The most likely problem to be raised by offenders was finding accommodation, with a few mentioning money problems. However, probation staff, when asked, could be seen as effective - almost half of those who had raised specific problems said that probation had sorted it out and the qualitative comments about, for example, finding accommodation were often positive.

When asked what else probation staff could have done to help, a majority could think specifically of nothing else (58 per cent), although others did mention specific practical matters, such as finding accommodation, financial and money difficulties, help with getting onto courses for qualifications or obtaining employment. It seems, however, that most of those being supervised were not raising practical difficulties with probation staff; despite the fact that a majority said they wanted to desist.

Facilitating a 'second start': the possible role of probation

Overall, our findings on the social and economic circumstances of our sample of persistent offenders make depressing reading. Though the majority of the sample did want to desist, it is very doubtful whether they would be able to take the steps necessary to lead a non-offending life in the community without practical advice and help. Our mainstream system for educating young people envisages that they will emerge from education and be able to start supporting themselves as adults at 18 (after school and vocational courses) or 21 (after higher/ further education or practical training). Community-based educational and social agencies mostly do not seem to be well equipped to help young adults at 21 with few or no qualifications or skills to acquire jobs, who also have a criminal record. Prison- and probation-based programmes, to their credit, are more aware of the poor educational base of those they house and supervise and many of our sample had taken up learning opportunities with them.

However, acquiring qualifications in prison does not sort out the practical matters of jobs, housing and money management when back in the community. Desisting is learning to lead a non-offending life in the community. However, a non-offending life without a job, activities or money is – as some desisters in our sample told us in later interviews – extremely boring and limited. Just sitting around the house, playing computer games, watching television and so forth is, mentally, a very unfulfilling life.

The implication is that it is important to deal with these practical issues; and that the probation service, amongst others, is probably in the best position to lead such efforts. Our emerging findings chime with those of the Tübingen study (Kerner 2006) and also with those of Deirdre Healy in the Republic of Ireland (Healy and

O'Donnell 2006, 2008). The Irish study was based on long qualitative interviews with male probationers, with an average age of 25.4 years and with 6.8 previous court convictions. The probationers in their study found the positive aspects of probation to be, first, practical assistance (with education, employment, and addiction) and, second, what Healy and O'Donnell described as a 'therapeutic alliance' (defined as a good relationship with one probation officer, to help offenders to cope with problems as they arise and to encourage positive behaviour). It is worth noting that the sessions with probation staff in Ireland seemed to be much longer than was the case for the Sheffield sample. For the Irish offenders, the key to a good therapeutic alliance was when officers treated them with respect, when officers were seen as approachable and when they appeared to be genuine and caring.

These findings parallel our own in relation to what offenders saw as best about their experiences with criminal justice – and most of our sample did find some positive things to say about some aspect of criminal justice, although they also said some very negative things as well. Positive elements focused around more helpful aspects of sentencing, but also included comments such as they 'seemed to care' and 'listened to me' when describing the responses by individual prison or probation staff to them. This is reminiscent of Tom Tyler's (2003) more recent work on procedural justice, in which he has usefully distinguished between the quality of the processes involved in decision making (for example, the sentencing and breach elements in our study) and what he calls 'quality of treatment', which is more personal (for example, 'am I treated with respect, as a human being', etc.). We used Tyler and Blader's (2000) fairness scale in our own study and found that, at both the first and second interviews, those in touch with community justice staff rated them more highly than did those in touch with prison staff.[19]

It seems, therefore, that probation supervision provides a real opportunity for building a relationship with offenders, whether on licence or on community sentences, and for addressing practical issues, which are key at this time of changing social and economic contexts for young adults (provided, of course, that both parties do meet up and talk about specific issues for reasonable periods). However, we have to report that, when asked a general overall question about how useful probation supervision had been, just 9 per cent of offenders at our second interview said 'very useful', 25 per cent said 'fairly useful', 19 per cent said 'a little useful' and 45 per cent said 'not at all useful'.

Those who said they had made a definite decision to desist were significantly more likely to find probation useful.[20] This could indicate that those trying to stop tended to ask probation to do more – and probation responded. It could, alternatively, mean that a positive feedback process took place, with probation activity and desistance playing off each other. We cannot yet know for certain the causal direction. Another factor is that probation could encourage the pro-desistance elements in offenders' lives, such as their parents, to be more influential.[21]

This suggests the need for a new – or the revival of an old – direction for supervision by probation staff, particularly for offenders in their early 20s. In recent years, we have seen an emphasis on the monitoring of supervision and on tightening up enforcement for probation in England and Wales. Both of these elements are important: a lax probation regime, for instance, will not be taken seriously by offenders and certainly not by the kinds of offenders in this sample. However, these aspects need, we think, to be balanced by more positive aspects. Monitoring and enforcement alone cannot provide the guidance, support and direction that people in their early 20s need as their lives change. Theoretically, Bottoms' (2002) theory of compliance would suggest that desistance needs (amongst other things) the reinforcement of a normative component based on relationships: supporting and encouraging positive relationships, such as those with parents, relatives, girl friends or partners, which discourage criminality and discouraging negative relationships.

As we have seen desistance also needs belief and hope that it is possible to earn a living other than through crime. Persistent offenders who are trying to desist in their early 20s need what we would call *'a second start'*; be that with employment, with obtaining some qualifications which will be relevant to employment and/or with managing debt or financial matters. In other words, they need to acquire the human capital that they did not acquire during schooling and adolescence. In addition, (previously) persistent offenders have few links to mainstream organisations or relationships they can draw on with people in these organisations to provide opportunities in mainstream society; as such, they have little bridging social capital (see Halpern 2005). If probation staff address these issues, they could become agents for helping to increase both the human capital and the social capital of would-be desisters (see also McNeill and Whyte 2007; Farrall 2004).

Ultimately, persistent offenders' decisions to desist will succeed or founder on whether habitual patterns of criminality can be replaced with other habits which bring a better life and the hope of attaining the goals our offenders expressed. The new possibilities aspired to may be different for different offenders, given the diverse patterns of social and economic contexts in which persistent offenders have been living. From our initial findings, it is when offenders have decided to try to desist that probation can be most useful. These findings have implications for the practice and management of probation services. Encouraging desistance through proactively providing support, guidance and advice on practical difficulties and through supporting pro-desistance relationships (alongside monitoring and enforcement) are case management tasks. They are, though, dependent upon probation officers spending time on casework and building relationships with offenders over periods of time. They require skills and experience from probation officers, which themselves take time to build and which are different from the management skills of mounting programmes, assessing risk or ensuring enforcement.

Notes

1 For the origins of this chapter, see chapter 1, and for a more recent overview of the Sheffield Desistance Study see Bottoms and Shapland (2011). We are also grateful to three colleagues in the Sheffield Desistance Study – Helen Atkinson, Deirdre Healy

and Deborah Holmes – who contributed valuably to the original version of this paper, as presented at the Cropwood Conference.

2 Although the shape of the curve has remained the same, it is interesting that for males in England and Wales the actual peak age has risen since the middle of the twentieth century (see Walker 1968: 29). A similar pattern has been observed in Germany (see chapter 2 of this volume).

3 This point is well made by Moffitt (1993), who postulates a 'dual taxonomy' theory that there are two main kinds of offenders: the 'adolescence-limited' and the 'life-course persistent'. The former, by definition, commit only relatively few offences in adolescence, and, she suggests, their criminality is the primary explanation for the shape of cross-sectional age–crime curves. By contrast, 'life-course persistent' offenders begin their criminal careers early and, it is suggested, continue offending in a relatively flat trajectory throughout adulthood.

4 The mean age of the delinquent sample at the time of selection for the research study was 14 years 8 months (Glueck and Glueck 1950: 37). By that date, the boys had an average of 3.5 court appearances resulting in a conviction (including violation of probation) (Glueck and Glueck 1950: 295).

5 For a recent literature review of this area, together with an extensive pilot research study in Peterborough, see Wikström and Butterworth (2006).

6 The study was conducted at the University of Sheffield, and funded by the Economic and Social Research Council, as part of the research network on Social Contexts of Pathways in Crime (ScoPiC). The SCoPiC network was co-ordinated by Professor P. O. Wikström at the University of Cambridge. Anthony Bottoms's more recent work on the study has been supported by an Emeritus Fellowship awarded by the Leverhulme Trust.

7 Further details of the research methodology and of the eventual sample interviewed are given in Bottoms and Shapland (2011).

8 It was originally intended to include females in the study, using the same selection criteria as for males. However, these procedures generated only a tiny handful of eligible females, so we reluctantly restricted the study to males only.

9 The second interview re-contact rate was 85 per cent. Since this paper was written we have also analysed responses from the third and fourth interviews; results in relation to perceptions of the criminal justice system are similar.

10 Or, for those in prison at the time of the first interview, the 12 months prior to going into prison. Aggregate offence totals are adjusted to reflect time at liberty.

11 Similarly, of those identified as Prolific and Other Priority Offenders by local criminal justice agencies, only 56 per cent said they were currently misusing drugs, whilst only 36 per cent said that obtaining drugs or drug use was a major occupation for them (Home Office 2007).

12 For instance, Stouthamer-Loeber *et al.* (2004) found that desistance in early adulthood seemed to be predicted by the following factors as measured at age 13–16: accountable (parents expecting to be told of the adolescents' whereabouts and actions); believing one is likely to be caught if one offends; low physical punishment from parents; having a good relationship with peers; and low peer substance abuse. Though the extent of parental supervision and associating with delinquent peers are protective factors for delinquency during adolescence, those predicting desistance are in general far more relational than are most protective factors for adolescent delinquency and tie up with our emerging findings that mending/extending relationships with parents, partners and other relatives is important in moving towards desistance (Shapland and Bottoms 2007; Bottoms and Shapland 2011).

13 The National Offender Management Service (NOMS) has declared that its aims are to protect the public, reduce re-offending, punish offenders, rehabilitate offenders, and ensure that victims feel justice has been done (http://noms.justice.gov.uk/).

14 $t = -2.202, df = 103, p = 0.030$, equal variances assumed. There was no significant relationship between perceptions of a greater likelihood of being caught and intention to desist.

15 Additionally, for those who did have a drug problem, prison can provide a setting to try to get off drugs (13 per cent of our sample indicated this was a major element of their time in prison).

16 Some probation staff are situated in prisons and YOIs to provide communication with mainstream probation work and to liaise in preparation for offenders' release. However, none of our sample mentioned prison-based probation staff as direct contacts, or included them within their category of 'probation'. 'Probation' to them meant probation service staff based in community criminal justice environments; whether as supervising officers for licence or community sentences, running unpaid work programmes or in specialist programme units.

17 Only a few of our sample were on POPs (Persistent Offender Programmes).

18 $T = 2.55, df = 42, p = 0.015$.

19 At first interview, $t = 8.73, df = 44.6, p < 0.001$; at second interview $t = 5.02, df = 95, p < 0.001$.

20 $t = -2.18, df = 49.79, p = 0.034$.

21 Usefulness of probation rated at the second interview was positively related to having a high factor loading on the parental-based social context factor at first interview (Spearman's $r = 0.43, n = 43, p = 0.004$), but unrelated to having a high factor loading on the other social context factors of unsettled, disadvantaged lifestyle or relying on alcohol/mates.

References

Barrow Cadbury Commission (2005) *Lost in Transition: a report of the Barrow Cadbury Commission on Young Adults and the Criminal Justice System.* London: Barrow Cadbury Trust.

Bottoms, A. E. (2002) 'Morality, crime, compliance and public policy', in A. E. Bottoms and M. Tonry (eds), *Ideology, Crime and Criminal Justice: a symposium in honour of Sir Leon Radzinowicz.* Cullompton, Devon: Willan.

Bottoms, A. E. and Shapland, J. (2011) 'Steps towards desistance among male young adult recidivists', in S. Farrall, S. Maruna, M. Hough and R. Sparks (eds), *Escape Routes: contemporary perspectives on life after punishment.* London: Routledge-Cavendish.

Bottoms, A. E., Shapland, J., Costello, A., Holmes, D. and Muir, G. (2004) 'Towards desistance: theoretical underpinnings for an empirical study', *Howard Journal of Criminal Justice*, 43: 368–89.

Canton, R. and Hancock, D. (eds) (2007) *Dictionary of Probation and Offender Management.* Cullompton, Devon: Willan.

Farrall, S. (2004) 'Social capital and offender reintegration: making probation more desistance-focussed', in S. Maruna and R. Immarigeon (eds), *After Crime and Punishment: ex-offender reintegration and desistance from crime.* Cullompton, Devon: Willan.

Farrington, D. (1989) 'Self-reported and official offending from adolescence to adulthood', in M. Klein (ed), *Cross-National Research in Self-Reported Crime and Delinquency.* Dordrecht: Kluwer.

Farrington, D., Lambert, S. and West, D. J. (1998) 'Criminal careers of two generations of family members in the Cambridge Study in Delinquent Development', *Studies on Crime and Crime Prevention*, 7: 85–106.

Farrington, D., Coid, J., Harnett, L., Jolliffe, D., Soteriou N., Turner, R. and West, D. (2006) *Criminal Careers up to Age 50 and Life Success up to Age 48: new findings from the Cambridge Study in Delinquent Development (Home Office Research Study 299).* London: Home Office.

Glueck, S. and Glueck, E. (1950) *Unraveling Juvenile Delinquency.* Cambridge, Mass.: Harvard University Press.

Halpern, D. (2005) *Social Capital.* Cambridge: Polity Press.

Healy, D. and O'Donnell, I. (2006) 'Criminal thinking on probation: a perspective from Ireland', *Criminal Justice and Behavior*, 33: 782–802.

Healy, D. and O'Donnell, I. (2008) 'Calling time on crime: motivation, generativity and agency in Irish probationers', *Probation Journal*, 55: 25–38.

von Hirsch, A., Bottoms, A. E., Burney, E. and Wikström, P. O. (1999) *Criminal Deterrence and Sentence Severity.* Oxford: Hart Publishing.

Home Office (1997) *Tackling Delays in the Youth Justice System: a consultation paper.* London: Home Office.

Home Office (2007) *Working Together: the Prolific and Other Priority Offender Programme and the Drug Interventions Programme.* London: Home Office.

Kerner, H. J. (2006) 'Crime prevention, prospects and problems: the case of effective institutional versus community-based treatment programs for prevention of recidivism among youthful offenders – lecture given at the 129th International Senior Seminar, United Nations Asia and Far East Institute for the Prevention of Crime and the Treatment of Offenders (UNAFEI)', in *UNAFEI Resource Material Series No. 68*. Tokyo: UNAFEI.

Laub, J. H. and Sampson, R. J. (2003) *Shared Beginnings, Divergent Lives: delinquent boys to age 70.* Cambridge, Mass.: Harvard University Press.

Mair, G., Burke, L. and Taylor, S. (2006) '"The worst tax form you've ever seen"?: probation officers' views about OASys', *Probation Journal*, 53: 7–23.

McNeill, F. and Whyte, B. (2007) *Reducing Reoffending: social work and community justice in Scotland.* Cullompton, Devon: Willan.

Moffitt, T. E. (1993) '"Life-course-persistent" and "adolescence-limited" antisocial behaviour: a developmental taxonomy', *Psychological Review*, 100: 674–701.

Pratt, T. C., Cullen, R. T., Blevins, K. R., Daigle, L. E. and Madensen, T. D. (2006) 'The empirical status of deterrence theory: a meta-analysis', in F. T. Cullen, J. P. Wright and K. R. Blevins (eds), *Taking Stock: the status of criminological theory.* New Brunswick, NJ: Transition Publishers.

Robinson, G. (2003) 'Implementing OASys: lessons from research into LSI-R and ACE', *Probation Journal*, 50: 30–40.

Sampson, R. J. and Laub, J. H. (1993) *Crime in the Making: pathways and turning points through life.* Cambridge, Mass: Harvard University Press.

Shapland, J. and Bottoms, A. (2007) 'Between conformity and criminality: theorctical reflections on desistance', in H. Müller-Dietz, E. Müller, K.-L. Kunz, H. Radtke, G.Britz, C. Momsen and H. Koriath (eds), *Festscrift für Heike Jung.* Baden-Baden: Nomos.

Shepherd, A. and Whiting, E. (2006) *Re-offending of Adults: results from the 2003 cohort (Home Office Statistical Bulletin 20/06).* London: National Statistics.

Stouthamer-Loeber, M., Wei, E., Loeber, R. and Masten, A. (2004) 'Desistance from persistent serious delinquency in the transition to adulthood', *Development and Psychopathology*, 16: 897–918.

Tyler, T. R. (2003) 'Procedural justice, legitimacy and the effective rule of law', *Crime and Justice: a review of research*, 30, 283–357.

Tyler, T. and Blader, S. (2000) *Cooperation in Groups: procedural justice, social identity, and behavioral engagement.* Philadelphia, PA: Psychology Press.

Walker, N. (1968) *Crime and Punishment in Britain (revised edition).* Edinburgh: Edinburgh University Press.

Warr, M. (2002) *Companions in Crime.* Cambridge: Cambridge University Press.

West, D. J. (1963) *The Habitual Prisoner.* London: Macmillan.

Wikström, P. O. and Butterworth, D. (2006) *Adolescent Crime: individual differences and lifestyles.* Cullompton, Devon: Willan.

9 Lost in transition?

A view from the Youth Justice Board

Rod Morgan

The conference for which this paper was first prepared took place in late January 2007 in the week preceding my resignation as Chairman of the Youth Justice Board (YJB). When I spoke to the conference I had already determined (though the audience did not know this) that I was going to resign. The factors precipitating that decision were tangentially connected to the questions discussed in this volume. For this reason, I will not fundamentally revise what I said to the conference that day, but, rather, spell out in greater detail than I did on that occasion the operational reasons that led me to take the decision I did. In an Addendum, I will then provide some more contemporary reflections on the current situation.

I should, therefore, begin with a few words about the statutory and operational responsibilities of the YJB. The Board is a non-departmental public body funded almost entirely by what until May 2007 was the Home Office, but whose responsibilities have now been transferred to the Ministry of Justice. It has been responsible since 1998 for overseeing youth justice in England and Wales, although it does not manage the youth justice system. Instead, youth justice services are devolved to, and delivered and managed by, the local authorities. Multi-agency youth offending teams (YOTs) assess child and young offenders (10 to 17 year olds) for the courts and also supervise and, directly or indirectly, provide programmes for them if they are subject to court orders, both community-based and, when following release, custodial.

The YJB provides all YOTs with a core grant (although the bulk of their budget comes from local government or key local services), monitors their performance, identifies and promotes good practice and advises ministers on all these issues. Since 2000, the YJB has also had an operational responsibility; namely, to commission and pay for sufficient custodial places to meet the needs of the courts as expressed through their remand and sentencing decisions. Approximately two thirds of the YJB's budget goes on the cost of custodial services which are principally provided by the Prison Service (and, less frequently, commercial providers of escort and residential services) and the local authorities in the form of secure homes that are generally used to accommodate younger children. This is the organisational and operational background to the stance that I, as Chairman of the YJB, adopted with regard to provision for young adult offenders (YAOs).

The YJB and young adult offenders

In July 2001 my predecessor as Chairman of the YJB, Lord Warner, made a fairly explicit bid (House of Lords, 11 July, Col 1105–08) for the YJB to take responsibility – along the same lines that the YJB had already taken over responsibility from the Home Office for commissioning provision for juveniles in April 2000 – for commissioning custodial provision for YAOs. His bid was not taken up, but in 2004 the Coulsfield Inquiry Report (2004: 77) suggested that this proposition be looked at again.

I want to revisit that proposition in the light of developments since the Coulsfield Report. In doing so, I shall take as given various issues which have already been reviewed by other contributors in this volume and which have long been acknowledged, namely:

- That a high proportion of 18 to 20 year olds have not achieved anything approaching economic independence.
- That the degree to which YAOs are emotionally, and in every other sense, mature varies enormously.

YAOs typically exhibit the same multiple deficits and problems that characterise older young offenders (15 to 17 year olds), namely: poor engagement in, and low attainment with regard to, education, vocational training and employment; high incidence of abuse of alcohol and illicit drugs; poor physical and mental health; and histories of fractured relationships, often involving experience of state care (Hazell *et al.* 2002; Social Exclusion Unit 2002; Galahad SMS Ltd 2004; Harrington and Bailey 2005; HMIP/YJB 2005; Morgan and Newburn 2007; Morgan and Liebling 2007: 1123–26).

The above characteristics are most acutely represented among those children and young offenders remanded or sentenced to custody; and the same is true for YAOs. It is for this reason, as well as because of its commissioning and financial responsibilities, that since 2000 the YJB has devoted such a large part of its energies towards improving custodial provision for juveniles. Let me begin, therefore, by describing both the current arrangements for custody and the ways in which custodial provision for young offenders – subject to scathing criticism by successive Chief Inspectors of Prisons (see HMIP 1997, 2001; HMIP/YJB 2005) – abuts that used for YAOs.

Most children and young persons in custody (80–85 per cent) are 15 to 17 years old and the overwhelming majority are housed in the 15 Young Offenders' Institutions (YOIs) which accommodate young offenders (i.e. those under 18). Of these, 12 are split-site; meaning that they are institutions which are shared by young offenders and YAOs (typically split between more-or-less self-sufficient compounds separated by some form of physical barrier).

The YJB (2005) has determined, however, that provision for young offenders should be, as far as is possible, in dedicated establishments. This means moving away from split-site establishments and/or making the young offender facilities in the remaining split-site establishments even more self-sufficient. The rationale for doing this is to ensure that regimes for young offenders are geared entirely to their needs and that the staff who work with them are specifically recruited and trained to work with young offenders. At present, all prison governors responsible for split-site YOIs must, on operational grounds (staff sickness, security needs, etc.), reserve the right to cross-allocate staff to both sides of each establishment. This means that whatever requirements or provision the YJB makes for the specialist training of staff working with young offenders, there will still be occasions when staff neither recruited nor trained for the purpose are responsible for the care of such offenders. Furthermore, the need to move away from split-site establishments was made more imperative by the prospect that YOI provision for YAOs might, as a result of the possible implementation of section 61 of the Criminal Justice and Court Services Act 2000, be diluted by the presence of adult prisoners (21 years old or more).

The YJB (2005) also plans to create several small, more intensively staffed, living units for those young offenders aged 15 to 17 years old who are more vulnerable than most (by virtue of their offences, stature, immaturity or any other factors). Furthermore, the YJB also aims to greatly enhance vocational training provisions in young offender institutions. This is especially important as it was found that a high proportion of school-age young offenders in custody were not attending school regularly and many had not attended at all for months or years prior to their incarceration (they were either excluded or not attending, with or without the collusion of the schools). Of those beyond school age, most were neither in employment nor had any form of training (many of them having left school with no qualifications). Indeed, high proportions of children and young offenders in custody actually have literacy and numeracy ages some 3 to 5 years below their chronological age (for a general review of the education and training evidence see Stephenson 2007). Any suggestion that such young people can simply be put in classrooms and/or given intensive tuition to be brought rapidly up to speed is clearly naive. For many, there is a need to first build up the motivation necessary to reverse the alienation, rejection, failure and humiliation that they associate with classrooms. Engagement in practical, vocational tasks is for many young offenders a necessary first step on the road to building up the will to acquire basic employment-enabling skills. However, most YOIs, let alone the Secure Training Centres (STCs) and local authority secure homes (LASHs), lack adequate workshops and other vocational training facilities and programmes.

The adverse regime comparisons that could be made when the YJB assumed responsibility for juvenile custodial provision in 2000 diminished in the period 2004–06. This was as a result of service level agreements between the YJB and the Prison Service specifying higher regime standards for young offenders and of substantial YJB investment in regime facilities and YJB programmes (see YJB 2005). This subsequently led to a disparity between provision for young offenders and the split-site YOIs that held YAOs (see HMIP 2001). In response, the Prison Service strove to match provision for YAOs with that for young offenders. However, the gap in provision for the two groups may now be opening up again because of overall prison system overcrowding against which the YJB is, to some extent, able to provide a commissioning bulwark. For example, while it is generally agreed that children and young offenders will not be held in police cells or adult establishments, there are no guarantees for YAOs.

The point is best illustrated by the fate of young offenders who, in the course of a Detention and Training Order (DTO), reach the age of 18. The YJB's policy has generally been to retain these young adults in designated accommodation for young offenders (for what is normally just the few weeks prior to their release; this is why there have typically been 300 to 500 18- or even 19-year-olds in YJB-commissioned establishments). The YJB's view is that it would be inhumane and counter-productive to transfer such offenders to a YAO-YOI establishment, for which they would technically be eligible. Transfers would inevitably disrupt participation in educational, vocational or offending behaviour programmes and would likely interfere with visiting and resettlement arrangements. However, in the wake of the surge in the child and young offender custodial population in 2006–07, the YJB was forced, for want of capacity, to require that more transfers be made at 18 years. The contrasts in provision were sometimes stark; for example, an 18-year-old-girl transferring from one of the five new Prison Service-managed small units for 17-year-old-girls might have to move from a facility with a highly active, positive regime and a staff-inmate ratio approaching 1:1, to a relatively impoverished facility in a wing with three officers for 60–70 young adult and adult women. In such cases, a transfer is the equivalent of falling off a regime cliff.

YJB constraints

As the YJB has repeatedly and emphatically made clear, the realisation of the Board's aspirations for the establishment of secure estate is dependent on two factors: one, sentencing trends (and, therefore, the overall numbers of children and young people in custody); and, two, the allocation of resources to the YJB from the relevant governmental ministry (now the Ministry of Justice). Current trends in both these areas do not provide grounds for optimism.

At the time that this paper was originally delivered, one of the YJB's stated targets was to 'reduce the size of the under-18 custodial population by 10 per cent through the implementation of minimising the use of custody work programme' by the end of March 2008, from a March 2005 baseline (YJB 2006: 11). The Board adopted this reductionist target because the accumulated evidence suggested that custody – except where it is a necessary response to protect the public from serious persistent and grave young offenders and however well organised and resourced – remains the least promising environment in which to achieve anything positive (see Liebling and Maruna 2006).

In this respect, there seems no reason to question the Home Office 'new realism' judgements which preceded the Criminal Justice Act 1991; namely, that sentencers are not justified in sentencing offenders to custody on the grounds that custody will in some sense enable them to be made better. They also went on to point out that treatment, training or rehabilitation were more likely to be accomplished by the offender remaining in the community (Home Office 1990: para. 2.7; Home Office 1991: para. 1.28). Further, deterrence in its individualistic calculative sense (as regards both potential offenders and offenders undergoing punishment, particularly a custodial sentence) was no longer given any credibility (Home Office 1990: para. 2.8; Von Hirsch *et al.* 1999).

Of course, to take up Michael Howard's line of argument, 'prison works' in the sense that during the typically transitory period that persistent offenders (particularly young offenders) are incarcerated, the public gains temporary respite from their depredations. However, the in incapitative impact of a higher custodial population is marginal. There seems no reason, therefore, to dispute the widely held judgement that imprisonment is largely an expensive way of making bad people worse. For the YJB, in particular, custody is extremely expensive. It currently costs approximately £55,000 to provide a YOI place per annum, £155,000 for a STC place and £195,000 for a LASH place. By comparison, the amount of money the YJB is able to allocate for early prevention work is pitifully small.

Regrettably, the YJB is not succeeding in its reductionist aim; indeed, it is actually going backwards. Between March 2005 and March 2006, for example, the population of children and young people in custody rose by 4 per cent (YJB 2006: 11) and the autumn and winter period of 2006–07 witnessed a further increase. During the winter of 2005–06, the Board – which was at that time applying for additional resources from the Home Office to cope with the increasing custodial demand – wrestled with the question of whether or not it should abandon its absolute custodial population target or replace it with a 'proportionate use of custody by sentences' target against which it might succeed. It would be more likely to succeed in the latter case because the overall proportionate use of custody for young offenders has marginally reduced in recent years (the near record numbers of young offenders in custody is largely explained by the very substantial increase in the numbers of young offenders prosecuted; see Morgan and Newburn 2007). In the end, and with the existing target having already been implicitly endorsed in a Home Office Five Year Plan (Home Office 2006: para. 3.31), the YJB decided it should be retain its absolute custodial population target. Their hope was that in subsequent months there would be public Home Office ministerial backing for the target. No such backing was forthcoming, however, and this was a major factor in my decision to resign. As a result, the number of children and young people criminalised continued to expand (see YJB 2007a).

All of which means that the YJB has little operational room to manoeuvre and that regimes for those young offenders held in YOIs (the STCs and LASHs are invariably close to being full) are under threat. In such circumstances, young offenders in custody are more likely to be held a distance away from their home, to have to share cells with other prisoners with whom they would not have requested to share and to have their programmes disrupted because of overcrowding transfers. The stresses on everyone concerned – the young offenders, their families and the staff who have to care for them – are also increased. Likewise, the risks of self-harm and other disturbances are inevitably raised in a system in which there have already been too many deaths in custody in recent years (Coles and Goldson 2005).

All of which means that the YJB is struggling to defend the progress it has made with custodial provision for young offenders (see YJB 2007b). The available capital and revenue monies available are currently being overwhelmingly spent on finding and managing additional accommodation, rather than on reconfiguring the estate in furtherance of the principles set out by the Board in 2005 (the principal exception to this is the commissioning of a new 48 bed unit for vulnerable young offenders at Wether by YOI). The time scarcely seems ripe, therefore, for the YJB to make a bid to take responsibility for YAOs, or even older offenders, especially given the absence of a clear Government commitment to stabilise or reduce resort to custody for offenders both young, young adult and adult.

The Cadbury Commission proposals

As regards the Cadbury Commission proposition that there be a flexible sentencing boundary between young offenders and young adults along similar lines to that used in Germany or Scandinavia (see Albrecht 2004; Janson 2004; Kyvsgaard 2004; and chapter 2 of this volume), I can see little prospect that this being introduced in the short to medium term. Further, given the direction of Government policy – with its emphasis on making juveniles more responsible for their actions (abolishing the doli incapax presumption in the Crime and Disorder Act 1998, encouraging courts to publicise the identities of juvenile anti-social behaviour offenders, and so on) – it would seem probable that were a flexible boundary to be considered, it would likely conform to the American rather than the German or Scandinavian approach; that is, it would allow juveniles to be dealt with as adults, rather than the reverse.

However, there is another more modest and administrative possibility. Given operational room to manoeuvre, there is no reason why young offenders who reach the age of 18 or even 21 during the course of their custodial sentences should not be retained in young offender YOIs so that specialist regimes can be provided for them. Were such an arrangement to be encouraged then it would clearly need to be adequately funded and the YJB strategy for the custodial estate would need to be amended accordingly. On one level, this might be seen to represent little more than what the YJB considers should ideally happen already, but, if considered more radically, it could also involve the creation of specialised facilities for young adults or adults who committed serious or persistent offences when juveniles.

Conclusion

Any discussion of policies and provision for young offenders and YAOs, and the relationship between the two, will arrive at different conclusions depending on whether one takes as one's starting point policies that seem politically feasible, or a tabula rasa. These were issues that I had to consider while still Chairman of the YJB, particularly as regards the current responsibilities of the Board and whether or not they were being met.

Overall, I am – given the considerable variation in maturation among young adults and the many problems which, like their junior counterparts, they typically exhibit – in favour of there being more flexible arrangements in how young adults are dealt with within the criminal justice system. In my judgement, young adults typically require provision more akin to that provided for young offenders than adults and I judge that the principles set out by the YJB for young offenders should ideally be applied to YOAs. However, I see little prospect of that happening in the current political and operational climate. Further, given the pressures currently within the system, I think that the YJB should focus its attention on preserving for children and young offenders a distinct system, rather than seek to extend that provision to a young adult population for which adequate resources are currently not provided and will not likely be. Granted, this pragmatic conclusion is not attractive, but then neither is current Government policy regarding penal policy for young people generally; which is why I am no longer Chairman of the YJB.

Addendum (2011)

In the four years since I wrote this essay there has been a sea change with regard to the number of children and young persons in custody. However, this has not yet fed through to the young adult and adult custodial populations and it is far from clear that the pressures which in 2007 provoked my underlying pessimism regarding the prospects for a radical restructuring of provision for young adult offenders will be alleviated in the short to medium term.

In spring 2007, there were more than 3000 10 to 17 year olds sentenced or on remand in custody and a few hundred more young adults in juvenile custodial facilities who had reached the age of 18 during their sentence, but had not been transferred to young adult institutions. Today the number of 10 to 17 year olds in custody has fallen to around 2, 150, whereas the young adult and adult custodial population remains resiliently at, or close to, an all-time high of over 80,000. The factors contributing to this dramatic reduction in the youth custody population have yet to be analysed in detail but the following are generally regarded as important:

- First, in late 2007, the Labour Government modified their numerical target for 'offences brought to justice' (OBTJs) to focus on more serious offences. A powerful incentive for the police to focus on and criminalise relatively minor young offenders was there by removed. Following the 2010 General Election, however, the incoming Coalition Government dispensed with the OBTJ target altogether. The result has been that the number of children and young people proceeded against and penalised both out of court and following prosecution either as first time entrants or as repeat offenders has decreased dramatically (Morgan and Newburn 2012).
- Second, the YJB, in collaboration with the Prison Reform Trust, has encouraged some youth offending team areas with relatively high incarceration rates to closely analyse local data and decision making with the aid of a consultant.

These exercises had a 'Hawthorne effect', leading to significant reductions in the proportionate use of custody locally.

- Third, the return to what was termed 'common sense policing' in the wake of the Flanagan review of policing (Flanagan Report 2008) – combined with local initiatives to divert young offenders by means of police station-based triage assessment and the resuscitation of youth offending 'bureaux', reminiscent of the arrangements made in some areas during the 1970s and 1980s (see Independent Commission 2010 and Smith 2010) – encouraged diversion of young offenders from either court appearances or criminalisation out-of-court.

Both across the country and within particular localities, the overall size of the youth justice system significantly shrank as a result of these initiatives.

In autumn 2010, the incoming Coalition Government announced deep public expenditure cuts (HM Treasury 2010) and the abolition of the YJB. It also published a Green Paper (Ministry of Justice 2010) with a chapter devoted to youth justice. Among the proposals on which consultation was sought was the setting up of local pathfinder projects designed to further drive down the use of custody for children and young persons. All the evidence suggests that further success in this regard will lead, as before, to a reduction in custodial capacity specifically designed for children and young persons; the remaining capacity being predominantly juvenile-specific rather than split-site. Further, most of the money saved is being used by the Treasury to ameliorate the public expenditure deficit, rather than being used to provide community-based provisions to facilitate the transition to law-abiding young adulthood.

Despite the encouraging nature of some of the developments in youth justice, then, there is unfortunately no sign that the Government will provide funds or support for the significant restructuring of the arrangements for young adults in the immediate future.

References

Albrecht, H-J. (2004) 'Youth justice in Germany', in M. Tonry and A. Doob (eds), *Youth Crime and Youth Justice*, Chicago: University of Chicago Press.

Barrow Cadbury Commission (2005) *Lost in Transition: A report of the Barrow Cadbury Commission on Young Adults and the Criminal Justice System*, London: Barrow Cadbury Trust.

Coles, D. and Goldson, B. (2005) *In the Care of the State? Child deaths in penal custody*, London: Inquest.

Coulsfield, Lord (2004) *Crime, Courts and Confidence: Report of an independent inquiry into alternatives to prison*, London: HMSO.

Flanagan Report (2008) *The Review of Policing by Sir Ronnie Flanagan: Final report*, London: HMIC.

Galahad SMS Ltd (2004) *Substance Misuse and the Juvenile Secure Estate*, London: YJB.

Harrington, R. and Bailey, S. (2005) *Mental Health Needs and Effectiveness of Provision for Young Offenders in Custody and in the Community*, London: YJB.

Hazell, N., Hagell, A., Liddle, M., Archer, D., Grimshaw, R. and King, J. (2002) *Detention and Training: Assessment of the Detention and Training Order and its impact on the secure estate across England and Wales*, London: YJB.

HM Chief Inspector of Prisons (1997) *Young Prisoners: A thematic review*, London: HMIP.
— (2001) *Young Offender Institutions*, London: HMIP.
HM Chief Inspector of Prisons/Youth Justice Board (2005) *Juveniles in Custody 2003–4: An analysis of children's experiences of prisons*, London: HMIP/YJB.
HM Treasury (2010) *Spending Review 2010, Cm 7492*, London: Stationery Office.
Home Office (1990) *Crime, Deterrence and Protecting the Public, Cmnd. 965*, London: HMSO.
— (1991) *Custody, Care and Justice: The way ahead for the Prison Service in England and Wales, Cmnd. 1647*, London: HMSO.
— (2006) *A Five Year Strategy for Protecting the Public and Reducing Re-offending, Cm 6717*, London: Stationery Office.
Independent Commission (2010) *Time for a fresh start: The report of the Independent Commission on Youth Crime and Antisocial Behaviour*, London: Police Foundation/Nuffield Foundation.
Janson, C. G. (2004) 'Youth justice in Sweden', in M. Tonry and A. Doob (eds), *Youth Crime and Youth Justice*, Chicago: University of Chicago Press.
Kyvsgaard, B. (2004) 'Youth justice in Denmark', in M. Tonry and A. Doob (eds), *Youth Crime and Youth Justice*, Chicago: University of Chicago Press.
Liebling, A. and Maruna, S. (eds) (2006) *The Effects of Imprisonment*, Cullompton: Willan.
Ministry of Justice (2010) *Breaking the Cycle: Effective punishment, rehabilitation and sentencing of offenders*, London: TSO.
Morgan, R. and Liebling, A. (2007) 'Imprisonment: an expanding scene', in M. Maguire, R. Morgan and R. Reiner (eds), *The Oxford Handbook of Criminology, 4th Edition*, Oxford: Oxford University Press.
Morgan, R. and Newburn, T. (2007) 'Youth justice', in M. Maguire, R. Morgan and R. Reiner (eds), *The Oxford Handbook of Criminology, 4th Edition*, Oxford: Oxford University Press.
— (2012) 'Youth Crime and Justice: rediscovering, devolution and discretion?' in Maguire, M., Morgan R. and Reiner R. (eds), *The Oxford Handbook of Criminology, 5th Edition*, Oxford: Oxford University Press.
Smith, D. J. (ed) (2010) *A New Response to Youth Crime*, Cullompton: Willan.
Social Exclusion Unit (2002) *Reducing Reoffending by ex-prisoners*, London: ODPM.
Stephenson, M. (2007) *Young People and Offending: Education, youth justice and social inclusion*, Cullompton: Willan.
Von Hirsch, A., Bottoms, A. E., Burney, E. and Wikström, P.-O. (1999) *Criminal Deterrence: An analysis of recent research*, Oxford: Hart.
Youth Justice Board (2005) *Strategy for the Secure Estate for Children and Young People*, London: YJB.
— (2006) *Annual Report and Accounts 2005/6*, London: YJB.
— (2007a) *Youth Justice Annual Statistics 2005/6*, London: YJB.
— (2007b) *Update on the Strategy for the Secure Estate for Children and Young People*, London: YJB.

10 Young adults in the English criminal justice system

The policy challenges

Rob Allen

The purpose of this chapter is to offer a series of reflections on the challenges that lie in the way of better policies on young adult offenders in England and Wales. The creation of the coalition government in May 2010 offered the opportunity for a fresh approach to criminal justice and the treatment of offenders in general, and in its recent Green Paper the government has spoken of a 'rehabilitation revolution' (Ministry of Justice 2010a). This outlook opens up the possibility of new measures for young adults being introduced which give greater attention both to evidence from research and experience from abroad – examples of which are contained in this volume (see also Allen 2010) – although, as will be seen, the new Green Paper actually says little specifically about the young adult age group.

The most systematic efforts to develop policy ideas in respect of young adults in the last few years have been undertaken by the Transition to Adulthood Alliance (T2A), a coalition of 14 voluntary organisations set up to: raise awareness of the specific developmental needs of young people as they reach adulthood; formulate better options for meeting those needs; and to test the best ways of implementing those policies on the ground through practical demonstration projects. The Alliance's work builds on the work of the Barrow Cadbury Trust Commission on Young Adults in the Criminal Justice System and their ground-breaking report *Lost in Transition* (Barrow Cadbury Trust 2005). Although their recommendation that greater focus should be given to the 18–24 year old age group received a warm welcome from government and other interested parties, progress in introducing measures tailored to the specific needs of this age group was initially slow (Allen 2008). In response, the Barrow Cadbury Trust decided in 2008 to reignite interest in this age group by funding a variety of research, policy development and practical work designed to identify what improvements were needed and to generate support. The portfolio of projects now includes three pilot schemes to test new approaches to the supervision of, and support for, young adult offenders; these schemes are operative in London, the West Midlands and West Mercia.

In November 2009, following a major consultation, the T2A published their *Young Adult Manifesto* which contained ten recommendations that were intended to make the way in which we deal with young adult offenders more effective, fairer and less costly (Barrow Cadbury Trust 2009). The work of the Alliance has built on an upsurge of interest in how young people in trouble fare during the transition to adulthood. In addition to the Barrow Cadbury Commission's *Lost in Transition* report, other important work has been undertaken by the voluntary sector. The Young Mind's (2006) *Stressed Out and Struggling* initiative looked at the mental health problems facing young people, while The Prince's Trust has mapped out the costs of youth disadvantage and emphasised the importance of engaging young people themselves in the development of answers to their problems (Prince's Trust 2007a, b).

The last Labour government was active too in this area and in November 2005, the Social Exclusion Unit (SEU) published a report entitled *Transitions – Young Adults with Complex Needs* (Social Exclusion Unit 2005). On top of this, a £115m Youth Opportunity Fund (YOF) and a Youth Capital Fund (YCF) were set up as part of a vision for empowering young people; 'giving them somewhere to go, something to do and someone to talk to' (Department for Education and Skills 2006: 1). While they were in opposition, the Conservative Party's Social Justice Commission also drew particular attention to the levels of addiction among the young (Conservative Party 2006) and, at the launch of a new Young Adult Trust, the Party Leader called for a national debate on how to give young people a new sense of duty and social responsibility. David Cameron also called for the intro-duction of a new National Service; 'not military, not compulsory, but built in the same spirit, mixing up classes and backgrounds, allowing youngsters to live and work together, developing into responsible adults' (Cameron 2007). This initiative subsequently resulted in an initiative to provide National Citizen Service pilots for 16-year-olds in the summer of 2011. This scheme will provide about 10,000 places for school-leavers to take part in activities which could include outdoor challenges and helping the local community and forms part of the coalition government's 'Big Society' agenda, which aims to give teenagers the chance to learn new skills that will help them to make positive contributions to their community.

Parliament has also taken an interest in young adults, with the Home Affairs Select Committee (HASC) producing an important report on black young people and the criminal justice system. This report expressed serious concerns about the prediction that three quarters of the young black male population will soon be on the DNA database as a consequence of disproportionate arrest rates; observing that 'the number of young black people in custody is growing at an alarming rate' (Home Affairs Select Committee 2007: para. 322). The Justice Select Committee's (2010a) *Cutting Crime* report on justice reinvestment further argued that:

> It does not make financial sense to continue to ignore the needs of young adult offenders. They will become the adult offenders of tomorrow. Particular effort should be made to keep this group out of custody. A multi-agency approach, akin to that applied to young offenders aged under 18, might bring similar benefits in terms of the reduction of re-offending to those aged 18 to 25.
>
> (para. 166)

In its last few months in office, the Labour government responded to the Justice Select Committee's report by expressing a commitment to improving the way that young adult offenders were managed. It also made reference to a project to develop a strategic approach for the management of offenders between the youth and adult criminal justice systems:

> This project will explore the feasibility of taking into account factors other than age (including maturity levels) when managing young adult offenders, and whether the classification of a young adult offender should remain as 18–20 years old. The project will also explore the possibility of developing a cost benefit case for changing the way we manage this group, and will look separately at the way information is shared between agencies in order to improve the service offered to those moving to the adult justice system.
>
> (Ministry of Justice 2010b: 29)

At the time of writing, however, it is not clear whether the coalition government will actually pursue this line of work.

The case for developing new measures for the young adult age group is overwhelming. Young adults aged 18–24 make up 9.5 per cent of the population, yet they commit approximately one-third of all crime, take up one-third of the probation caseload and represent almost one-third of those sentenced to prison each year. Their rate of re-offending is higher than other adult age groups and many experience high levels of need and vulnerability; something which looks to have been exacerbated by the recent economic recession. Indeed, a study by the University of York estimated the cost of young adult crime to be £20 billion per year (Bowles and Praditpyo 2004). As the Council of Europe Human Rights Commissioner put it after his visit to the UK in 2004:

> The importance of this age group is not merely quantitative. The peak age of offending is around 18. Reconviction rates for 18–20 year olds stand at 71 per cent. Effectively addressing the needs of this age group whilst in detention is consequently central to reducing crime. It is vital, in short, that young adults should leave prison with something other than advanced degrees in criminality.
>
> (Gil-Robles 2004)

Despite a manifesto promise by Labour in 2001 to extend aspects of the youth justice reforms to young adults, little has in fact happened in the subsequent period since; not withstanding a range of international norms which encourage such an approach. The UN Committee on the Rights of the Child has noted with appreciation for example that, 'some State parties allow for the application of the rules and regulations of juvenile justice to persons aged 18 and older, usually till the age of 21, either as a general rule or by way of exception' (United Nations 2007: para. 38). More recently, the Council of Europe, in its *Rules for Juvenile Offenders*, has argued that young adult offenders aged 18–21 may, where appropriate, be regarded as juveniles and dealt with accordingly (Council of Europe 2008; see also chapter 2 of this volume).

As such, there is at present a real opportunity for a change of direction in criminal justice which could sensibly start with this age group. Arguably, the overall aim should be to work towards producing the advances that were sought by the Advisory Council on the Penal System (1974) when it reported on young adults 35 years ago. To quote from a summary by the Council's Chairman (Younger 1974: 98), these desirable goals included:

> Reducing the numbers of young adults who are kept in custody, reducing the social isolation of those who still have to be committed to custody and strengthening the supervision which can be provided for offenders who remain in the community after conviction.

Dame Anne Owers has, more recently, re-affirmed these goals too, noting that 'the high rate of reoffending among young adult men is unlikely to reduce without significant changes in approach, funding and focus' (HM Chief Inspector of Prisons 2010: 64).

Key policy questions

Discussions of policy questions relating to young adult offenders seems to be primarily framed by two central issues. The first is the crisis in the criminal justice system brought about by stubbornly high levels of recidivism and a seemingly inexorable rise in prison numbers. Indeed, on the day of the conference at which the papers in this volume were originally delivered, news came in that a wing in a prison and Young Offender Institution (YOI) which had recently closed down because it had been deemed unfit for human habitation, was being re-opened. Population pressures were so great that although it was 'on the edge of decency' it was going to have to accommodate up to 100 remand prisoners from all over the country. On that day too, the then Prime Minister, Gordon Brown, was forced to defend a letter sent the previous night from the Home Secretary, Lord Chancellor and Attorney General to the Lord Chief Justice urging judges and magistrates to jail only the most dangerous and persistent criminals in a bid to ease prison overcrowding. Four years on and the problems of overcrowding have been eased somewhat by a prison building programme, although problems remain for young adults. For example, in her final annual report as Chief Inspector of Prisons, Dame Anne Owers described young adults as 'a neglected and under resourced age group' (HM Chief Inspector of Prisons 2010). Such neglect is reflected perhaps in the concern of the Independent Monitoring Board for Rochester YOI – the largest prison for young adults in the country – 'that for the fourth year running it has [had] to raise the issue of inadequate provision of full-time purposeful activities for all prisoners' (Kent Online 2010).

The second major issue relates to the paradoxical finding that the operation of the criminal justice system exercises a somewhat limited role in affecting levels and types of offending by this age group. As Ian Loader has argued, 'policing, criminal justice and punishment have an important but ultimately small and peripheral part to play in the production of orderly societies' (Loader 2006). Indeed, whether young people who become persistently involved in crime chose to give it up seems to depend not so much on how much they are punished, but on a range of other factors, including; whether they have work which provides an adequate income, a decent place to live, a lifestyle without addiction to drink or drugs and a healthy set of relationships with family and friends. Moreover, there is growing evidence that the impact of the recession may have been particularly severe on young people.

This chapter now turns to a discussion of the need for policy change within criminal justice before moving on to look at some of the wider questions of social policy outside criminal justice which particularly impact on the involvement of this age group in crime. The chapter then closes with some suggestions about promising areas for policy development.

Criminal justice

In England and Wales, young people in conflict with the law are dealt with in the youth justice system until the age of 18 and the adult system there after. Although under 18's can, on occasion, be dealt with in the adult courts, there are (unlike in some countries) no possibilities for young adults in England and Wales to be dealt with in the youth system. Indeed, in recent years, young people serving sentences in the youth justice system have, upon reaching the legal age of majority, been transferred ever more rapidly into the adult system.

Under 18s

Youth Justice has been subject to a radical overhaul since 1997, with new court powers and infrastructure of services, which the Audit Commission described as representing an improvement on the old system (Audit Commission 2004), being introduced. A more recent assessment by the author has, however, characterised the current arrangements for youth justice as 'the good, the bad and the ugly' (Allen 2007). Certainly, there are aspects of recent reforms which have had a positive impact and there is much to admire in the development of projects working with children at risk of being drawn into crime, in the creation of multi-disciplinary teams committed to addressing the personal, social and educational deficits which underlie so much offending and in the increasing involvement of both victims of crime and the wider public in youth justice arrangements. Substantial declines in the use of custodial sentences since 2008 have also been highly encouraging, with fewer than 2000 under-18's locked up at the end of 2010; a third fewer than had been convicted three years earlier (Allen 2011).

However, there are other elements that are less admirable. These include the tendency to criminalise young people involved in minor delinquency and, until

2008 at least, the stubbornly high use of custodial remands and sentences. Likewise, there are some developments in juvenile justice of which we really should be ashamed; particularly, as regards the way we lock up children and demonize young people involved in anti-social behaviour along with the general coarsening of the political and public debate about how to deal with young people in trouble (Allen 2007). Although there are important signs of a shift in emphasis from the new coalition government – with the Green Paper (Ministry of Justice 2010a: 70) arguing that 'too many young people whose offences are not the most serious and whose behaviour does not pose a risk to the public are sent to custody' – little detail has actually emerged at the time of writing about any changes the government intend to introduce. They have given sole responsibility for youth justice to the Ministry of Justice, but whether this signals a view that the policy of shared responsibility with the Department for Children, Schools and Families introduced in 2007 had been a failure or whether this is simply a collateral consequence of the disbanding of that Department, is not yet clear.

Certainly, the kind of changes which would be needed to build on current evidence and bring England and Wales further into line with international norms and standards would have to involve activities which fall well beyond the responsibility of the Ministry of Justice. They might include: greater investment in prevention, with an emphasis on addressing the educational and mental health difficulties underlying much offending behaviour; the placing of limits on the way we criminalise young people by raising the age of criminal responsibility and introducing a more appropriate system of prosecution and courts; and the development of a wider range of community-based and residential provision for the most challenging young people along with a phasing-out of prison custody for those of compulsory school age.

Young adults

In contrast to those in the juvenile age range, young adults have been relatively neglected by policy-makers. Indeed, the only area within the criminal justice system in which the special status of young adult offenders is recognised is the sentence of Detention in a Young Offender Institution, available for young people aged 18–21. This sentence is served in specialist YOIs and, in contrast with practices for older adults, all sentences, however short, are followed by a period of supervision on licence in the community. This relatively modest protection for this age group would have disappeared if the statutory provision to end this special sentence contained in the Criminal Justice and Courts Services Act 2000 had been implemented;[1] but the Labour government decided against doing so. Instead, it set in motion a 'suite of proposals' to address the specific needs of a wider group of young adults aged 18–24. The national young adult offenders' project, set up in the Home Office following the Barrow Cadbury report in December 2005, concluded that the age range for young adults should be extended to the age of 24 and recommended that separate regimes established in prisons and enhanced supervision, mentoring and programmes in the community should be implemented (National Offender Management Service 2007). In part, the project represented a rather belated effort to give effect to the government's 2001 manifesto commitment to 'build on our youth justice reforms to improve the standard of custodial accommodation and offending programmes for 18- to 20-year-old offenders' (Labour Party 2001). In reality, however, little progress was actually made until a new prison and YOI was finally opened in August 2010 at Isis, within the curtilage of Belmarsh Prison in south-east London.

The T2A Alliance has mapped out an altogether more systematic agenda for criminal justice reform (Barrow Cadbury Trust 2009, Transition to Adulthood Alliance 2011). The first objective is to divert more young adults away from the formal criminal justice system and into measures which can help address the causes of offending and provide reparation to victims. While there are well established systems (which have been substantially extended since 2007–08) for diverting under 18's away from prosecution, cautioning rates for young adults are much lower. Almost half of 15–17 year olds are formally diverted away from prosecution in England and Wales, whereas for 18–20 year olds it is nearer a third. This figure also masks enormous variations between police forces – from 61 per cent in Northamptonshire, to 22 per cent in Greater Manchester – suggesting that there remains substantial scope for more diversion. Matrix Consulting, who undertook work to cost a number of the Manifesto's recommendations (in response to questions about their afford ability), estimated that diverting young adults away from community orders to pre-court Restorative Justice conferencing schemes would be likely to produce a lifetime cost saving to society of almost £275 million (£7,050 per offender), with the costs of conferencing likely to be paid back within the first year of implementation. During the course of two parliaments, implementation of such a scheme would be likely to lead to a total net benefit to society of over £100 million (Matrix 2009). Diversion to mental health or drug treatment is also likely to entail up-front costs, but successful interventions in this area should also produce dividends. Young adult offenders are three times more likely to have a mental health problem than someone of the same age who is not an offender (Young People in Focus 2009) and outside the criminal justice system the young adult age group is seen as a priority group for proactive early intervention, with evidence showing that early prognosis and treatment of mental health issues can save long-term costs (McCrone *et al.* 2008).

T2A's second set of recommendations concerned sentencing. Here they wanted to see the replacement of short prison sentences for non-violent offenders with constructive community sentences. Until very recently, young adults have scarcely received a mention in any of the work by the Sentencing Advisory Panel or Sentencing Guidelines Council. By contrast, sentencing in several European countries takes much greater account of the developing maturity among this age group; most notably in Germany where the law allows sentencers a level of discretion, depending on the seriousness of the crime and the maturity of the offender, in trying young adults up to age 21 under juvenile law (see chapter 2 of this volume). When T2A consulted the general public about its proposals, approximately 80 per cent of respondents agreed that maturity rather than age should be taken into account in sentencing. This is an area to which the new Sentencing Council, which started work in April 2010, has also given much consideration. For example, the definitive guideline on assault that the Council produced in March 2011 clearly states that 'age and/or lack of maturity where it affects the responsibility of the offender' should be one of the factors reducing seriousness or reflecting personal mitigation (Sentencing Council 2011: 5). It remains to be seen what impact this will have, however, as the Chairman of the Magistrates Association told the Justice Committee that he thought that 'maturity' would be a difficult concept to apply 'because first how are you going to measure it and secondly who is going to measure it and what specific information are you going to give the court in terms of black and white decisions as to the maturity of the individual in front of you?' (Justice Committee 2010b: Q17). By contrast, Lord Justice Leveson, the Chair of the Sentencing Council, took the view that 'this is something we've done forever... judges have been assessing the maturity of defendants as long as they've been passing sentence' (Justice Committee 2010c: Q58).

The third challenge is to make the experience of custody much more educational for those who really do need to be locked up. At present, the Prison Service admits on its web site that: 'Prison life for a young offender held in a Young Offenders Institution (or YOI) isn't that different to prison life for adult prisoners' (HM Prison Services 2011). The latest Prison Inspectorate report confirms this, finding that 'busy and overcrowded local prisons struggle to deal with their specific needs and even specialist YOIs lack the resources, support and training to do so' (HM Chief Inspector of Prisons 2010: 64). On this issue, T2A would like to see YOIs twinned with Further Education Colleges to ensure that education is enshrined at the heart of their regimes. This may currently seem unlikely given the present squeeze on spending facing the prison service. However, the coalition government has explicitly espoused a 'rehabilitation revolution' (Ministry of Justice 2010a), and this could realistically and sensibly begin with the young adult age group; building on all the leads previously described in this chapter.

The final priority is to intensify efforts at reintegrating those young people who do need to be locked up after their release back to the community. Bottoms and Shapland's (2011) research with young adult persistent offenders in Sheffield has found that the great majority of these young adults indicated a wish to desist from crime and that factors relating to their social and lifestyle circumstance were important in determining whether or not they succeeded in this (see also chapter 8 of this volume). Through-the-gate peer mentoring combined with a national employment initiative (along the lines of that already in place for young people leaving care) could potentially impact on those circumstances and give young adults a real chance to reform.

At each of these stages, T2A is clear that measures need to be in place to address the disproportionate involvement of young people from black and minority ethnic (BME) groups in the criminal justice system. In 2008, for example, 27 per cent of young offenders aged 15–29 in prison were from a BME background; this represents a 10 per cent increase over the last decade. It is also important that the distinctive needs of young women are met because, although relatively small in number, they require special attention from all of the agencies in the system.

These proposals chime with many other recent proposals for change in criminal justice, including: the Corston (2007) and Bradley reviews, the Justice Committee's Justice Reinvestment inquiry and the reports from think tanks like the Centre for Social Justice. The same is also true for the recent government Green Paper (Ministry of Justice 2010a), which places much emphasis on rehabilitation. It is, therefore, particularly disappointing that, as T2A noted in its response to the Green Paper, 'more attention is not given to the particular issues that relate to young adults'. In this respect, T2A mentioned two issues that they regarded as being 'very significant', neither of which were addressed in the Green Paper: first, the extent to which various criminal justice processes such as prosecution and sentencing take proper account of the developing maturity of young adults and, second, the need for the agencies and institutions which make up both the youth and adult criminal justice systems to provide more flexible approaches which meet the transitional status of people in the young adult age range (Transition to Adulthood Alliance 2011).

T2A is, however, convinced that while such changes to the criminal justice system are necessary, they are not by themselves sufficient as the roots of offending by young adults extend beyond the reach of criminal justice agencies. It is the systems of education, health and social care and the policies in respect of training, employment and housing that need attention as much as, what the Americans refer to as, the 'cops, courts and corrections.'

Social policies

Responding to young offenders in ways which are most likely to encourage desistance from crime requires the involvement of a wide range of agencies outside the justice system. The evidence about how well children and young people in general are faring in the UK is not hugely reassuring. For example, a recent international survey placed the UK near the bottom of a league table of child well-being in the EU (Bradshaw *et al.* 2006). Similarly, analyses of Offender Assessment System (OASys) results for young adult offenders found lower educational achievement, higher problematic alcohol and substance misuse, higher incidence of mental health issues and more significant deficits in attitudes, thinking and social skills in this age group (National Offender Management Service 2007).

The Social Exclusion Unit report on young adults with complex needs also found that 'there are relatively few examples of public services that address the needs of 16- to 25-year-olds in the round or ensure an effective transition from youth services to adult services' (Social Exclusion Unit 2005: 8). The Home Affairs Select Committee's report on black young people (2007: para. 221) also concluded it was not just a question of making services more appropriate, accessible and targeted; stating that 'there is also some need for extra resources in areas such as mental health services, drug treatment and housing policy'. Shortfalls in services like these for young people are likely to impact particularly severely on young offenders.

In terms of housing, in 2004 the Youth Justice Board (YJB) found that 15 per cent of all young offenders were identified as having housing need, but in a more detailed recent study of a sample of offenders all were found to have a housing need (YJB 2007). Three quarters of this sample had lived with someone other than a parent at some time and 40 per cent were, or had been, homeless or had sought formal housing provision and/or support. Today, young adults represent a greater proportion of those accepted as homeless by local authorities than in 1997. The Corston Report (2007) has also drawn attention to the specific problems that young women face in trying to find appropriate housing. Efforts have been made to provide greater assistance to children leaving care, many of whom are at risk of becoming involved in criminal justice, and legislation passed in 2001 stipulated that a Local Authority will provide help until a young person reaches the age of 21, and in some cases 24. The response on the ground has been mixed, however, with some local authorities setting up 'systems to try to avoid responsibility' (Cragg 2007).

The economic downturn since 2008 and the forthcoming cuts in public spending look set to make the prospects for young adults considerably bleaker. Figures released in August 2010 revealed that 72,000 people in the age range 18–24 had been unemployed for 24 months or longer in the three months up to June 2010. This represented an increase of 42 per cent on the corresponding figure in 2009 and an increase of more than 10 per cent on the previous quarter. It was also revealed by the Office for National Statistics that an additional 184,000 young workers in the UK had been unemployed for more than 12 months in the three-month period up to June 2010.

In respect of lifestyle issues, evidence about the use of drugs and alcohol is of particular concern. Admissions to hospital for alcohol-related problems have risen by a third for under-16's and doubled for adults in the last ten years, and it is estimated that one in ten of those aged 16–24 have used hard drugs in the last month. Cocaine is used by 1.75 million young adults; a number which has doubled in seven years. In response, the Conservative Party's Social Justice Commission concluded that 'the current scale of prevalence of alcohol and drugs is historically unprecedented and that young adults are engaging in a new culture of intoxication' (Conservative Party 2006: see also chapter 3 of this volume). It is certainly true that assessments of young adult offenders show that alcohol misuse is one of the factors that distinguishes them from older offenders and several sentences told Baroness Corston that they had noted an increase in young women appearing before them who had clearly abused alcohol (Corston 2007). It is also widely accepted that there is a shortfall of services in this area.

Moving forward

What follows are suggestions of four areas in which concrete change might be possible; suggestions which would improve responses for this age group. The first two relate to criminal justice; the second two to the mode of organising services.

Reducing imprisonment

The first priority is to make a concentrated effort to reduce the use of imprisonment for this age group. At the end of June 2010, 10,037 young people under 21 were in prison; an increase of 14 per cent since 2000. Of those sentenced, over a thousand were serving sentences of less than 12 months. There is no easy recipe for bringing down prison numbers, although some lessons can be drawn from the experiences of the 1980s – when there was a dramatic fall in the number of male juveniles sent to custody – and from the recent falls in the juvenile custodial population (Allen 1991; Allen 2011). Increasing the extent to which first-time and less serious young offenders are dealt with outside the formal system is a particularly promising strategy and the greater use of informal methods may serve, over time, to curtail the development of a delinquent career more effectively than a formal caution or prosecution. Additionally, the development of informal measures effectively delays the criminalisation of those young people who do continue to offend. Moreover, extending the range of pre-court options both increases the opportunity for young people to turn away from crime and dilutes their criminal histories (which courts might take into consideration if they eventually do come to be sentenced).

As for those young people who do come to be sentenced, research by the Centre for Crime and Justice Studies has suggested that full use is not being made of the Community Order which was introduced in 2005, with requirements for alcohol or mental health treatment hardly used at all (Stanley 2007). Given the level of need in these areas, additional investment of at least some of any savings made from reductions in prison numbers could usefully be used to increase their availability.

Use Restorative Justice (RJ)

If a more sparing use of criminal justice is to be made, then an alternative way of responding to the harms caused by young adult offenders needs to be put in its place. While aspects of RJ have been developed in youth justice, its availability in the adult system is currently very limited. Research is increasingly showing the benefits of RJ to victims and while the impact on offenders is more mixed, there is sufficient positive evidence to justify some investment (see for example Shapland *et al.* 2008). A good deal of the most positive evidence comes from experimental and other work involving young offenders (Sherman and Strang 2007). The coalition government has also expressed interest in developing RJ, with the Ministry of Justice publishing a 'Structural reform plan' pledging to consider the use of Restorative Justice for adult and youth crimes. A sensible starting point might be the age group that falls between these two categories.

Localise responses

The third area for exploration relates to the way that services are organised. Evidence is increasingly showing high geographical concentrations of offenders known to the criminal justice system. For example, a study in Scotland found that while the imprisonment rate for men as a whole in Scotland was 237 per 100,000, the rate for men from the 27 most deprived wards was 953 per 100,000. For men aged 23 from those wards the rate was an astonishing 3,427 per 100,000 (Houchin 2005). Likewise, a study in Gateshead found that almost a quarter of the offenders who became known to the service in 2005–2006 lived in 2 out of 22 electoral wards, while a half lived in just 5 wards (Allen *et al.* 2007). Half of the wards account for 80 per cent of the known offenders and in 4 wards more than one in a hundred residents is under probation supervision (in the others the rate is less than one in a thousand). Furthermore, the distribution of the 322 probation cases in Gateshead who (as of August 2005) were, or had been, in prison shows a slightly higher concentration with just over a quarter coming from the top two wards.

One way of addressing these geographical concentrations is for the probation service and other agencies to develop more of a presence in the neighbourhoods where their caseload is concentrated. Mapping work in the US has led some probation services to reorganise their work on a geographical basis, with small groups of officers assigned responsibility for all of the cases from a particular locality. Such an approach enables the probation service to get to know the strengths and resources within particular neighbourhoods as well as the problems. In England patch-based probation services were developed in the 1970s, but recent practices have militated against such a localised approach. Instead, programmes tend to be delivered according more to the type of offender than on a geographical basis. The Probation Service's 'estates strategy' – through which decisions are made about the location and staffing of buildings and facilities – has reduced the flexibility that probation services have about the use of property; although the recent creation of Probation Trusts could restore a much needed local ownership to the work of the service (Allen *et al.* 2007).

Another approach would be to create a more systematic and comprehensive multi- agency response through a locally managed Adult Offending Team (AOT); modelled on Youth Offending Teams and first proposed in the Local Government Association's 2005 report *Going Straight* (Local Government Association 2005). One option would be to initially limit the responsibility of the AOT to the young adult age group (those aged 18–24) as most of the caseload of the successful Priority and Prolific Offender Schemes – which provide targeted and intensive help – were in their 20s; suggesting that this is an age group that can respond well to such a distinctive approach.

Young offender participation

The final suggestion is that greater efforts need to be made to involve young adult offenders themselves in the development of policy and practice. Suggestions made by young people to The Prince's Trust have included: making more mentors and workers with similar experiences available to support them; providing greater incentives to take on education courses in prison; establishing tailored, in-depth pre-release programmes in every prison; investing in schemes, led by ex-offenders, that provide training and supported employment for ex-offenders; and providing more opportunities for young people to put something back into their communities. A Task Force established by the organisation Clinks has considered various ways in which the voices of service users can be better incorporated (Clinks 2008). These included enabling young adult offenders to have a greater say in the recruitment and training of staff of criminal justice organisations (and providing more opportunities for ex-offenders themselves to obtain employment in the sector), allowing them to contribute more systematically to the development of policies by government and criminal justice agencies and giving them the opportunity to participate in the commissioning of services by the National Offender Management Service and other relevant bodies. Such an approach is consistent with the responsibility model of desistance and the emerging criminological evidence which stresses the importance of seeing offenders as active contributors to their own rehabilitation (Raynor 2004).

Conclusion

Whether the kind of policy suggestions made in this chapter are taken forward in the coming years depends partly on whether governments can free themselves from the straitjacket of punitive populism and partly on whether they take seriously the developmental needs of the young adult age group. Given the growing body of evidence about the needs of adolescents and young adults, it can only be hoped that policy makers respond to the challenges laid down by the contributions in this volume, and other recent work, especially by T2A. The need for cuts in spending will of course exercise a strong influence on policy development in the coming years, but it should be borne in mind that a more sparing use of prosecution and a greater use of punishment organised through more locally responsive and accountable structures could increase benefits and reduce costs.

Note

1 See Criminal Justice and Court Services Act 2000, section 61(1). The section was enacted to assist the Prison Service at a time of population pressures and states that adults sentenced to imprisonment may not, under the existing law, serve that sentence in a YOI. Hence, abolishing the special sentence of Detention in a YOI would have revoked this prohibition, allowing greater flexibility in the allocation of prisoners to institutions.

References

Advisory Council on the Penal System (1974) *Young Adult Offenders*, London: H. M. S. O.
Allen, R. (1991) 'Out of jail: the reduction in the use of penal custody for male juveniles 1981–88', *Howard Journal of Criminal Justice*, 30: 30–52.
— (2007) 'From punishment to problem solving', in Z. Davies and W. McMahon (eds), *Debating Youth Justice*, London: Centre for Crime and Justice Studies.
— (2008) *Lost in Transition: Three years on*, London: Barrow Cadbury Trust.
— (2010) 'On prisons, Ken Clarke shows real reforming spirit', *Guardian*, 30 June.
— (2011) *Last Resort? Exploring the reduction in child imprisonment 2008–11*, London: Prison Reform Trust.

Allen, R., Jallab, K. and Snaith, E. (2007) 'Gateshead: the story so far', in R. Allen and V. Stern (eds), *Justice Reinvestment: A new approach to crime and justice*, London: International Centre for Prison Studies.

Audit Commission (2004) *Youth Justice 2004: A review of the reformed youth justice system*, London: Audit Commission.

Barrow Cadbury Commission (2005) *Lost in Transition: A report of the Barrow Cadbury Commission on Young Adults and the Criminal Justice System*, London: Barrow Cadbury Trust.

Barrow Cadbury Trust (2009) *Young Adult Manifesto*, London: Barrow Cadbury Trust.

Bottoms, A. E. and Shapland, J. (2011) 'Steps towards desistance among male young adult recidivists', in S. Farrall, S. Maruna, M. Hough and R. Sparks (eds), *Escape Routes: Contemporary perspectives on life after punishment*, London: Routledge-Cavendish.

Bowles, R. and Praditpyo, R. (2004) *Commission on Young Adults and the Criminal Justice System: Summary of costs and benefits*, York: Centre for Criminal Justice Economics and Psychology.

Bradshaw, J., Hoelscher, P. and Richardson, D. (2007) 'An index of child well-being in the European Union', *Journal of Social Indicators Research*, 80: 133–177.

Cameron, D. (2007) 'Young Adult Trust will make a constructive difference', a speech delivered on 30 October 2006 [online], accessed at:
http://www.conservatives.com/tile.do?def = news.story.page&obj_id = 133290& speeches=1.

Clinks (2008) *Unlocking Potential*, York: Clinks.

Conservative Party (2006) *Breakdown Britain: Social Justice Policy Group*, London: Conservative Party.

Corston, Baroness (2007) *The Corston Report*, London: Home Office.

Council of Europe (2008) *Recommendation CM/Rec(2008) 11 of the Committee of Ministers to member states on the European Rules for juvenile offenders subject to sanctions or measures Rule 17*, Strasbourg: Council of Europe.

Cragg, S. (2007) 'Legislation update', *The Times*, 19 June.

Department for Education and Skills (2006) *Youth Green Paper: Next Steps Match 2006*, London: The Stationery Office.

Gil-Robles, A. (2004) *Report by Mr Alvaro Gil Robles on his visit to the United Kingdom 4th–12th November 2004*, Strasbourg: Council of Europe.

HM Chief Inspector of Prisons (2010) *HM Chief Inspector of Prisons Annual Report 2008–9*, London: The Stationery Office.

HM Prison Service (2011), 'Prison, Probation and Rehabilitation: Young Adult Offenders' [available online], accessed at: [https://www.justice.gov.uk/guidance/prison-probation-and-rehabilitation/types-of-offender/young-adult-offender.htm].

Home Affairs Select Committee (2007) *Black Young People and the Criminal Justice System*, London: The Stationery Office.

Houchin, R. (2005) *Social Exclusion and Imprisonment in Scotland: A report*, Glasgow: Glasgow Caledonian University.

Justice Select Committee (2010a) *Cutting Crime: The case for justice reinvestment*, London: The Stationery Office.

— (2010b) *Draft sentencing guideline on assault – uncorrected evidence – 23 November 2010HC 637-i*, published 26 November 2010, evidence given by John Thornhill, Chair, Magistrates' Association, London: The Stationery Office.

— (2010c) *Draft sentencing guideline on assault – uncorrected evidence – 14 December 2010HC 637-ii*, published 26 November 2010, evidence given by Lord Justice Leveson, Chairman, Sentencing Council, London: The Stationery Office.

Kent Online (2010) *Rochester youth jail suffers violent outbreaks* [available online], accessed at: http://www.kentonline.co.uk/kentonline/news/2010/august/10/rochester_youth_jail_violence.aspx.

Labour Party (2001) *Election Manifesto*, London: Labour Party.

Loader, I. (2006) 'Rebalancing the Criminal Justice System?', in *Contribution to Our Nation's Future*, [available online], accessed at: www.pm.gov.uk/output/page97q1.asp.

Local Government Association (2005) *Going Straight*, London: Local Government Association.

McCrone, P., Dhanasiri, S., Patel, A., Knapp, M. and Lawton-Smith, S. (2008) *Paying the Price: The cost of mental health care in England to 2026*, London: King's Fund.

Matrix (2009) *Economic Analysis of Interventions for Young Adult Offenders*, London: Barrow Cadbury Trust.

Ministry of Justice (2010a) *Breaking the Cycle: Effective punishment, rehabilitation and sentencing of offenders*, London: The Stationery Office.

— (2010b) *Government Response to the Justice Committee's Report: Cutting crime: the case for justice reinvestment*, London: The Stationery Office.

National Offender Management Service (2007) 'London's Young Adult Offenders (18–24)', (unpublished report), London: NOMS.

Prince's Trust (2007a) *The Cost of Exclusion: Counting the cost of youth disadvantage in the UK*, London: Prince's Trust.

— (2007b) *Breaking the Cycle of Offending: Making the views of young people count*, London: Prince's Trust.

Raynor, P. (2004) 'Rehabilitative and reintegrative approaches' in A. Bottoms, S. Rex and G. Robinson (eds), *Alternatives to Prison*, Cullompton, Devon: Willan Publishing.

Sentencing Council (2011) *Assault: Definitive Guideline*, London: Sentencing Council.

Shapland, J., Atkinson, A., Atkinson, H., Dignan, J., Edwards, L., Hibbert, J., Howes, M., Johnstone, J., Robinson, G. And Sorsby, A. (2008) *Does Restorative Justice Affect Reconviction? the fourth report from the evaluation of three schemes. Ministry of Justice Research Series 10/08*, London: The Stationery Office.

Sherman, L. and Strang, H. (2007) *Restorative Justice: The evidence*, London: Esmee Fairbairn Foundation.

Social Exclusion Unit (2005) *Transitions – Young Adults with Complex Needs*, London: Cabinet Office.

Stanley, S. (2007) *Young Adult Offenders and the Community Order*, London: Centre for Crime and Justice Studies.

Transition to Adulthood Alliance (2011) 'Transition to Adulthood Response to "Breaking the Cycle"', [available online] accessed at: www.t2a.org.uk/wp-content/uploads/2011/09/T2A-Alliance-response-to-Breaking-the-Cycle.pdf.

United Nations (2007) *General Comment No. 10 (2007): Children's Rights in Juvenile Justice*, Geneva: UN.

Young Minds (2006) *Stressed Out and Struggling – Emerging Practice: Examples of mental health services for 16–25 year olds*, London: Young Minds.

Young People in Focus (2009) *Young Adults Today*, Brighton: Young People in Focus.

Younger, K. (1974) 'Introducing the report', *Probation Journal*, 21: 98.

Youth Justice Board (2007) *Housing Needs and Experiences*, London: Youth Justice Board.

Index